# MONUMENTS, MEMORIALS, & MARKERS

Photo David C. Kasserra

*An* ILLUSTRATED GUIDE *to*

# MONUMENTS, MEMORIALS, &MARKERS

*in the* KINGSTON AREA

**Kingston Historical Society Plaque Committee**
John H. Grenville, David C. Kasserra,
Jennifer McKendry, William J. Patterson,
Edward H. Storey

A Millennium Project of the Kingston Historical Society

© 2000
Kingston Historical Society
P.O. Box 54
Kingston, Ontario  K7L 4V6
Canada

*web:* www.HeritageKingston.on.ca


ISBN 0-919770-10-X

Graphic Design: Peter Dorn RCA, FGDC

**Canadian cataloguing in publication data**
Main entry under title:
An illustrated guide to monuments,
memorials & markers in the Kingston
Area
Includes bibliographical references.
ISBN 0-919770-10-X
1. Monuments – Ontario – Kingston
Region – Guidebooks. 2. Memorials –
Ontario – Kingston Region – Guidebooks.
3. Historical markers – Ontario – Kingston
Region – Guidebooks. I. Grenville, John
H. II. Kingston Historical Society (Ont.).
Plaque Committee
FC3099.K5Z54 2000
917.13'72044
C99-901690-3
F1059.5.K5154 2000

FRONT COVER
*Sir John A. Macdonald's statue in City Park,
Kingston, 1999.*
Photo David C. Kasserra

BACK COVER
*The unveiling of Sir John A. Macdonald's
statue in City Park, Kingston, 1895.*
Queen's University Archives

2000
Canada

DEDICATED
TO THOSE MEMBERS OF THE
KINGSTON HISTORICAL SOCIETY
WHO HAVE BEEN RECORDING
KINGSTON'S HISTORY FOR MORE
THAN ONE HUNDRED YEARS.
THEY CLEARED THE PATH FOR US,
AND MADE IT EASIER
TO FOLLOW IN THEIR FOOTSTEPS.

# Contents

# List of Markers *

* Index of Markers, pp 243-244

# List of Maps

# List of Illustrations

# Foreword

AT THE THIRD meeting of the Kingston Historical Society in March 1894, a motion was approved to ask the City Council to place markers "where the old forts and buildings stood so that visitors might have the opportunity of seeing [what] our city [was like] in the early days." Although the City Council did not support funding this worthy idea, the Society began erecting markers by 1916 at the latest. As the work proceeded, the city did provide valuable assistance with the actual installation of plaques and markers. By the 1960s, so many plaques of various kinds had been raised by various sponsors that the Society and the *Kingston Whig-Standard* published a small book listing and describing them. In the book's preamble, the following sentiment was expressed: "this interesting and informative book should prove to be of invaluable historical and educational interest and a guide to the citizens of Kingston and vicinity and to our visitors."

As President of the Kingston Historical Society, I can confidently echo that sentiment in regard to this new, expanded, and illustrated guide to heritage markers throughout our city. The Society's plaque committee – John H. Grenville (chair), Jennifer McKendry, William J. Patterson, and Edward H. Storey – engaged David C. Kasserra for this project as part of the federal government's Career Edge program. They have provided guidance and worked diligently with David on recording, organizing, adding supplementary material, editing, and illustrating the guide. Financial contributions by the Millennium Bureau of Canada and by many life members of the Kingston Historical Society have also been of real importance in this enterprise. We also deeply appreciate the co-operation of the City of Kingston which, through its Strategic and Long-Range Planning Group, provided the detailed maps needed for this publication. This book has been produced using state-of-the-art technology such as digital photography, scanning, word processing, desktop designing, and printing directly from computer disks. Technically, this is far removed from the then state-of-the-art methods of the 1890s when the Society promoted the photography of landmarks to create a visual record – a relatively slow and cumbersome procedure by our standards, as was printing books with traditional typesetting and plates. The pleasure of reading, however, remains timeless and this volume is intended not only as a repository of information on Kingston history but also as a source of satisfaction and pleasure to all who read it.

Desmond O'Meara
President, 1998-1999, Kingston Historical Society

*The Kingston Historical Society always welcomes new members. Please contact:*
*Kingston Historical Society*
*P.O. Box 54*
*Kingston, ON K7L 4V6 Canada*

# Acknowledgements

EW BOOKS are published that present, as this one does, the work of so many writers. Each of the 193 texts on monuments, memorials, and markers presented herein reflects the work of one or more people dedicated to expressing recognition of and respect for our social, economic, cultural, military, medical, educational, recreational, and architectural heritage. To all these people who, individually and through committee work, have contributed over the span of a century to our understanding and appreciation of significant events, people, and places, we owe our gratitude.

The Plaque Committee of the Kingston Historical Society also gratefully acknowledges the many contributions of individuals, organizations, institutions, and corporations for financial support, information, illustrations, and knowledgeable assistance.

The Kingston Historical Society Council and Executive, in designating this book as the Society's millennium project, provided encouragement and financial support. President Desmond O'Meara, and Vice-President Brian Osborne worked closely with our committee. Warren Everett graciously accepted responsibility for advertising and distribution. Life members of the Society, at the suggestion of Margaret Angus, generously contributed supporting funds, which enabled an enhanced production of this book.

Peter Dorn provided creative and aesthetic guidance in the book's design, and Hugh Gale and Daryl J. Martin of the Strategic and Long-Range Planning Group of the City of Kingston provided maps. The Government of Canada provided financial support through the Millennium Partnership Program and the employment of David C. Kasserra under the Career Edge Internship Program. Corrections Canada provided space for several committee meetings. Parks Canada provided office space for this project, as well as space for committee meetings at Bellevue House National Historic Site. We thank the staff at Bellevue House National Historic Site for all of the support and assistance that they provided throughout the entire project. We thank Paul Litt and Jeremy Diamond of the Ontario Heritage Foundation for their contribution of photographs, knowledge, information, and never-ending patience. We are grateful for the many hours of assistance the Queen's University Archives and in particular George Henderson gave the committee in researching and illustrating this guide.

Generous assistance of information and photographs was provided by the Archives of James Richardson and Sons Limited, Winnipeg; Archives of Ontario; Derek Bechthold, Marine Museum of the Great Lakes at Kingston; Buffalo and Erie County Historical Society; Jennifer Bunting, County of Lennox and Addington Museum and Archives; Benoit Cameron, Massey Library, Royal Military College of Canada; Canada Post Corporation; Robert Cardwell; Department of Manuscripts and Archives, Cornell University; Dorothy Duncan; Paul Evoy, City of Kingston; J. B. Fitsell; Patsy Fleming; Chris Grace, Molson Breweries Canada; Jack Granatstein; Carrie Holden, Hotel Dieu Hospital; John Deutsch University Centre Staff, Queen's University; Major E.F. Joyner; David C. Kasserra; Kingston Historical Society; Kingston Public Library, Main Branch; *Kingston Whig-Standard*; John Langton; George Lilley; Loyalist Township; Blake McKendry; Jennifer McKendry; Ross Mackenzie, Royal Military College of Canada; National Portrait Library, London, England; Newberry Library, Chicago; Nor'wester Museum, Glengarry Historical Society, Martintown; Tony O'Loughlin, Irish Commemoration Association; Ontario Heritage Foundation; Parks Canada; Princess of Wales' Own Regiment; James Purser, City of Kingston; Ron Ridley, Fort Henry National Historic Site; Royal Ontario Museum, Toronto; St Joseph Province Archives; St Mark's Church, Barriefield; David St. Onge, Corrections Canada Museum, Kingston; Toronto Reference Library; Isobel and Bogart Trumpour; and Herbert Walsh.

The Kingston Historical Society Plaque Committee

# Introduction

*A land without memories is a land without history.\**

IN 1957 at the unveiling of a provincial plaque to Bishop Alexander Macdonell (128-9), Kingston mayor F.P. Boyce expressed the hope "that when their project of placing markers in the area is completed a booklet describing them and their locations would be published for distribution to the general public." Eight years later the *Kingston Whig-Standard*, in association with the Kingston Historical Society, did publish a 56-page booklet on historic sites and monuments of Kingston and district – *A Catalogue of Markers, Tablets, Memorials and Museums in Historic Kingston and in the Circulation Area of the Kingston Whig-Standard*. It was reprinted with corrections in 1968 and was available for some time into the 1970s. It has now been, however, out of print for more than twenty years. As a Millennium Project the Kingston Historical Society has produced this book and contributed to a web-based version (www.HeritageKingston.on.ca) that incorporates information taken from and expanding upon heritage markers in and around the City of Kingston, reflecting the geographical area encompassed by amalgamation in 1998. We are hoping that this collection will help visitors and researchers alike to find spots of historical interest – reminders of Canada's roots as we enter the new millennium. Mayor Boyce predicted correctly the creation of such a guide but did not foresee that the installation of markers was endless as history continues to unfold and continues to need to be recorded. We hope that the current guide will be in need of revision during this new century as other aspects of Kingston's history are commemorated.

When the Kingston Historical Society plaque committee began to record markers in the Kingston region, we were uncertain about how many existed. The quantity and diversity pleasantly surprised us. While a metal plaque on a stand is the usual image of a marker, in fact they come in many forms including stone sundials (199), benches (30), statues (157, 205), memorial arches (78-79), and Celtic crosses (137).

We have collected information for this book on more than 190 heritage markers, yet this is by no means a comprehensive list. Because of the overwhelming quantity of markers we had to be selective in order to control the book's length and to be able to publish it in a reasonable length of time. There are, for example, a large number of markers in cathedrals, churches, chapels, and synagogues. These often explain aspects of the particular history of the institution or memorialize the contributions of individual members. This situation also applies to the numerous plaques found in or on educational and military buildings and on their grounds such as Queen's University and the Royal Military College. We chose markers that best represented different elements of the heritage of Kingston, especially those with an impact on the province and country. Our aim is to deepen the reader's appreciation of and to provide information to researchers on Kingston's place in Canadian history from its beginnings to the end of the Second World War. There are other factors that influenced the selection process: certain plaques have been lost through theft and fire, for example, more than 80 memorials were destroyed during the burning of St George's Cathedral in 1899. Others are in interior locations that are difficult to access.

The sponsors of most of the markers we recorded are the Historic Sites and Monuments Board of Canada (markers of national significance), the Ontario Heritage Foundation (provincial significance), and the Kingston Historical Society (regional significance).

A federal body called the Historic Landmarks Association of Canada was established by the Royal Society of Canada in 1907. The Association was interested in identifying historic sites in Canada and during the next few years it prepared an inventory of important historic sites in Canada. In 1919, as a result of representations from individuals both inside and outside government service, the federal government organized a special board called the Historic Sites and Monuments Board

---

\* Abram J. Ryan (1834-1886), "A Land Without Ruins."

1

of Canada. The Board, assisted by Parks Canada, considers any aspect of Canada's human history for ministerial designation of national historic significance. To be studied for designation, a place, a person, or an event has to be assessed as having a nationally significant impact on Canadian history or illustrating a nationally important aspect of Canadian history. Kingston is well represented with federal plaques on Sir John A. Macdonald (37, 62-3, 123, 125, 126, 130, 157, 186, 202, 203), Sir Richard Cartwright (24), the Murney Martello Tower (142), Legislature of the Province of Canada (165), Fort Frontenac (72-73), etc. In the first twenty years of the Board's existence almost 300 markers were erected at various locations across the country. Today across the nation there are more than 1,600 commemorative plaques, which one can recognize because they are cast in bronze with raised lettering and a maroon background colour. The text is in the two official languages. In the top left corner there is a casting of the Arms of Canada.

The Ontario Heritage Foundation, founded in 1967 as a not-for-profit agency of the Government of Ontario, builds upon the achievements of its predecessor, the Archaeological and Historic Sites Board of Ontario. The latter was organized in 1953 to advise the Minister of Tourism and Information on archaeological and historical matters within the Province of Ontario. In 1956 the Board began a program of marking places, events, and persons of importance in the history of the province, as well as to stimulate public awareness of and pride in Ontario's past. The first two decades of the Archaeological and Historic Sites Board of Ontario and the Ontario Heritage Foundation were fruitful: from 1957 until 1974 they erected between forty and sixty markers per year. There are now approximately 1,100 plaques across the province. Kingston gained numerous provincial plaques, for example, St Mark's Church (112), the King's Royal Regiment of New York (25), Molly Brant (55), Charles Sangster (148), and Government House (189). Since 1992 the Foundation has also assisted communities in the erection of almost 300 markers across Ontario through its local marking program – most recently for this area in July 1999 with the unveiling of the Kingston Historical Society's plaque on Portsmouth Village's history (193, 234). The prosperity of the postwar period led to a sudden increase in property development that threatened many archaeological sites.[1] The Archaeological and Historic Protection Act of 1953 (superceded in 1974 by the Ontario Heritage Act) set out a legal process whereby sites could be designated. Designation protected the architectural, historical or archaeological integrity of a site by controlling access in some instances, safeguarding artifacts, and imposing legal controls on certain aspects of its development, alteration, and demolition. Plaques have become a successful and important tool that the Foundation has used to supplement designation. Marking raises public awareness of and thus gives some protection for historic and heritage sites.[2] The Foundation's plaques are cast in royal blue with raised lettering – bilingual since 1982 – and at the top is a horizontal oval containing the provincial coat-of-arms.

The Kingston Historical Society, founded in 1893, considers the raising and maintaining of plaques to be a very important part of its mandate to explore, record, and explain regional history and heritage. At the Society's third meeting in March 1894 markers for old forts and buildings were proposed, but the City Council did not support the idea. It was not until 1916 that the Society erected its first marker – a memorial to the Rev. John Stuart (41) placed inside St George's Cathedral. Because of the war effort the timing was not propitious to raise further markers. The Society had hoped to commemorate Governor Simcoe's house, Sir John A. Macdonald's house on Brock Street, old Fort Frontenac, and the first parliament of the Province of Canada (held in the Kingston General Hospital). From 1923 to 1959, however, the pace of plaquing picked up, and 17 were erected by the Society on such subjects as Kingston City Hall (16), Market Battery (27), Fort Frontenac (73), Colonel Bradstreet's Landing (183), and Sir John A. Macdonald's Law Office (37). This number compared well with the 16 raised in the area by 1959 by the Archeological and Historic Sites Board of Ontario and the 13 by its federal counterpart. In its 1965 catalogue the Kingston

Historical Society recorded 17 plaques; there are now 22 plaques in place. Given the ever-increasing cost of erecting plaques (about $2,000 for a large bilingual bronze plaque with artwork in 1999), it is encouraging that partners are showing an interest in sharing the funding, for example the Ontario Heritage Foundation and the Portsmouth Villagers contributed towards the Society's Portsmouth Village plaque, while the City of Kingston looked after the actual installation. This book, published by the Society, is the only current inventory of plaques, which have been sponsored by a variety of organizations and individuals. Its importance is recognized by a contribution from the Canada Millennium Partnership Program.

ALL THREE ORGANIZATIONS – federal, provincial, and regional – share common aspects in producing plaques. This holds true as well for many other sponsors, such as the City of Kingston, Fort Henry, the Pittsburgh Historical Society, the Princess of Wales' Own Regiment, the *Kingston Whig-Standard*, Queen's University, and the Royal Military College. When one looks at subject matter, for example, one suspects that it is influenced by a marker's unusual form of communication – a concise summary of events located in a particular site for public scrutiny. There is a tendency for citizens to request markers on subjects related to a specific location rather than to a broad heritage subject. Similarly, the tangible predominates over the abstract. Ideas, cultural trends, and other such cerebral themes are rarely suggested. On the other hand, people associated with such subjects are often recognized, and houses and institutional structures are marked because of their inhabitants or incidents that took place there.[3] We want to stand on the very spot where a past event occurred. The recent growth of interest in genealogy has served to increase this aspect.

The content of various plaque programs has changed over time in response to shifting pressures from various interests and changing perspectives on history. From the beginning, the plaque programs have likely been influenced most strongly by influential persons in society: academics, amateur and professional historians, and governing politicians. The historical consciousness of these groups is heightened by natural curiosity about society's origins. People, who are descendants of original families in an area, often display a special interest in the community's early history.[4] Some may be motivated by a desire to elevate social standing on the basis of antecedents, to stress the unbroken chain of relatives to the present or to reveal the harsh or unfair conditions that ancestors faced and survived. If a cultural group feels that its position in society is underrated or under threat as conditions change, the wording of a marker may attempt to redress the situation. In 1894, for example, Bishop Cleary (who emigrated from Ireland in 1881) of St Mary's Roman Catholic Cathedral felt the need – perhaps because of the on-going Irish religious and political troubles – to sponsor a statue (205) remembering the deaths by typhoid of Irish emigrants almost half a century earlier. A more recent example is the plaque at Fort Henry on the internment of Ukrainian Canadians (101). Citizens, concerned about the persuasive homogeneity of today's world, may desire markers to recognize local community identity and history, for example markers recording the history of Pittsburgh Township before amalgamation with the new City of Kingston (114, 116). Sentiment can play a large role in some subjects where heroes are involved. The emotions evoked by the inscriptions and carvings on war memorials seem the least survivors can do for those who died in foreign lands: "your memory hallowed in the land you loved."*

The depth and extent of Kingston's military past is expressed in no less than 60 markers, memorials, and monuments, about one-third of the total. The military theme encompasses not only the supreme sacrifice of those who died on active service but also all those who served in the defence of Canada in war and peace: "they also serve who only stand and wait."**

In the 1950s and 1960s professional historians in Canada were mainly concerned with recording a national history especially

* John S. Arkwright (1872-1954), "The Supreme Sacrifice."
** John Milton (1608-1674), "On His Blindness."

as the 100th anniversary of Confederation approached. Spurred on by the aftermath of the Second World War, it was an era of national pride, self-awareness, and the creation of a Canadian identity.[5] This is the style of rhetoric fashionable in the 1950s: "We are too apt to forget that citizenship brings duties and responsibilities as well as privileges and we must be alert to maintain the freedom for which our ancestors fought," spoken by Professor T. F. McIlwraith of the Archeological and Historic Sites Board of Ontario at the Kingston City Park unveiling of the plaque commemorating the events of 1837-1838 (153). Canadian historians explored Canada's difficult journey from British colony to an independent nation. In Kingston the obvious candidate for honouring was Sir John A. Macdonald, Canada's first Prime Minister who spent much of his career in or representing the city. Bellevue House, where Macdonald lived for a relatively short time, was restored as a National Historic Site and opened to the public in 1967 (186). During its early years the Historic Sites and Monuments Board of Canada's recommendations emphasized military history, politics, and exploration, areas then fashionable in historical studies.

In the early years of the Archaeological and Historic Sites Board of Ontario, the ideology of its board members fit nicely with the outlook of local history advocates around the province. The Board wanted to give an account of colonial settlement and the early political and economic development of the province. The plaque program may not have been consciously conceived with this political expression in mind but it was well aligned with it.[6] Certain subjects – usually geared around how society and history were affected by males from New England and the British Isles – dominated. At the unveiling in 1957 of the provincial plaque to Bishop Macdonell (128-9), the Hon. W.M. Nickle described him as "one of those great men in the history of the province who gave us the heritage of the way of life, which we enjoy today." In the last two decades nationalist historiography has been waning while a new form of historiography has become well established. In recent years the Ontario Heritage Foundation has broadened its recognition of aspects of Ontario heritage to include the histories of women, First Nations, Franco-Ontarians, workers, and various ethnic groups.

The work of the Historic Sites and Monuments Board of Canada focussed increasingly on heritage buildings. Since the 1980s the Board has extended its definition of built heritage to include streetscapes, districts, gardens, and cultural landscapes. This interest has manifested itself in numerous markers commemorating buildings and sites and, as well, in recommendations for cost-sharing to preserve and restore historically significant buildings such as Kingston City Hall (17) and Elizabeth Cottage (47). The 144 National Historic Sites within the Parks Canada system are a tribute to its belief in, and concern for, historic conservation and presentation. The Kingston Historical Society, while primarily interested in history rather than architecture, opens Murney Tower, a National Historic Site, to the public during the tourist season. One should note, however, that the Society as early as 1894 expressed concern about the disappearance of "many old landmarks of the city," for example the War of 1812 blockhouse on Sydenham Street. The Society's museum committee arranged to record it in a photograph. By the early 1920s the Society was negotiating a lease from the federal government for Murney Tower. After six arduous years of negotiations, the tower was finally opened on 1 August 1925 as a museum run by the Society. By 1996 the Ontario Heritage Foundation held 165 properties (such as the Cartwright House in Kingston, 132) in the Heritage Conservation Easement Program, as well as owning 26 built properties and 37 natural heritage properties. Through publications, awards, plaques and conferences, the federal government and the provincial foundation have taken leading roles within the heritage community in advocating the preservation and restoration of public buildings.

Public concern about new developments intensified greatly during the late 1960s and early 1970s. Saving old buildings, the most obvious and tangible evidence of the past in the modern landscape, became a focus of concern[7] (for example the creation of Upper Canada Village near Morrisburg in 1961). As previously noted, the Kingston Historical Society attempted in the late 19th century to raise awareness of the need to preserve old buildings, notably those associated with important military or political events. During the second half of the 20th century historians spoke in favour of preserving a wider sweep of buildings that explained how ordinary Canadians had lived. Architecture gave tangible shape to the past, especially during the sentimental fervour of 1967 as Canadians celebrated one hundred years as a nation. Heritage Canada, a national organization, was incorporated in 1973 and, in Kingston, the Frontenac Historic Foundation in 1972. A year earlier the city was in the forefront of the process to designate certain buildings worthy of protection because of their architectural or historic significance. Thus, a new link between political and local history interests was forged, which would by the mid-1970s reshape the political and bureaucratic context within which the plaque programs operated.

Government policy on multi-culturalism in the 1970s introduced a substantial change in the nature of plaque subjects. A new era began for topics of a more inclusive nature. Early markers concentrated on the nation's military, political, and economic heritage. Today, they cover a much broader range of subjects, including science, nature, and culture. More sensitivity is demonstrated with the languages used on plaques: English, French, and First Nations have appeared when appropriate to the subject matter (for example the federal plaque on Molly Brant is trilingual, 64). Subjects for plaquing were broadened again in the 1990s with the addition of labour history, for example the provincial plaque on the Workers on the Rideau (120) in 1993.

A similar movement has been seen in the 1990s within the Historic Sites and Monuments Board of Canada. It has taken initiatives in those areas of heritage, which have become more prominent in Canadian historiography and society: the histories of Aboriginal Peoples, women, and cultural communities. In Kingston the Board's recent plaque (1996) to Molly Brant (64) made her active role in influencing the politics and historical events more tangible by citing specific actions. In contrast the earlier provincial plaque of 1975 (55) summarized these aspects as a "leading role." The federal plaque of 1999 for the Ann Baillie Building honours the nursing profession (161), while the plaque for Dr Jenny Trout (19) commemorates the first woman licensed to practice medicine in Canada. Heritage markers often fall captive to older attitudes toward the past. Those markers commemorate subjects chosen according to the historical priorities of past eras, and may display texts that from today's perspective appear inaccurate, offensive or questionable.[8] Kingston, fortunately, has little evidence of this type of text, and may sin more by omission, for example the histories of manufacturing (such as Kingston's important role in manufacturing locomotives) and workers are areas that have been largely neglected. It was only in 1997 that Kingston Penitentiary's nationally significant contribution to the reform penitentiary movement was finally recognized (192, 220), while the national importance of Rockwood Lunatic Asylum as an innovative building type and state-of-the art hospital (for the 1870s) has yet to be noted on a marker.

As historic interpretations and sensibilities change with the times, what should be done about the older "dated" interpretation of history? Despite recent initiatives, the sheer volume of markers with traditional subject matter produced during the first years of commemoration ensures their exposure to the public,[9] and creates problems in revising their texts. It is also questionable whether we should be revising older texts, because the wording is itself part of the changing tide of history. For this reason it is desirable that the date of erection be included in the plaque wording. The onus is on us to consider carefully the topics of forthcoming markers to redress neglected events and people. There will likely be more debate about the need to record the typical and ordinary as opposed to the unusual and heroic in history and heritage.

The physical appearance of plaques has changed over the years. Those raised in the first half of the 20th century tended to be plain in appearance and brief in message, although examples with more ornamental aspects and sometimes made of brass with enameled detailing, were placed inside buildings and thus protected from weathering. In the second half of the century, the overall size increased reflecting longer texts. Plaques from the late 20th century are often quite large with bilingual messages and artwork. This may necessitate more than one plaque mounted on a common base, for example there are three panels for the Kingston Penitentiary marker of 1997 (220). Site plans, architectural schemes, and historical views help to explain written descriptions. High-relief artwork cast in bronze, as on the Portsmouth plaque of 1999 (193, 234), add to the aesthetic appeal of plaques. In this century we are likely to see a proliferation of large ceramic markers, capable of displaying long texts and numerous detailed illustrations in colour.

In the 1980s increasing consideration was given to installing plaques on freestanding posts, even if buildings relevant to the plaque text existed. Architectural conservators and historians were concerned that plaques attached to walls were damaging and distracted from the aesthetic appearance of historic buildings. Although attached plaques are being replaced, especially as bilingual versions

are cast, there are still examples in Kingston: Kingston Custom House (39), City Hall (16), and Bellevue House (186).

Monuments, memorials, and markers summarize our communal memories; they show the rich diversity of our history and tell us stories that should not be forgotten. Kingston can trace its marking program back into the 1820s, when the congregation of St Andrew's Presbyterian Church raised a stone monument (61) to mark the untimely death of their young minister the Rev. John Barclay. We can look to two statues raised in the 1890s: one to more than 1,400 persons who perished from an epidemic in the 1840s (205) and the other to the passing of one man, Sir John A. Macdonald, who meant so much to thousands of his fellow citizens (157). His memory is kept alive for millions of Canadians and visitors from other countries in part because of monuments and markers dedicated to his life and achievements. In 1950 a public appeal was made to add explanatory plaques on the pedestal of his statue to ensure the handing on of knowledge of "our Sir John," as he was affectionately known to his contemporary Kingstonians. In 1952 the federal government responded with the installation of a bronze plaque, which was replaced by a bilingual version in 1977. As recently as June 1999 a panel (203) with information regarding Macdonald's life and accomplishments and accompanied by a Canadian flag was placed at his gravesite in Cataraqui Cemetery as part of the national program of Parks Canada to honour the grave sites of Canadian Prime Ministers. By the end of the twentieth century there were more than 190 significant markers in the Kingston region, and it is apparent that we can look forward to this number increasing in this new century.

[1] Paul Litt, "Pliant Clio and Immutable Texts: The Historiography of a Historical Marking Program," *The Public Historian* 19 (1997): 7-28.

[2] Ibid., 8.

[3] Ibid., 14.

[4] Ibid., 15-16.

[5] Ibid., 18.

[6] Ibid., 19-21.

[7] Ibid., 22.

[8] Ibid., 7-8.

[9] Ibid., 26.

# Table of Markers by Installation Date and Sponsor

| YEAR | KINGSTON HISTORICAL SOCIETY | ONTARIO HERITAGE FOUNDATION | HISTORIC SITES AND MONUMENTS BOARD OF CANADA | OTHER |
|---|---|---|---|---|
| 1826 | | | | The Reverend John Barclay |
| c1834 | | | | Mechanics' Institute of Kingston |
| 1843 | | | | City Hall medallion |
| 1844 | | | | Commissariat Stores, Fort Henry |
| 1892 | | | | Kingston Collegiate Institute (KCI): KCI cornerstone; KCI at 100 Years |
| 1894 | | | | Angel of the Resurrection |
| 1895 | | | | Sir John A. Macdonald statue |
| 1900-04 | | | | Lord Sydenham; George M. Grant; Fleming Building cornerstone; Sir Sandford Fleming bust; Sir George A. Kirkpatrick fountain |
| 1905-09 | | | | |
| 1910-14 | | | | |
| 1915-19 | The Rev. John Stuart | | | 21st Battalion Memorial Cross; Frontenac Club Honour Roll |
| 1920-24 | First Queen's College; First Parliament of United Canada; Alwington House*; Stone Frigate*; Count Frontenac* | | First Meeting of the Executive Council; First Steamship on Lake Ontario | Memorial Hall; WWI Memorial in City Hall; Frontenac County WWI Memorial; Royal Military College (RMC) Memorial Arch; Laying of City Hall Cornerstone |
| 1925-29 | | | Fort Frontenac; Sir John A. Macdonald (110-112 Rideau St) | Cross of Sacrifice |

* Marker no longer in place

| YEAR | KINGSTON HISTORICAL SOCIETY | ONTARIO HERITAGE FOUNDATION | HISTORIC SITES AND MONUMENTS BOARD OF CANADA | OTHER |
|---|---|---|---|---|
| 1930-34 | | | Sir Charles Bagot; Lord Sydenham; Crawford Purchase | Royal Canadian Horse Artillery (RCHA) Memorial; 21st Battalion War Memorial; Henry W. Richardson; Samuel Dwight Chown; Sir Alexander Campbell |
| 1935-39 | | | Kingston Navy Yard; *Pro Patria*; Early Land Survey; Sir James Lucas Yeo | |
| 1940-44 | | | | The Rev. Robert McDowall |
| 1945-49 | | | Sir Richard Cartwright | Book of Remembrance (City Hall); 100 Years of Daily Newspaper Publication in Kingston; Queen's University War Memorial Room; Students' Memorial Union |
| 1950-54 | Bradstreet's Landing; Naval Engagement of 1812; John A. Macdonald (Bellevue House); Macdonald's First Law Office; Murney Tower* | | Murney Tower; Sir John A. Macdonald | 21st Canadian Infantry Battalion; Princess of Wales' Own Regiment (PWOR); RMC Astronomical Observatory; Garrison at Fort Henry; James A. Richardson |
| 1955-59 continued on next page | Kingston City Hall; Market Battery; Strange House; Sir George A. Kirkpatrick; Fort Frontenac; St Paul's Churchyard; Sir Richard Cartwright | Hillcroft; Government House; Fort Henry; Sir R. Bonnycastle; Heathfield; Bishop A. Macdonell; Stone Frigate; Rideau Canal; | | Stormont, Dundas & Glengarry (SD&G) Highlanders; Canadian Press Association; Fort Frontenac |

\* Marker no longer in place

| YEAR | KINGSTON HISTORICAL SOCIETY | ONTARIO HERITAGE FOUNDATION | HISTORIC SITES AND MONUMENTS BOARD OF CANADA | OTHER |
|---|---|---|---|---|
| **1955-59** continued | | La Salle; Summerhill; Militia Garrison; Daniel Fowler; Hawley House; Bath Academy | | |
| **1960-64** | Kingston Gas Light Company; Lt Col C.M. Strange*; Robert Rogers | The Rev. John Stuart; The Rev. John Langhorn; Sir Oliver Mowat; St Mark's Church; Escape of the *Royal George*; Founding of Queen's University*; Charles Sangster; RMC | | Royal Canadian Corps of Signals Memorial; Royal Canadian Electrical and Mechanical Engineers Memorial |
| **1965-69** | | René-Amable Boucher; Typhus Epidemic; Rush-Bagot Agreement; Rockwood Villa; Regiopolis College | Bellevue House; Kingston City Hall | Confederation Park; Canada's Centennial; Royal Canadian Air Force War Memorial; Fort Henry Guard Honour Roll; Tribute to the Planners, Builders and Restorers of Fort Henry |
| **1970-74** | | Madeleine de Roybon D'Allonne; Count Frontenac | Roselawn; Site of the First Legislature | Queen's Royal Charter; Tercentennial Sundial; Kingston's Tercentenary; Robert Sutherland; Donald Gordon Centre; RCHA Memorial; *HMCS Cataraqui* |
| **1975-79** | | Lt Col Edwin A. Baker; Molly Brant | Point Frederick Buildings | Dockyard Bell; 97-101 Yonge Street; Shoal Tower |
| **1980-84** | Women's Medical College; Meagher House; Molson Breweries | Loyalist Landing at Cataracoui; Founding of Bath; Point Frederick | Kingston Custom House; Kingston Post Office; Fort Henry; Sir E.P.C. Girouard; Sir John A. Macdonald | Sir John A. Macdonald gravesite; Sir Alexander Campbell; Orphans' Home; Loyalist Parkway; Kingston Collegiate Vocational Institute (KCVI) |

* Marker no longer in place

9

| YEAR | KINGSTON HISTORICAL SOCIETY | ONTARIO HERITAGE FOUNDATION | HISTORIC SITES AND MONUMENTS BOARD OF CANADA | OTHER |
|---|---|---|---|---|
| 1985-89 | | Kingston Observatory*; King's Royal Regiment of New York | Kingston Dry Dock; Frontenac County Court House | Queen's Medical Quadrangle; Ronald Way |
| 1990-94 | | | Queen's University; Kingston Fortifications; Wolfe Island Township Hall | First Hockey Game; Queen's University Sesquicentennial; Sir John A. Macdonald (Hazeldell, 79-81 Wellington Street, 180 & 194 Johnson Street, 343 King Street East, 134 Earl Street); KCVI (KCVI, Cornerstone, KCVI at 200 Years); Century of Engineering at Queen's; Sir John A. Macdonald gravesite; Workers on the Rideau; Naval Memorial; PWOR; Internment of Ukrainian Canadians; "Old Red Patch"; Freemasonry in Kingston |
| 1995-99 | Molly Brant; Portsmouth Village; Kingston: A City Since 1846 | | Molly Brant; Kingston General Hospital; Kingston Penitentiary; Ann Baillie Building; Elizabeth Cottage; Dr Jenny Trout | Burma Star War Memorial; King's Mills; Royal Canadian Artillery 125th; The Irish Famine; Robert Sutherland Memorial Room; Sir John A. Macdonald gravesite; Fairfield House |
| 2000- | | | | John Bennett Marks; Reeves of Pittsburgh Township; Pittsburgh Township 1787-1997; Hawthorn Cottage |

* Marker no longer in place

I T IS LIKELY that the rate of installing markers is affected by broad social, political, and economic factors in society, as well as local particular ones. Markers are the manifestation of society's fluctuating interest in the past. Previous to 1890 a large number of memorials were erected but of a special nature, namely to reflect the contribution of parishioners to their place of worship. Headstones in cemeteries and graveyards were another special category of memorial. It was only with the 1890s in this region that memorials took on a more public character both in location and in sentiment. During this decade there was a strong provincial and local interest in the past – more than one-hundred years, for example, having passed since Loyalist settlement in the first half of the 1780s and one-hundred years since the creation of Upper Canada in 1791. Kingstonians had only to look around to observe fewer and fewer landmarks surviving from that early era. They realized the generation who had lived through those pioneering days was no longer alive to tell their stories. The formation of the Kingston Historical Society in 1893 comes out of this context. Nationalism was an ever-growing phenomenon as Canada now existed "from sea to sea."

Marking activities were almost certainly curtailed during both World Wars when more pressing issues were in ascendancy. Times were also not auspicious for historical expenditures and ceremonies during economic set-backs such as

# Commentary on the Table of Markers by Installation, Date, and Sponsor

the Great Depression of the 1930s. The greatest peak of activity for marking occurred during the boom post-war years in the 1950s. Across the province there was a growth in urban centres and in industry. This was reflected in the strong sponsorship of plaques by the province, as well as by the Kingston Historical Society. Prosperity was accompanied by renewed anglophone nationalism. Kingston expressed confidence by expanding its boundaries to take in large areas of Kingston Township in 1952. Its industrial base was growing. Industrial production, however, began to shrink in the 1970s. In this decade there was a drop in the rate of installing markers. In the 1990s almost as many markers were installed as in the other peak period of the 1950s, but in the '90s the main sponsorship was from a variety of organizations. An ageing constituency of those who had served in the World Wars showed a particular interest in recording and commemorating traditional military groups and events. Other sponsors marked previously neglected and often disadvantaged groups and individuals. While the provincial government held back as a sponsor, the federal government erected nine bilingual plaques. One consistent figure picked out for commemoration from the 1890s to the 1990s was John A. Macdonald who holds a special place in the hearts of Kingstonians.

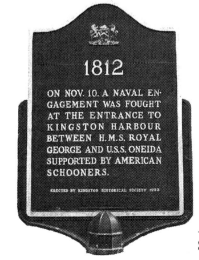

*Kingston Historical Society plaque.*
See also p. 141. Photo David Kasserra

# Directory of Markers

## How to Use the Directory

**Map** The entries are organized into 12 geographic sections, each with a map on coloured paper at the beginning. The map number links the entry with the appropriate map.

**Shaded Text Box** This part contains the text for the marker, memorial, or monument. In most cases, it has been transcribed directly. In a number of instances, adjustments have been made in the capitalization and punctuation (but without changing the wording of the inscription) to make it clearer for the reader. This was particularly true with monuments, which were usually written in upper case letters without any punctuation.

**Location** To assist in locating the marker, the civic address is usually provided. At larger locations such as Fort Henry and the Royal Military College, a more detailed description of the location is also given. Readers should use the section map in conjunction with the description of the location.

**Sponsor** The name of the organization responsible for erecting each plaque, monument, or memorial is recorded here. In most cases, this is recorded somewhere on the marker. Provincial plaques were initially erected by the Archaeological and Historic Sites Board of Ontario. In 1975, this responsibility was taken over by the Ontario Heritage Foundation. All plaques erected under provincial authority are shown as "Ontario Heritage Foundation" regardless of the date or name of the organization at the time the plaque was erected.

**Date** The date when the marker was first erected is recorded here. In the case of the Historic Sites and Monuments Board of Canada plaques, most of the early markers were replaced in the 1970s and 1980s with a bilingual version. In most cases, the text for the plaques was changed at the same time. The book contains only the current text. An example of the two versions of the plaque can be seen at 110-112 Rideau Street (62-3), where the 1927 plaque remained *in situ* when the new version was erected in 1982.

**Additional Information** This section provides further information on the person, event or site being commemorated. In some cases, there is additional information about the erection of the monument or marker.

**Readings** The reader can find more information on the subject of the commemoration by following up on the readings in the Bibliography. This section contains a list of readings, which is linked to the Bibliography by the author's name and year of publication. The entries in the Bibliography are arranged alphabetically by author. For example, Angus 1966 in the Readings section, refers to the entry in the Bibliography: Angus, Margaret. *The Old Stones of Kingston: Its Buildings before 1867*. Toronto: University of Toronto Press, 1966.

**Related Markers** The page numbers for markers which have related subject matter are noted here.

# I

# CITY HALL *and* CONFEDERATION PARK

# Map I

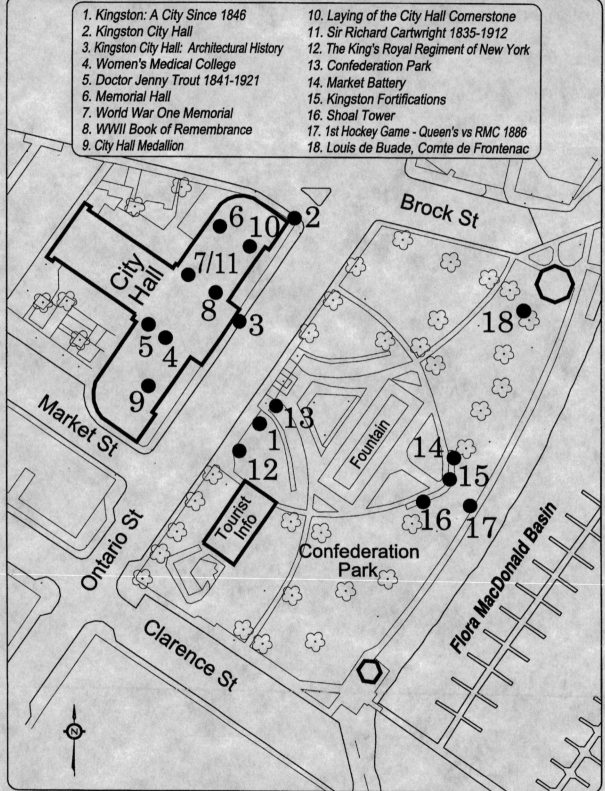

1. Kingston: A City Since 1846
2. Kingston City Hall
3. Kingston City Hall: Architectural History
4. Women's Medical College
5. Doctor Jenny Trout 1841-1921
6. Memorial Hall
7. World War One Memorial
8. WWII Book of Remembrance
9. City Hall Medallion
10. Laying of the City Hall Cornerstone
11. Sir Richard Cartwright 1835-1912
12. The King's Royal Regiment of New York
13. Confederation Park
14. Market Battery
15. Kingston Fortifications
16. Shoal Tower
17. 1st Hockey Game - Queen's vs RMC 1886
18. Louis de Buade, Comte de Frontenac

Strategic & Long-Range Planning - DJMartin

**Map I – 1**

# Kingston: A City Since 1846

*Location:* Confederation Park, opposite City Hall, 216 Ontario Street, Kingston

*Type:* Bronze plaque on post

*Sponsor:* Kingston Historical Society

*Date Erected:* 1996

*Additional Information:* Until census returns became available in the mid-nineteenth century, it was difficult to determine the population of Kingston. According to Preston, Kingston was little more than a village for the first 25 years after the Loyalist arrival. In 1792 Kingston had only 50 houses, a number which had increased to 150 at the start of the war in 1812. In the early 19th century Kingston was the premier town in Upper Canada with a population of about 2,500 in the early 1820s and 3,587 in 1830 (compared with 2,800 in Toronto). However by mid-century the population of Kingston was 11,585 while Toronto had increased to 30,775. By the end of the century Kingston's population was almost 18,000 while Toronto's had exceeded 200,000. In terms of geographic size Kingston was originally laid out within the area bounded by West Street, Rear Street (now Bagot) and North Street. With the expansion of Kingston in 1998 to take in Kingston and Pittsburgh Townships, Kingston now has a population of 112,605 (1996) within an area of 447 square kilometres.

*Related Markers:* 66, 72, 73, 154, 165

*Readings:* Roy 1952; Preston 1959; Rollason 1982; Mika 1987; Smith 1987; Osborne and Swainson 1988.

Successively an Indian encampment, a French fort and trading post, a United Empire Loyalist settlement and a British garrison town, Kingston owed its continuing military and commercial importance to its strategic position at the head of the St Lawrence River and the foot of the Great Lakes. Founded as Cataraqui in 1673, it became known as Kingston in 1788. It was the site of the first school and the first successful daily newspaper in Upper Canada. From 1841 to 1844 Kingston was the capital of the United Province of Canada. Late in the nineteenth century Kingston declined as a port and transportation centre; it has become a city of institutions and service industries – recreation, education, military, penal and health-care.

*View of Kingston from Fort Henry in 1855.* By Edwin Whitefield. Queen's University Archives

# Kingston City Hall

**Map I – 2**

Built during the mayoralty of John Counter, when Kingston was the capital of the Province of Canada. The corner stone was laid by the Governor General, Sir Charles Metcalfe, on June 5th, 1843, and the building was completed by November 21, 1844. The architect was George Browne.

*Location:* City Hall, 216 Ontario Street, Kingston, at the top of the exterior stairs on the Brock Street corner
*Type:* Aluminum plaque on wall
*Sponsor:* Kingston Historical Society
*Date Erected:* 1955
*Related Markers:* 17, 20, 22, 23, 186, 190, 196
*Readings:* Angus 1966; Stewart and Wilson 1973; Kingston City Hall 1974; Osborne and Swainson 1988; McKendry 1995.

*City Hall c1929.* National Archives of Canada, C-27705

Map I – 3

# Kingston City Hall: Its Architectural History

*Location:* City Hall, 216 Ontario Street, Kingston, main entrance
*Type:* Bronze plaque on building
*Sponsor:* Historic Sites and Monuments Board of Canada
*Date Erected:* 1967
*Additional Information:* Architect George Browne (1811-1885) emigrated in 1830 from Ireland to Quebec. As government architect he practised in Kingston from 1841 to 1844 when it was the capital of the United Province of Canada. He designed many important Kingston buildings including Rockwood Villa, the Commercial Mart, Wilson's Buildings, Hales' Cottages, Bellevue House (attribution) and Roselawn (attribution). The initial functions of the City Hall included, in addition to corporate offices, offices for lawyers and brokers, the post office, police quarters, shops, housing for welfare recipients, a newsroom, saloon, meat market, the Merchant's Exchange, and a Town Hall for meetings and dances. Since the amalgamation of the Townships of Pittsburgh and Kingston with the City of Kingston in 1998, the Corporation's space requirements have exceeded the capacity of this historic building.
*Related Markers:* 16, 20, 22, 23, 186, 190, 196
*Readings:* Angus 1966; Stewart and Wilson 1973; Kingston City Hall 1974; Osborne and Swainson 1988; McKendry 1995.

In 1843 the architect George Browne was commissioned to design a town hall in keeping with Kingston's status as a provincial capital. This building, one of the most ambitious examples of nineteenth century Canadian municipal architecture, was completed in 1844 at a cost of almost £20,000. It housed the municipal offices, the council chambers, and the town market, and also contained shops, other offices, and a saloon. A fire in 1865 destroyed part of the rear wing. The portico, removed in 1958, was rebuilt in 1966 by the City with the financial assistance of the federal government.

*City Hall, Market Square c1900.* Queen's University Archives

# Women's Medical College

Map I – 4

On June 8, 1883 the citizens of Kingston in City Hall assembled, founded Canada's first Women's Medical School. The City Council voted on August 6th, 1883 to donate the lease of Ontario Hall and the room above it to the Women's Medical College of Kingston for teaching purposes. When the College left City Hall in 1890, twenty-three young ladies had graduated MD CM from Queen's University to which the W.M.C. (K) was affiliated. Chairman: Sir Richard Cartwright, Vice-Chairman: W.W. Harty, Esq., President: Dr. Michael Lavell, Registrar: A.P. Knight, Esq.

*Location:* City Hall, 216 Ontario Street, Kingston, south interior stairway to third floor
*Type:* Brass plaque on wall
*Sponsor:* Kingston Historical Society
*Date Erected:* 1983
*Additional Information:* In 1883, after the Royal College of Physicians and Surgeons at Kingston refused women entry into their affiliation, the Women's Medical College was established. The college was originally located in the south wing of the City Hall, before moving to a house at 75 Union Street in 1890. In 1894, due to lack of students, the college closed its doors. The few women who were studying medicine were attracted to the larger medical schools in Toronto and Montreal. Queen's University did not allow women to be admitted to the Faculty of Medicine until 1943.
*Related Markers:* 19, 161
*Readings:* Hacker 1974; Travill 1982.

*Women's Medical College graduating class of 1889.* Queen's University Archives

**Map I – 5**

# Doctor Jenny Trout 1841-1921

*Location:* City Hall, 216 Ontario Street, south interior stairway to third floor, Kingston
*Type:* Bronze plaque on wall
*Sponsor:* Historic Sites and Monuments Board of Canada
*Date Erected:* 1999
*Additional Information:* Jenny Trout attended the 1871-1872 winter session of the Toronto School of Medicine. Although she survived the hostility of the men towards medical education for females, she transferred the following year to the Women's Medical College in Philadelphia. She returned to Toronto in 1875 and passed the licensing exams of the Ontario College of Physicians and Surgeons, thereby becoming the first woman licensed to practise medicine in Canada. In her efforts to encourage and support the medical education of young women, Dr Trout offered to donate $10,000 towards the establishment of a medical college for women in Toronto. Because of disagreements with the men who were proposing to run the Toronto facility, she withdrew her offer. Instead she pledged her support to the Kingston Women's Medical College which not only provided medical education for women but also had women represented on the College's management and faculty.
*Related Markers:* 18, 161
*Readings:* Hacker 1974; Travill 1982.

In 1875 Jenny Trout became the first woman licensed to practise medicine in Canada. Made famous by the event, Dr. Trout was a role model for women. She encouraged them through public lectures, private financial support, tutoring and counseling to follow her profession. The prejudice Dr. Trout faced in obtaining her own degree convinced her to advocate a separate medical college for women. Funded in part by Dr. Trout, the Kingston Women's Medical College, opened here in 1883, provided a segregated environment for study, and helped women overcome restrictions imposed by a male profession.

*Dr Jenny Trout, a benefactor of the Kingston Women's Medical College and the first woman physician who took the Medical Council licence in Canada.*
Queen's University Archives

# Memorial Hall

Map I – 6

On this the fourteenth day of December in the year of Our Lord 1921 and in the twelfth year of the reign of King George V, General, His Excellency The Lord Byng of Vimy, Governor-General of Canada unveiled the memorial tablets in this Hall and the Hall was dedicated as a Memorial Hall. Hugh C. Nickle, Mayor.

*Location:* City Hall, 216 Ontario Street, Kingston, to the left of the stage in Memorial Hall
*Type:* Bronze plaque on wall
*Sponsor:* City of Kingston
*Date Erected:* 1921
*Additional Information:* Previously known as the Town or City Hall, the north half of the second floor of Kingston City Hall was renovated in 1921 as Kingston's memorial to the fallen in the First World War. In the main the work consisted of replacing the ordinary glass in the hall's twelve windows with stained glass memorials of the war. The windows were constructed by Robert McCausland Ltd. Of Toronto. The topics and their relevance are (on one side): Ypres 1915, Canada's first battle; St Eloi, Engineers in war; Amiens 1918, Canadian cavalry; Somme 1916, Canadian industry; Jutland 1916, Royal Navy's biggest battle; Sanctuary Wood 1916, Family at home; (on the other side) Mons 1917, 42nd Canadian Infantry Battalion, Royal Highlanders; Scapa Flow 1918, Surrender of German Navy; Passchendaele 1917, Canadian artillery; Vimy 1917, Canadian soldiers' greatest victory; ; Lens 1917, Nurses at war; Cambrai 1918, Royal Flying Corps. After the Second World War the City of Kingston's war memorial took the shape of the Kingston Community Memorial Centre (a hockey arena) erected in the fair grounds. The cornerstone was laid by the Governor General, Field Marshal, Viscount Alexander of Tunis on 6 October 1950. The Kingston Naval Veteran's Association erected a plaque in the Centre's entrance foyer in remembrance of those from Kingston and District who gave their lives while serving with the Canadian Naval Forces in the Second World War.
*Related Markers:* 21, 151, 179
*Readings:* Kingston City Hall 1974; Cohoe 1995.

*"Canada! Ypres: April 22-24, 1915."* This cartoon was used in the design of the Ypres window in Memorial Hall, Kingston City Hall.
Drawing by Bernard Partridge, *Punch*, 5 May 1915.

**Map I – 7**

*Location:* City Hall, 216 Ontario Street, Kingston, Memorial Hall
*Type:* Two brass plaques on wall
*Sponsor:* City of Kingston
*Date Erected:* 1921
*Additional Information:* The names of the fallen are on the plaque.
*Related Markers:* 20, 151, 179
*Readings:* Nicholson 1962; Wilson 1977; Morton 1981; Rollason 1982.

**Map I – 8**

*Location:* City Hall, 216 Ontario Street, Kingston, Memorial Hall
*Type:* Book
*Sponsor:* City of Kingston
*Date Erected:* 6 August 1946
*Additional Information:* The names of 2,600 Kingstonians who served in the Second World War are listed in the Book of Remembrance, which is displayed under glass in a custom-made ornate wooden chest. It is decorated with five shields: one with the text above together with the Canadian Coat of Arms; one to each of the Services: Army, Navy, Air Force; and one to the Medical Services. The Book of Remembrance, which is highly decorated, was the work of George Wakeling.
*Related Markers:* 20, 151, 179
*Readings:* Nicholson 1962; Wilson 1977; Morton 1981; Rollason 1982.

# World War I Memorial

In honour of Kingston's Sailors, Soldiers, Airmen and Nursing Sisters who served overseas in The Great War 1914-1918.

In memory of those who fell in the Great War 1914-1918.
*Their name liveth for evermore*

# World War II Book of Remembrance

Kingston Centennial 1846-1946
Book of Remembrance 1939-1945

Photo David Kasserra

*George Wakeling, who designed and lettered Kingston's Book of Remembrance, is shown holding the book while Canada's governor general, Field Marshal Viscount Alexander reads aloud from the printed page.*
*Kingston Whig-Standard*

# City Hall Medallion

Map I – 9

On the [blank] day of [blank] in the year of Our Lord 1843 being the anniversary of the birthday of Queen Victoria and in the sixth year of her reign, the Right Hon. Sir Charles Theophilus Metcalfe, Bart., &c., Governor General of British North America, laid the first stone of this building, undertaken by the Common Council of Kingston. John Counter, Mayor. Aldermen: Henry H. Benson, Edward Noble, Joseph Thirkell, John A. Macdonald. Com.ⁿ Councilmen: Samuel Phippen, John H. Greer, John Shaw, Robert Anglen. George Browne being the Architect and Joseph Milner, Robert & James Fisher and Thomas C. Pidgeon being the Builders. Officers of the Common Council: Francis M. Hill, Clerk C.C.; James J. Burrowes, Treasurer; Richard Brassington, City Surveyor; Andrew Mayne, Collector; George Clarke, Assessor. A.D. 1843. G.E. Searle, Sc.

*Location:* City Hall, 216 Ontario Street, Kingston, second floor near Mayor's office
*Type:* Pewter medallion in case on wall
*Sponsor:* City of Kingston
*Date Erected:* 1843
*Additional Information:* This 8-inch diameter pewter medallion, engraved by G.E. Searle, was re-discovered during the City Hall renovations of the early 1970s. Its original location is unknown, and it appears never to have been used. One of the aldermen noted was John A. Macdonald, later the first Prime Minister of Canada. He served as an alderman from 1843-1846. From 1841-1844 Kingston was the first capital of the United Province of Canada.
*Related Markers:* 14, 15, 20, 23
*Readings:* Angus 1966; Kingston City Hall 1974; Osborne and Swainson 1988; McKendry 1995.

*Pewter medallion commemorating the laying of the foundation stone, 1843.* Queen's University Archives

Map I – 10

# Laying of the City Hall Cornerstone

*Location:* City Hall,
216 Ontario Street, Kingston,
Memorial Hall
*Type:* Bronze plaque on wall
*Sponsor:* City of Kingston
*Date Erected:* 1921
*Additional Information:* This plaque was unveiled by Lord Byng (1862-1935) who was governor general of Canada from 1921 to 1926. He had a British military background, and commanded the Canadian Corps in the attack on Vimy Ridge in April of 1917. In 1921 Memorial Hall was dedicated to the dead of the First World War.
*Related Markers:* 14, 15, 20, 22
*Readings:* Angus 1966;
Kingston City Hall 1974;
Osborne and Swainson 1988;
McKendry 1995.

On this the fifth day of June in the year of Our Lord 1843 and in the sixth year of the reign of Queen Victoria, His Excellency the Rt. Hon. Sir C. Theophilus Metcalfe, Bart., G.C.B. Governor General of British North America, laid the first stone of this building, undertaken by the Common Council of Kingston for the public accommodation and ornament of the City of Kingston. John Counter, Mayor.

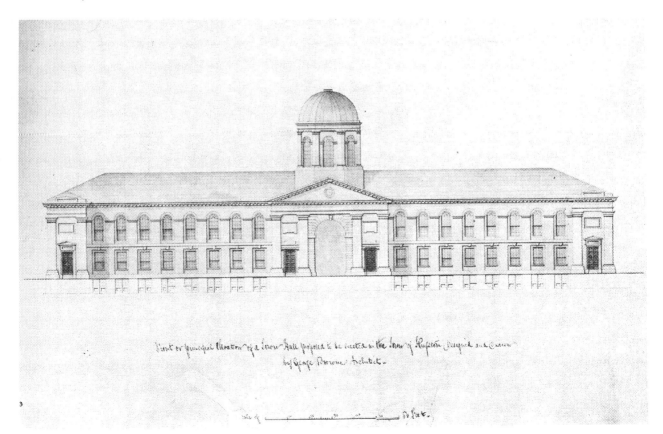

*Proposed elevation for Kingston town hall by architect George Browne in 1842.*
National Archives of Canada, Map Division, C-47411

# Sir Richard Cartwright
# 1835-1912

Map I – 11

Grandson of a prominent Loyalist merchant, Richard John Cartwright was born in Kingston, Upper Canada, and became a successful businessman. A Conservative in the Legislative Assembly of Canada (1863-67), he was later a Liberal member of the House of Commons for thirty-seven years (1867-1904), until appointed to the Senate. He served as Minister of Finance in the Mackenzie cabinet (1873-78) and under Laurier as Minister of Trade and Commerce (1896-1904). A renowned orator and free trader, he was the architect of the Liberal election policy of 1891 favouring unrestricted reciprocity with the United States. He died at Kingston.

*Location:* City Hall, 216 Ontario Street, Kingston, Memorial Hall
*Type:* Bronze plaque
*Sponsor:* Historic Sites and Monuments Board of Canada
*Date Erected:* 1948
*Related Markers:* 132
*Readings:* Cartwright 1912; Swainson 1968; DCB vol. 14.

*Sir Richard Cartwright.*
Queen's University Archives

Map I – 12

# The King's Royal Regiment of New York

**Location:** Confederation Park opposite City Hall,
216 Ontario Street, Kingston
**Type:** Aluminum plaque on post
**Sponsor:** Ontario Heritage Foundation
**Date Erected:** 1987
**Additional Information:** The 1st Battalion was disbanded on 24 December 1783; the following year 1,462 men, women, and children were settled in the five Royal Townships centred on Cornwall. The 2nd Battalion was disbanded on 21 July 1784, and 310 men, women, and children were settled in Cataraqui Townships 3 and 4 (Fredericksburg and Adolphustown).
**Related Markers:** 40, 41, 76
**Readings:** Cruikshank 1984.

The largest Loyalist Corps in the Northern Department during the American Revolution, the King's Royal Regiment of New York was raised on June 19, 1776 under the command of Sir John Johnson. Originally composed of one battalion with ten companies, it was authorized to add a second battalion in 1780. The regiment, known as the "Royal Yorkers," participated in the bitter war fought on the colonial frontier. It conducted raids against settlements in New York and was also employed in garrison duty. When active campaigning ceased in 1783, the regiment assumed various responsibilities, notably the establishment of a base here, in preparation for the settlement of the Loyalists. It was then fully disbanded, its officers and men settling near New Johnstown (Cornwall) and in the Cataraqui townships.

*Officer's sword-belt plate, c1780*
Nor'wester-Loyalist Museum, Glengarry Historical Society, Martintown, Ontario

# Confederation Park

Map I – 13

Established in 1967 in honour of Sir John A. Macdonald, First Prime Minister of Canada and Member of Parliament for Kingston. A special grant provided by the Government of the Province of Ontario made possible the construction of the Park.

*Location:* Confederation Park, Ontario Street, Kingston, on the retaining wall directly in front of the stage
*Type:* Brass plaque
*Sponsor:* City of Kingston
*Date Erected:* 1967
*Additional Information:* The evolution of the functions of this site, from the Market Battery to its present recreational purpose reflects significant stages of Kingston's history. The Market Battery, built to defend Kingston in 1848 during the fortification construction period, was dismantled in 1875. The Kingston and Pembroke Railway Station (once known as the "Kick and Push," now the Tourist Information Centre) was built in 1885 by architect William Newlands. Purchased by the Canadian Pacific Railway Company in 1913 it served as Kingston's "Inner Station" until 1961. The area was redesigned as a centennial project and named Confederation Park in 1967.
*Related Markers:* 27, 143
*Readings:* Roy 1952; Preston 1959; Bennett 1981; Mika 1987; Smith 1987; Osborne and Swainson 1988.

*The basin fronting Confederation Park was constructed in 1968. The additional breakwater to the south was completed in 1988, and the entire marina complex named the Flora MacDonald Confederation Basin.*
Photo David Kasserra

Map I – 14

# Market Battery

**Location:** Centre of Confederation Park, Ontario Street, Kingston, on a reconstruction of the Market Battery wall
**Type:** Aluminum plaque
**Sponsor:** Kingston Historical Society
**Date Erected:** 1955
**Additional Information:** The Market Battery was designed to complement the Shoal Tower and Fort Frederick in protecting the water approaches to the entrance of the Rideau Canal. Nine guns (2-32 pdrs., 7-24 pdrs.) were mounted in the battery. Structurally, it was a walled area that included most of what is now Confederation Park. In 1875 the wall along Ontario Street, the gates and guardroom were demolished and a park for civic celebrations was created. In 1885 the remainder of the battery was taken down and the area was given over to the railway. Stone from the Market Battery was used for the construction of the gatehouses at the Military College and for the railway station that remains on the site of the Market Battery. When the railway no longer needed access to the waterfront, the City acquired the land in the 1960s and transformed it into Confederation Park.
**Related Markers:** 26, 28, 29, 88, 94, 95, 142
**Readings:** Walkem 1897b; Lavell 1936; Parks Canada 1976; Mika 1987; Osborne and Swainson 1988; McKendry 1995.

Stood on this site from 1848 to 1875. With Shoal Tower opposite it defended Kingston harbour and the Rideau Canal. From 1875 this was a public park. In 1885 the Kingston and Pembroke Railway station was built.

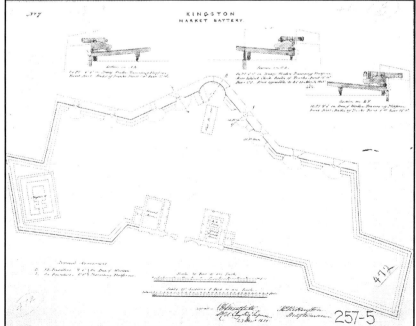

*Plan of the Market Battery, 1851.*
By Pilkington. National Map Collection, National Archives of Canada, C-51520

# Kingston Fortifications

Map I – 15

The site of the Royal Naval Dockyard during the War of 1812, Kingston assumed even greater strategic importance as the southern terminus of the Rideau Canal, which was built between 1826 and 1832. An extensive fortification plan of redoubts, towers, and batteries was developed to protect the dockyard and entrance to the canal, but only Fort Henry was actually built. In response to the Oregon Crisis with the United States in 1845-1846, four Martello towers and the Market Battery, which stood on this site, were constructed between 1846 and 1848.

*Location:* Centre of Confederation Park, Ontario Street, Kingston, on a reconstruction of the Market Battery wall
*Type:* Bronze plaque
*Sponsor:* Historic Sites and Monuments Board of Canada
*Date Erected:* 1992
*Additional Information:* Although the War of 1812 ended without Upper Canada falling into American hands, there was concern about what might happen in the future and a recognition that the Americans were unlikely to make the same mistake again of not cutting off the connection to the sea via the St Lawrence River. The British began to develop plans for better protection of Kingston not only because of the Royal Naval Dockyard but also as the southern terminus of the Rideau Canal, an inland water supply route. In addition to Fort Henry, the fortification plan for Kingston called for a further five redoubts, six towers and three batteries at an additional cost of £200,000. Kingston would have been a well defended town with three redoubts similar to Fort Henry planned to defend the western land approaches to Kingston and Fort Henry plus two others protecting the eastern approaches.
*Related Markers:* 27, 29, 88, 94, 95, 142
*Readings:* Walkem 1897b; Lavell 1936; Parks Canada 1976; Patterson 1981; Osborne and Swainson 1988, Fort Henry.

*Looking out to Cathcart Tower on Cedar Island from Fort Henry.*
Photo David Kasserra

Map I – 16

# Shoal Tower

**Location:** Centre of Confederation Park, Ontario Street, Kingston, on a reconstruction of the Market Battery wall
**Type:** Bronze plaque
**Sponsor:** Parks Canada
**Date Erected:** 1977

**Additional Information:** Because the Shoal Tower was completely surrounded by water, its construction was a challenge to the contractor William Murray and the sub-contractor John Greer. A coffer dam was constructed on the ice in March 1846 – a dam which was 90 feet in diameter and 7½ feet high. According to Harris (p. 176) it took 15 pumps, manned by six or seven men each, to pump out the coffer dam. It was mid-June before the interior was pumped dry and construction could begin. Remnants of the coffer dam remain submerged in the water around the tower.

**Related Markers:** 27, 28, 88, 94, 95, 142

**Readings:** Walkem 1897b; Lavell 1936; Parks Canada 1976; Osborne and Swainson 1988.

The massive round tower rising from the bottom of the harbour in front of you is a reminder of less peaceful days along the Canadian-American border. The threat of war in 1845 prompted British military engineers to expand the existing fortifications at Kingston. Strategically located at the entrance of the Rideau Canal as well as at the juncture of the St. Lawrence and the Great Lakes, Kingston was considered the key city in the defence of Upper Canada. By 1848, the Victoria (commonly known as Shoal) Tower and three other Martello Towers had been added to the city's defences. If an attack had occurred, British gunners could have defended the approaches to the harbour, behind stone walls up to 14 feet thick. The guns of the Shoal Tower with the nearby Fort Frederick and the Market Battery effectively blocked the entrance to the Rideau Canal. While 16 towers were built in British North America, the Shoal Tower is unique as it is the only one completely surrounded by water. By the 1860s, the Shoal Tower became obsolete because of new improvements in artillery. It continued to serve for a few years afterwards as married quarters for the Royal Canadian Rifle Regiment. Today, the Shoal Tower is preserved for present and future generations by Parks Canada.

*Shoal Tower, with the Royal Military College and Fort Frederick in the background.*
Queen's University Archives

# First Hockey Game
# Queen's vs RMC 1886

Map I – 17

First Hockey Game – Kingston – Queen's vs. Royal Military College March 10 1886.
International Hockey Hall of Fame and Museum.

*Location:* Confederation Park, Ontario Street, Kingston, near the waterfront pathway
*Type:* Stone bench
*Sponsor:* International Hockey Hall of Fame and Museum
*Date Erected:* 1990
*Additional Information:* The earliest printed reference to "hockey" played on ice refers to a game played by British soldiers garrisoned in Kingston in 1843. It is generally believed that hockey was conceived in Halifax, and born as an organized game with rules in Montreal in 1875. The first game played in Kingston under organized rules was in 1886, on harbour ice near Shoal Tower. Queen's defeated RMC 1-0. On 7 November 1990, Mayor Helen Cooper unveiled the grey granite bench commemorating the first hockey game between the Royal Military College and Queen's University, March 1886. The bench overlooks the waters of Confederation Basin, the location of this first game. The International Hockey Museum is located at York and Alfred Streets in Kingston.
*Related Markers:* 82, 174, 175
*Readings:* Fitsell 1982; Fitsell 1987.

*Historic hockey re-enactment of first game played on Kingston Harbour ice, 10 March 1886. These games have been held annually since 1969.* Painting by Irene McKim, courtesy J.W. Fitsell

Map I – 18

# Louis de Buade, Comte de Frontenac et de Palluau 1622-1698

**Location:** Confederation Park, Ontario Street, Kingston, in the north-east corncr near the tour boat ticket booth
**Type:** Aluminum plaque on post
**Sponsor:** Ontario Heritage Foundation
**Date Erected:** 1973
**Additional Information:** A small plaque near the bottom of the main post commemorates the unveiling of this plaque by Queen Elizabeth II. See also p. 32.
**Related Markers:** 68, 72, 73, 154
**Readings:** Eccles 1959; DCB vol. 1; Le Sueur 1964; Syme 1969; O'Brien 1975.

One of the most influential and controversial figures in Canadian history, Frontenac was born at St-Germaine-en-Laye, France. As a member of the noblesse d'épée he was able in 1672 to secure the appointment as Governor-General of New France. Devoted largely because of self-interest to promoting the colony's territorial expansion, Frontenac established a series of fortified fur-trading posts extending into the interior of North America, the first of which, Fort Frontenac, was constructed near here in 1673. He quarreled incessantly with other officials, however, and as a result was recalled in 1682. Reappointed seven years later, Frontenac successfully defended New France from attacks by the Iroquois and English and continued, until his death in Quebec, to expand the western fur trade.

*A modern painting by A. Sherriff Scott of Frontenac at Cataraqui 1673.*
Agnes Etherington Art Centre, Queen's University

*Dr Margaret Angus, President of the Kingston Historical Society, applauds as Queen Elizabeth II unveils the Ontario Heritage Foundation plaque for Count Frontenac in Confederation Park, Kingston 27 June 1973.* See also p. 31.

*Historic Kingston*, vol.22 (March 1974), Kingston Historical Society

# II

# DOWNTOWN KINGSTON

**Map II**　　　　　　　　　　**Downtown Kingston**

1. HMCS Cataraqui
2. Macdonald's Law Office
3. Macdonald's First Law Office
4. First Meeting of the Executive
   Council of Upper Canada
5. Kingston Custom House
6. The Rev. John Stuart 1740-1811
7. The Rev. John Stuart
8. Charles Edward Poulett Thomson
9. René-Amable Boucher 1735-1812
10. Kingston Post Office
11. Freemasonry in Kingston
12. Regiopolis College
13. Elizabeth Cottage
14. Queen's Sesquicentennial

Map II – 1

# HMCS Cataraqui

**Location:** Holiday Inn, 1 Princess Street, Kingston, just inside the lobby

**Type:** Two brass plaques on wall

**Sponsor:** Royal Canadian Naval Reserve Division

**Date Erected:** 1972 (upper)

**Additional Information:** The site of the present Holiday Inn is a dock on which the Richardson feed mill and grain elevator were located. The Naval Reserve was housed in the building during the Second World War. In August 1945 *HMCS Cataraqui* was moved to the Wellington Street School where it remained until 1958. It then moved into new quarters at the Royal Military College where it stayed until 1972 when the building was incorporated into RMC's new gymnasium complex. *HMCS Cataraqui* next moved to the Kingston Armouries sharing accommodation with the Princess of Wales' Own Regiment until 1992. That year a new facility for *HMCS Cataraqui* was built on the east bank of the Cataraqui River at the La Salle Causeway.

**Related Markers:** 20, 135

**Readings:** Rollason 1982; German 1990; Halford 1994; Crickard 1996.

This site was the first location of H.M.C.S. Cataraqui, Kingston's Naval Reserve Division, commissioned on 13th February 1940. The plaque was unveiled on the occasion of the 50th anniversary of the Canadian Naval Reserve by Commander W.C. Rigney (Retired).

Between September 1939 and August 1945 Kingston's Royal Canadian Naval Training Division occupied this site, W.C. Rigney, 1st Commanding Officer. During the course of World War II 3,211 men and women went forth from here to serve with distinction wherever duty called. This memorial is testimony to these volunteers and to those who made the supreme sacrifice in defence of the freedom we now enjoy.

*Porta lacum, portus classis*

*HMCS Cataraqui Ship's Badge.*
*Badges of the Canadian Forces*

# Macdonald's Law Office
# 343 King Street East

Map II – 2

Sir John A. Macdonald
Father of Confederation, First Prime Minister of Canada.
343 King Street East
In this building John A. Macdonald and his partners had a law office from 1849 until 1860. The firm then moved to 93 Clarence Street. Macdonald maintained a law practice throughout his political career.

*Location:* 343 King Street East, Kingston
*Type:* Bronze plaque on wall
*Sponsor:* Parks Canada
*Date Erected:* 1992
*Additional Information:* After the dissolution of his law partnership with Alexander Campbell in 1849, Macdonald moved his law office to this location. In September 1854 he took on a new partner, Archibald J. Macdonell. They remained in this building until 1860 when they moved their offices to a nearby building owned by Macdonell at 93 Clarence Street. Throughout his legal career, although he had a number of different offices in Kingston, he remained in the heart of the city, never moving more than a few blocks.
*Related Markers:* 37, 62, 123, 125, 126, 130, 157, 186, 187, 195, 201, 202, 203
*Readings:* Creighton 1952; Creighton 1955; Newman 1974; Angus 1984; Swainson 1979; Swainson 1989; DCB vol. 12.

*John A. Macdonald in 1865.* Queen's University Archives

Map II – 3

# Macdonald's First Law Office

*Location:* 171 Wellington Street, Kingston
*Type:* Aluminum plaque on wall
*Sponsor:* Kingston Historical Society
*Date Erected:* 1954
*Additional Information:* Legal training in Upper Canada in the early 19th century was done on an apprenticeship basis with qualifying exams administered by the Law Society of Upper Canada. When only fifteen years old, Macdonald was articled to George Mackenzie, a Kingston lawyer. In 1831 Mackenzie's office, with home above, was located near the corner of Store and Quarry Streets (now Princess and Wellington Streets) in the heart of the business section of Kingston and only a short distance from the waterfront. Within a short time, Macdonald was in Napanee opening a branch office for Mackenzie and then to Picton to help in the law office of his ill cousin. In the summer of 1834 his mentor Mackenzie died of cholera but Macdonald did not return to Kingston until the following summer. Although he opened his first law office in August 1835, it was not until February 1836 that he was finally "called to the degree of Barrister at Law."
*Related Markers:* 36, 62, 123, 125, 126, 130, 157, 186, 187, 195, 201, 202, 203
*Readings:* Creighton 1952; Creighton 1955; Newman 1974; Angus 1984; Swainson 1979; Swainson 1989; DCB, vol. 12.

In this building, John A. Macdonald, Father of Confederation and first Prime Minister of the Dominion of Canada, began the practice of law in 1835.

---

**JOHN A. MACDONALD,**

ATTORNEY, &c.

HAS opened his office, in the brick building belonging to Mr. Collar, opposite the Shop of D. Prentiss, Esq., Quarry Street, where he will attend to all the duties of the profession.

Kingston, 24th August, 1835. 17cw

National Library of Canada, NL-9790

# The First Meeting of the Executive Council of Upper Canada

Map II – 4

Because of the loyalist influx into the western part of Quebec after the American Revolution, the province was divided into Upper and Lower Canada (now Ontario and Quebec). The Constitutional Act of 1791 provided for representative government in each of the new provinces. On July 8, 1792, John Graves Simcoe, Lieutenant Governor of Upper Canada, met his Executive Council in St. George's Church which once occupied this site. In the following three weeks the Council divided the province into counties and allocated representation to the Assembly that was to meet at Newark (later Niagara-on-the-Lake) in September.

*Location:* 346 King Street East, Kingston [Not presently in place]
*Type:* Bronze plaque on wall
*Sponsor:* Historic Sites and Monuments Board of Canada
*Date Erected:* 1923
*Additional Information:* With the creation of Upper Canada in 1791, the citizens of Kingston hoped that, as the leading community in the province, it would become the seat of government. Although the government was proclaimed at St George's Church, the subsequent meetings of the Executive Council were probably held in the Commanding Officer's House (later known as Government House) which stood in the intersection of the present-day Queen and King Streets. Simcoe moved on to Newark where the legislature met until it was eventually moved to York, now known as Toronto. The Commanding Officer's House stood until 1821 when it was removed because it was blocking Queen Street.
*Readings:* Cruikshank 1924; Preston 1959; DCB vol. 5; Mecredy 1984

*St George's Church 1792.*
Queen's University Archives

Map II – 5

# Kingston Custom House

*Location:* 294 King Street East Kingston
*Type:* Bronze plaque on wall
*Sponsor:* Historic Sites and Monuments Board of Canada
*Date Erected:* 1981
*Related Markers:* 44
*Readings:* McKendry 1995.

Designed by the Montreal architectural firm of Hopkins, Lawford and Nelson, the Kingston Custom House was built in 1856-59 for the government of the united Canadas. The symmetrical composition of the two-storey ashlar building, surmounted by a restrained cornice and parapet, draws on the British classical tradition. The orderly design is achieved through repeated use of semi-circular forms for doors and windows. The Custom House and the nearby Post Office are fine examples of the architectural quality of mid-nineteenth century administrative buildings.

*The Custom House decorated for the diamond jubilee of Confederation in July 1927.*
National Archives of Canada, PA-57417

# The Reverend John Stuart
# 1740-1811

Map II – 6

Born in Pennsylvania, Stuart was ordained in 1770 and sent to Fort Hunter, N.Y., as missionary to the Mohawks. An ardent Loyalist he came to Canada in 1781 where he was appointed chaplain to the 2nd Battalion King's Royal Regiment of New York. In 1785, having settled at Cataraqui (Kingston), he became the first resident Anglican clergyman in what is now Ontario. Stuart ministered to the white and Indian settlers of this area and visited as far west as Niagara and the Grand River. He was the first chaplain of the legislative council of Upper Canada and was responsible for the building of Kingston's earliest church, St. George's, in 1792.

*Location:* St George's Cathedral, King Street East and Johnson Street, Kingston, on the front lawn
*Type:* Aluminum plaque on post
*Sponsor:* Ontario Heritage Foundation
**Date Erected:** 1960
*Additional Information:* The Reverend John Stuart's church was a small frame building erected in 1792 facing the market square on King Street East. In 1825, a second St George's was built in stone by his son the Reverend George Stuart (1776-1862). The church became a cathedral in 1862.
*Related Markers:* 25, 38, 41
*Readings:* Stewart 1973; Carruthers 1975; Swainson 1991.

*Plaque unveiling 9 October 1960. From left to right: The Hon. W.M. Nickle; The Most Rev. W.L. Wright* DD DCL *Archbishop of Algoma; The Very Rev. A.T. Briarly Brown,* DD, *Dean and Rector of St George's Cathedral; Alderman E. Watts of Kingston; Prof. G.F.G. Stanley of RMC; and B.W. Trumpour of the Kingston Historical Society.* Photo courtesy Bogart Trumpour

Map II – 7

# The Reverend John Stuart

**Map II – 7**

*Location:* St George's Cathedral, King Street East and Johnson Street, Kingston, inside the nave
*Type:* Ceramic tile in marble frame on wall
*Sponsor:* Kingston Historical Society
*Date Erected:* 1916
*Additional Information:* This is one of the earliest surviving plaques raised by the Kingston Historical Society who contributed $100 towards the project. Funds were also raised by the sales of George Starr's book *Old St George's: Being the Story of a Church and its Ministers in a Historic Centre of Upper Canada* (Kingston: Uglow, 1913). The plaque's wording follows closely that of the one lost during the cathedral's burning in 1899. Starr was the Dean of St George's and President of the Kingston Historical Society. The large horizontal plaque with its curved top is unusual because of its materials: ceramic coloured tile forming a mosaic and bordered by a reddish-purple marble frame. There is an inner border formed by ceramic pieces – green with a blue lozenge on each section, the latter are subdivided by narrow gold bands, and in the four main corners are red squares. The inner border curves over a gold cross near the top of the plaque. Gray tiles form the background for the text, which has been baked onto the tile itself.
*Related Markers:* 25, 38, 40
*Readings:* Flynn 1964; Stewart 1973; Carruthers 1975; Swainson 1991.

In sacred memory of the Reverend John Stuart D.D., 1740-1811, who came to this Province in 1784 as a United Empire Loyalist, and was known as "The Father of the Church in Upper Canada." He founded this cathedral (the first parish in the Province) and also the first school. He was Chaplain to the Garrison, and to the first Legislative Council, and for 27 years was Rector of Kingston. Associated with Tyendenaga (Chief Brant), he translated the Gospels and Book of Common Prayer into the Mohawk tongue. He was instrumental in founding many important missions throughout the province from Cornwall to York. *Universally Beloved this Intrepid Herald of the Gospel Fell Asleep August 15th, 1811.*
W.L. Grant, Secretary. G.L. Starr, President.

*Erected in 1916, this is one of the earliest surviving plaques placed by the Kingston Historical Society.* Photo David Kasserra

# Charles Edward Poulett Thomson, Baron Sydenham

Map II – 8

In the vault of this church rest the remains of the Right Honourable Charles Poulett Thomson, Baron Sydenham of Sydenham, Kent, Eng. and Toronto, U.C. Born at Waverly, Surrey, Eng. 13th Sept. 1799. Died at Kingston, Upper Canada, 19th Sept. 1841. First Governor General of British North America, 1839 to 1841. Erected by the Government of Ontario in 1901, on petition of the National Council of Women of Canada, to replace the original tablet destroyed by fire 1st January 1899.

*Location:* St George's Cathedral, corner of King Street East and Johnson Street, Kingston, inside, over the nave door

*Type:* Marble plaque on wall

*Sponsor:* Government of Ontario

*Date Erected:* 1901

*Additional Information:* Lord Sydenham arrived in Kingston in late May 1841 to take up official residence in Alwington House, where he lay dying only a few months later after a fall from his horse. The monument of 1901 is a handsome elaborate affair with a classical frame surrounding an inscribed rectangular panel. The frame features Ionic columns and a broken pediment that has a shield with the arms of Lord Sydenham at the apex. The large sum of $500 was spent on the tablet in 1900. Professor J. Douglas Stewart has argued that it is a replica of one made in England in 1843 to the design of architect George Browne (and lost in the fire of 1899) (Stewart 1991, pp 100-101).

*Related Markers:* 163, 189

*Readings:* Scrope 1844; Machar 1908; Shortt 1926; Angus 1967; Careless 1967; DCB vol. 7; Stewart 1991.

*Lord Sydenham.* Queen's University Archives

*St George's Cathedral 1791-1956.* (1953)

Map II – 9

# René-Amable Boucher 1735-1812

*Location:* Boucher Park, Clarence Street (between King Street East and Wellington Street), Kingston
*Type:* Aluminum plaque on post
*Sponsor:* Ontario Heritage Foundation
*Date Erected:* 1965
*Readings:* Preston 1959; DCB vol 5.

Boucher was born at Fort Frontenac (Kingston) where his father, an officer with the French colonial regular troops, was stationed. René-Amable also chose a military career and served in the Seven Years War with the French defenders of Canada. During the American Revolution, he was captain of a volunteer company of French Canadian militia and fought with the British under General John Burgoyne. In Quebec, and later in Lower Canada, Boucher sat on the legislative council; he also served as a magistrate of the Mecklenberg (later Midland) District of Upper Canada. From 1782 until his death he devoted much time and energy to managing and developing his seigneury of Boucherville, a community of more than 2,000 inhabitants located near Montreal.

*Plaque commemorating René-Amable Boucher with St George's Cathedral's dome in the background.*
Photo David Kasserra

# Kingston Post Office

Map II – 10

In 1856-59 the government of the united Canadas erected the Kingston Post Office. Designed by the Montreal architectural firm of Hopkins, Lawford and Nelson, this limestone building shows the influence of the British classical style, particularly as it derived from Italian Renaissance palace architecture. The pronounced rustication of the ground storey contrasts with the refined details of the upper level to create a balanced, harmonious composition. Planned in conjunction with the nearby Custom House, the Post Office contributes to the dignified quality of this nineteenth century streetscape.

*Location:* 86 Clarence Street, Kingston
*Type:* Bronze plaque on wall
*Sponsor:* Historic Sites and Monuments Board of Canada
*Date Erected:* 1981
*Additional Information:* John Power (1816-1882) supervised the construction of the post office. The builders were Matthew and Overend. Today the building houses various federal government offices.
*Related Markers:* 39
*Readings:* Stewart and Wilson 1973; McKendry 1995.

*Kingston Post Office before the addition on Wellington Street.* Queen's University Archives

Map II – 11

# Freemasonry in Kingston

*Location:* 126 Wellington Street, Kingston
*Type:* Marble plaque on wall
*Sponsor:* M.W. Bro. C. Edwin Drew, Grand Master
*Date Erected:* 1994
*Additional Information:* Freemasonry is an international fraternity for mutual help and fellowship with elaborate secret rituals. It claims precursors among the medieval building corporations, but its modern origins began in the British Isles in the early eighteenth century. By the close of the nineteenth century there were 10,000 lodges and one million members. Certain United Empire Loyalists who settled in the Kingston region in the 1780s, were masons. John Collins who surveyed this area, was the Provincial Grand Master of the Province of Quebec (which included modern Ontario). The first formal meeting of Kingston masons took place 7 August 1794 in Freemason's Tavern, run by John Daley, on King Street East at Barrack Street. Those attending included Richard Cartwright, Christopher Danby, John Daley, John Walker, and John C. Stewart. The membership grew to 18 by early 1795. Freemasonry enhanced social standing and cemented business and political interests. Significant members included Captain Bonnycastle of the Royal Engineers (later Sir Richard Bonnycastle) who was initiated in 1827 and John A. Macdonald (later Prime Minister of Canada) initiated in 1844.
*Related Markers:* 36, 37, 62, 96, 123, 125, 126, 130, 157, 158, 186, 187, 195, 201, 202, 203
*Readings:* Robertson 1900.

Presented to the Ancient St. John's Lodge No. 3 A.F. & A.M., G.R.C. Kingston, Ontario August 6, 1994 to commemorate two hundred years of Masonry 1794-1994. M.W. Bro. C. Edwin Drew Grand Master Grand Lodge A.F. & A.M. of Canada in the province of Ontario.

*Since 1794 lodges have been held in various buildings including the St John's Masonic Hall from 1825 to 1833. This was Brother John McArthur's stone house (now demolished) on Princess Street. On the gable wall was the compass and square ensignia associated with Freemasonry.* By W.J. Thomson. National Archives of Canada, C-20886

# Regiopolis College

Map II – 12

Regiopolis College, incorporated March 4, 1837, by an Act of legislature of Upper Canada, opened in the central portion of this building. Its corner-stone was laid by the school's founder, Bishop Alexander Macdonell, on June 11, 1839. In 1866 the College was given full degree-granting powers, although these were rarely used. Financial difficulties forced its closing in 1869. In 1892 the building was acquired by the Religious Hospitallers of St. Joseph who opened here the Hôtel Dieu Hospital. The school re-opened on King Street in 1896 and, in 1915, moved to the northern part of the city. In 1931 the diocesan clergy transferred the College to the Jesuit Order.

*Location:* Hotel Dieu Hospital, 123 Sydenham Street, Kingston
*Type:* Aluminum plaque on post
*Sponsor:* Ontario Heritage Foundation
*Date Erected:* 1969
*Additional Information:* "The College of Regiopolis at Kingston is located in a handsome and spacious, but unfinished stone edifice, termed the Seminary in the midst of what was once called Selma Park, the property of the late Bishop Macdonell, and which he devoted during his life time to religious purposes. The number of scholars of all ages, and of all classes, is nigh to a hundred, and the Teachers, Professors, we should say, are numerous in proportion." *Daily British Whig,* 13 April 1850.
*Related Markers:* 128
*Readings:* Roy 1952; Mika 1987; Osborne and Swainson 1988; Regiopolis College.

*Regiopolis College (now part of Hotel Dieu Hospital) in 1871.*
From a photograph by H. Henderson reproduced in *Canadian Illustrated News,* 17 June 1871.

Map II – 13

# Elizabeth Cottage

*Location:* 251 Brock Street, Kingston

*Type:* Bronze plaque

*Sponsor:* Historic Sites and Monuments Board of Canada

*Date Erected:* 1999

*Additional Information:* In 1846 Edward Horsey (1809-1869) acquired the post of architect of Kingston Penitentiary. He then turned to designing Elizabeth Cottage as his architectural office and home for his wife Jane and their seven children. He sought the ideas for the Gothic Revival Style in American pattern books, as did architect William Newlands (1854-1926), when he converted the house into a double in 1883 for Horsey's son-in-law, Dr Fyfe Fowler. In 1954 Fowler's daughter, Louisa, donated the property for use as a retirement home.

*Readings:* Angus 1966

Elizabeth Cottage is a charming example of the Gothic Revival style. Reputedly built in the 1840s with a later addition, it is the work of Kingston architect, Edward Horsey, and originally served as his residence. The lively design features steeply pointed gables, projecting bays, and oriel windows which accentuate the play of light and shadow on the smooth stucco walls. Applied Gothic decorative details such as crockets, finials, and drip moldings heighten the picturesque effect. The Gothic Revival was particularly fashionable for residences in Ontario in the mid-19th century.

*Elizabeth Cottage c1870.* Queen's University Archives

# Queen's University Sesquicentennial 1841-1991

Map II – 14

The following members of the Synod of the Presbyterian Church in Canada in connection with the Church of Scotland are honoured for their role in the founding of Queen's University. They obtained an Act of Incorporation from the Upper Canada Legislature on February 10, 1840. This act was replaced with the bestowal of the name "Queen's College" by the granting of a Royal Charter from Her Majesty Queen Victoria on October 16, 1841. These members who initially met in St Andrew's Church at Kingston on May 20, 1840 formed the first Board of Trustees, under the chairmanship of the Hon. William Morris.

The Rev. Robert McGill; The Rev. Alexander Gale; The Rev. John McKenzie; The Rev. William Rintoul; The Rev. William T. Leach; The Rev. James George; The Rev. John Machar; The Rev. Peter Colin Campbell; The Rev. John Cruickshank; The Rev. Alexander Mathieson; The Rev. John Cook; The Rev. Robert J. McDowall; The Hon. John Hamilton; The Hon. James Crooks; The Hon. William Morris; The Hon. Archibald McLean; The Hon. John McDonald; The Hon. Peter McGill; Edward W. Thomson; Thomas McKay; James Morris; John Ewart; John Steele; John Mowat; Alexander Pringle; John Munn; John Strang.

*Location:* St Andrew's Presbyterian Church, 130 Clergy Street East at Princess Street, Kingston, in the nave
*Type:* bronze plaque on wall
*Date Erected:* 1991
*Sponsor:* St Andrew's Presbyterian Church
*Related Markers:* 168, 174, 175
*Readings:* Neatby 1978; Gibson 1983; Queen's University Alumni Association 1990.

*St Andrew's Church and Manse c1850.*
National Archives of Canada, C-20881

# WEST *of the* GREAT CATARAQUI RIVER

1. Strange House
2. Stormont, Dundas & Glengarry Highlanders
3. The Meagher House
4. St Paul's Churchyard 1783
5. Molly Brant
6. 21st Canadian Infantry Battalion
7. 21st Battalion Memorial Cross
8. Princess of Wales' Own Regiment
9. PWOR Memorial
10. The First Location of Queen's College
11. The Reverend John Barclay
12. Sir J.A.Macdonald
13. Mary (Molly) Brant (Tekonwatonti)
14. Molly Brant (Konwatsi'tsaienni Degonwadonti)
15. One Hundred Years of Daily Newspaper Publication in Kingston
16. The Canadian Press Association

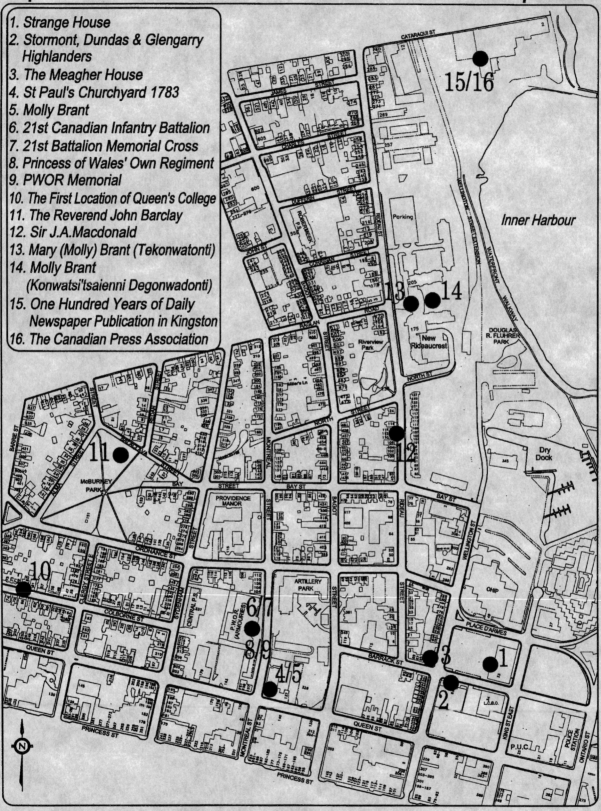

Map III– 1

# Strange House

**Location:** 55 Barrack Street, Kingston, facing the parking lot

**Type:** Aluminum plaque on wall

**Sponsor:** Kingston Historical Society

**Date Erected:** 1957

**Additional Information:** The Strange House, a handsome two-storey stone building in the neo-classical style, stood on the corner of King and Barrack Streets until the mid-1950s. One of John Strange's descendants, Lt Col Courtlandt MacLean Strange (1867-1958), son of Orlando and Ann Strange, was acting president of the Kingston Historical Society between 1941 and 1951, and president until his death in 1958. He advocated for the restoration of Fort Henry in the 1930s. A marker for Lt Col C.M. Strange was erected by the Kingston Historical Society in 1961. This plaque was located in Murney Tower, Macdonald Park, but has since been removed. It read "Born in Kingston Courtlandt Strange served in the Princess of Wales' Own Regiment and in the Westmount Rifles. For many years he was the president of the Kingston Historical Society and curator of the Murney Tower Historical Museum."

**Readings:** Anonymous 1958.

On this site stood a cut limestone house built 1824-26 by Captain John Strange 1788-1840, of the Frontenac Militia, father of Maxwell William Strange, M.L.A., 1820-1880 and of Orlando Sampson Strange, M.D., 1826-1909.

*The Strange House built by Captain John Strange.* Kingston Whig-Standard

51

# Stormont, Dundas and Glengarry Highlanders

Map III – 2

In remembrance of those who served with the Stormont, Dundas & Glengarry Highlanders and who gave their lives during the Second World War.

*They shall not grow old in our memory.*

**Location:** 64 Barrack Street, Kingston, in front of the No 9 Legion building
**Type:** Bronze plaque on wall
**Sponsor:** 1st Battalion, Stormont, Dundas & Glengarry Highlanders Association
**Date Erected:** c1956
**Additional Information:** This plaque was originally mounted in the Kingston Community Memorial Centre, which is situated on the fair-grounds, the location where the 1st Battalion concentrated after being mobilized on 18 June 1940. Formed from the Prince of Wales Rangers (Peterborough), Princess of Wales' Own Regiment (Kingston), Brockville Rifles (Brockville), and the parent regiment (Cornwall), the unit went into action on D-Day as part of the 9th Highland Brigade, 3rd Canadian Infantry Division. It was the first Allied unit into the City of Caen, the linchpin of the German defences in Normandy. By the end of the war it had won 10 battle honours: Normandy, Caen, Falaise, Boulogne 1944, The Scheldt, Breskin Pocket, The Rhineland, The Hochwald, The Rhine, and Leer. The Regiment, an active unit of the Canadian Militia, has its origins in the Upper Canadian militia units of the United Counties of Stormont, Dundas and Glengarry in eastern Ontario. Its formal lineage dates from 3 July 1868 with the formation of the 59th Stormont and Glengarry Battalion of Infantry. In the First World War it formed the basis of the 154th Overseas Battalion (Highlanders) which, although broken up for reinforcements, was granted three battle honours: Ypres 1917, Amiens, and Pursuit to Mons. The Regiment's present title dates from 15 February 1922 when it adopted the Macdonell of Glengarry tartan, in tribute to its first Honourary Colonel, Lieutenant General Sir A.C. Macdonell, who was Commandant of the Royal Military College (1919-1925) and also President of the Kingston Historical Society from 1921 to 1926.
**Related Markers:** 58, 59
**Readings:** Boss and Patterson 1995.

*Regimental badge of the SD&G Highlanders, with their motto "Faithful unto Death" written in Gaelic.*

# The Meagher House

Map III – 3

*Location:* 85 Barrack Street, Kingston
*Type:* Aluminum plaque on post
*Sponsor:* Kingston Historical Society in co-operation with Meagher's Distillery Limited
*Date Erected:* 1984
*Additional Information:* Pointed arches in the fanlight add a Gothic Revival touch to this otherwise traditional two-storey Kingston house, with its parapet endwalls and finely worked front stone work.
*Readings:* City of Kingston vol. 2; Fitsell 1985.

John Meagher (1816-1878), third son of Major James Meagher of Tipperary, Ireland, built this stone residence on Lot E, Barrack at Wellington Streets, in 1855. A produce agent and wine merchant he was a partner with his brothers, Jeremiah and James, M.D., in Meagher's Distillery of neighbouring Napanee, 1862-63. Five of his 13 children were pioneer figure skaters and won gold medals for performances throughout North America and Europe. John, Jr. (1847-1909) and Joseph G.C. (1849-1911) moved to Montreal in 1873 and established Meagher Brothers Distillery, which became Meagher's Distillery Limited, Canada's largest producer of fine liqueurs, and marketers of other spirits. From 1876 to 1892 the House was owned by Samuel Anglin (1843-1920) and S. Anglin and Co., Kingston.

Photo David Kasserra

# St Paul's Churchyard 1783

Map III – 4

Formerly St. George's burial ground, this cemetery is the oldest in the Kingston district. Among the distinguished persons buried here are Molly Brant, Reverend John Stuart, Lieutenant Hugh Earl (Provincial Marine), Colonel Sir Richard Bonnycastle, and the Honourable Richard Cartwright.

*Location:* St Paul's Churchyard, 137 Queen Street, Kingston
*Type:* Aluminum plaque on post
*Sponsor:* Kingston Historical Society
*Date Erected:* 1958
*Additional Information:* The first burial in this graveyard was likely in 1783 and in the following years the grounds were enclosed by a wooden fence. In the first decade of the 19th century St George's (Anglican) Church built a stone fence in part to establish their rights over the burial ground. St Paul's (Anglican) Church was built in 1845 in the graveyard and when the Parish Hall was built in 1872, a number of gravestones disappeared from view. In the 1930s seventy-one memorials were identified in the graveyard, but Molly Brant's (c1736-1796) was not found.
*Related Markers:* 24, 40, 41, 55, 64, 96, 132
*Readings:* Long 1955; Preston 1956; Anderson 1963.

Photo David Kasserra

Map III – 5

# Molly Brant

**Location:** St Paul's Churchyard, 137 Queen Street, Kingston

**Type:** Aluminum plaque on post

**Sponsor:** Ontario Heritage Foundation

**Date Erected:** 1975

**Additional Information:** Parishioners of St George's were buried in the graveyard located on the property now known as St Paul's Churchyard. Molly Brant was a staunch supporter and generous contributor to St George's Church (now Cathedral). The Reverend John Stuart, the first minister at St George's and a friend of Molly Brant, had been a missionary to the Mohawks at Fort Hunter (New York), and had conducted services at Sir William Johnson's church in Johnstown. It was the Reverend John Stuart who conducted her funeral service on 16 April 1796 as he had conducted Johnson's when he died in 1774 in Johnstown. Molly Brant is buried in an unmarked grave (her marker may have been lost during a church fire in 1854) along with other Loyalists who settled in Kingston. There are no known portraits of Molly Brant during her lifetime.

**Related Markers:** 40, 41, 54, 64

**Readings:** Preston 1959; Wilson 1976; DCB vol. 4; Thomas 1989; Thomas 1996; Bazely 1997; Benedict 1997; Maracle 1997.

Born about 1736, Molly Brant (Degonwadonti) was a member of a prominent Mohawk family. About 1759 she became the wife of Sir William Johnson, Superintendent of Indian Affairs in the Province of New York and a powerful figure in that colony. Well-educated and a persuasive speaker, Molly Brant wielded great influence among the Iroquois and was responsible for much of Johnson's success in dealing with them. Following the outbreak of the American Revolution she and her younger brother Joseph played a leading role in persuading the Confederacy to support Britain. In 1777 she fled to Canada and after the war, in recognition of her services, was granted a pension by the government. She settled in Cataraqui (Kingston), where she died in 1796.

*On Sunday 21 September 1975, a historical plaque commemorating Molly Brant was unveiled on the grounds of St Paul's Anglican Church. Shown from left to right after the unveiling are: Mr Bogart Trumpour, President, Kingston Historical Society; His Worship G. N. Speal, Mayor of Kingston; Mrs W.G. Simmons; Mr Keith Norton MPP (Kingston and the Islands); The Right Reverend Jack Creegan, former Bishop of Ontario; Mr Ian Wilson, President, Ontario Historical Society; Mrs Marian Bradshaw, representative of the Ontario Heritage Foundation; and Mrs W.G. Stinson.*
Ontario Heritage Foundation

# 21st Canadian Infantry Battalion

Map III – 6

This tablet commemorates the mobilization of the 21st Canadian Infantry Battalion under the command of Lieut. Col. (later Brig.-General) W. St. Pierre Hughes, D.S.O., V.D., in the armouries 19th October 1914. The Battalion proceeded overseas 6th May 1915, to France 15th of September 1915, was demobilized on returning to Kingston 24th May 1919. Other Commanding Officers: Lieut. Col. Elmer W. Jones, D.S.O., Lieut. Col. F. Elmitt, D.S.O., Lieut. Col. H.E. Pense, D.S.O., M.C. The Battalion is perpetuated in the Princess of Wales' Own Regiment, Kingston Ont. This tablet further records with gratitude the spirit of loyalty and comradeship that prevailed among all ranks during the war and still endures.

*To all those who made the supreme sacrifice we pay our humble tribute. They shall grow not old as we that are left grow old; age shall not weary them nor the years condemn. At the going down by the sun and in the morning we will remember them.*

**Location:** Kingston Armouries, 100 Montreal Street, Kingston, inside on the west wall
**Type:** Bronze plaque
**Sponsor:** 21st Battalion Association
**Date Erected:** 1950
**Additional Information:** The 21st Battalion was one of the most famous Canadian infantry battalions of the First World War. Formed around a nucleus of the 14th Regiment, The Princess of Wales' Own Rifles, the 21st became part of the 4th Canadian Infantry Brigade, 2nd Canadian Division. In action from 15 September 1915 until 11 November 1918, 830 men were killed and over 2,000 wounded. For its outstanding record it led the 2nd Division's triumphant march over the Rhine.
**Related Markers:** 57, 155
**Readings:** Mackenzie-Naughton 1946.

*21st Battalion crossing the Rhine at Bonn, 13 December 1918.*

Map III – 7

# 21st Battalion
# Memorial Cross

*Location:* Kingston Armouries, 100 Montreal Street, Kingston, inside on the west wall
*Type:* Painted wooden cross
*Sponsor:* 21st Battalion Association
*Date Erected:* 1917
*Additional Information:* On 9 April 1917 the 21st Battalion was part of the Canadian Corps, which successfully attacked and captured Vimy Ridge, one of the outstanding victories of the First World War. This cross was originally erected on Vimy Ridge shortly after the battle, but was brought back to Kingston by the 21st Battalion in 1919 and erected on the grounds of the Royal Military College. In 1994 it was moved to this location.
*Related Markers:* 56, 155
*Readings:* Mackenzie-Naughton 1946.

In memory of the officers, N.C.O.'s and men of the 21st Canadian Infantry Battalion killed in action April 9th, 1917.

Photo courtesy Major E.F. Joyner

# Princess of Wales' Own Regiment

Map III – 8

This plaque is dedicated to the members of the Princess of Wales' Own Regiment (MG) who served in the Stormont, Dundas and Glengarry Highlanders First Battalion and to their comrades, who gave their lives for their country in the Second World War, by the Officers and Senior Non-Commissioned Officers of the Princess of Wales' Own Regiment, on 12 November 1994. *These men were infantry. They fought the hard way — yard by yard, and mile by bloody mile. Who would have thought that they'd have come out with a smile, knowing the hell they'd left behind and carried with them in their heart.* T. Saunders

*Location:* Kingston Armouries, 100 Montreal Street, Kingston, inside on the west wall
*Type:* Wooden plaque
*Sponsor:* Princess of Wales' Own Regiment
*Date Erected:* 1994
*Additional Information:* This plaque acknowledges the services of members of the Regiment who formed 'A' Company of the SD&G Highlanders upon its mobilization in 1940. For its service the Regiment was awarded an Honourary Distinction. The badge of the SD&G Highlanders with the dates 1944-1945 is emblazoned on the bottom centre of the Regimental Colour.
**Related Markers:** 52, 59
*Readings:* Mackenzie-Naughton 1946; Boss and Patterson 1995.

*The Regimental Colour of the Princess of Wales' Own Regiment.*
Princess of Wales' Own Regiment

Map III – 9

# Princess of Wales' Own Regiment Memorial

*Location:* Kingston Armouries, 100 Montreal Street, Kingston, inside on the west wall
*Type:* Bronze plaque
*Sponsor:* Princess of Wales' Own Regiment
*Date Erected:* 1950
*Additional Information:* The Regiment, an active unit of the Canadian Militia, perpetuates the 21st Battalion, Canadian Expeditionary Force, and includes ten of its battle honours on the Regimental Colour. In addition the Regiment is entitled to the battle honour, South Africa, 1901, and an honourary distinction, the badge of the SD&G Highlanders, 1944-1945.
*Related Markers:* 52, 58
*Readings:* Mackenzie-Naughton 1946.

This tablet is erected in commemoration of the formation of the First Volunteer Militia Company of Kingston, 16 August 1855, and the organization of the Volunteer Rifle Companies into the 14th Battalion, 16th January 1863, and designated the Princess of Wales' Own Rifles and re-designated the Princess of Wales' Own Regiment 20th March 1920. In proud recollection of the services of officers and other ranks of the Regiment during the Fenian Raid 1866, The Red River Expedition 1870, The North-West Rebellion 1885, The South African War 1900-1901, The First Great War 1914-1918, The Second Great War 1939-1945.
*And in abiding memory of those who gave their lives on active service in defence of Canada and the Empire. Then Lord, in thy Mercy, grant them safe lodging, a holy rest and peace at the last. Amen*

*The regimental badge of the PWOR, with the mottoes "Nunquam cede" (Never Yield) and "Ich Dien" (I Serve)*

# The First Location of Queen's College

Map III – 10

The first classes of Queens College met in this building in March 1842.

*Location:* 67 Colborne Street, Kingston
*Type:* Bronze tablet on wall
*Sponsor:* Kingston Historical Society
*Date Erected:* 1923
*Additional Information:* On 7 March 1842 the first classes of Queen's College (now Queen's University) were held in a small rented house at 67 Colborne Street. There were 13 students and two professors, Principal Thomas Liddell and Peter Colin Campbell. The College stayed here for only six months, the first of many locations. In 1854 classes were held in a building – Summerhill – that was purchased by the College and that became the core of the university campus that we know today.
*Related Markers:* 169, 174, 175
*Readings:* Angus 1972; Neatby 1978; Gibson 1983; Osborne and Swainson 1988.

*An early photograph of 67 Colborne Street.* Queen's University Archives

Map III – 11

# The Reverend John Barclay

*Location:* McBurney Park, Balaclava Street , Kingston
*Type:* Stone monument
*Sponsor:* St Andrew's Presbyterian Church Congregation
*Date Erected:* 1826
*Additional Information:* This stone grave marker is the only surviving example from an early graveyard, once divided by fences into the last resting places for Anglicans, Presbyterians, and Roman Catholics. Headstones and remains were moved by families over the years to Cataraqui Cemetery. In 1893 the neglected graveyard became a public park, known as Frontenac Park, Skeleton Park, and now McBurney Park.
*Readings:* Edmison 1953; Ross; Stewart 1991.

Sacred to the memory of The Rev'd John Barclay M.A., first Minister of St. Andrew's Church Kingston who departed this life the 26 Sept. 1826 in the 30th year of his age and 5th of his ministry.

*The Barclay monument is the largest marker in this late 19th-century view of the Upper Burial Ground.*

# Sir John Alexander Macdonald

Map III – 12

Statesman and patriot. His boyhood days, those critical years that decide the character of the man, were spent here in the old town which has seen more than a century of Canadian history.

Born in Scotland, Macdonald's formative years were spent here in the historic old town of Kingston. His superb skills kept him at the centre of public life for fifty years. The political genius of Confederation, he became Canada's first prime minister in 1867, held that office for nineteen years (1867-73 and 1878-91), and presided over the expansion of Canada to its present boundaries excluding Newfoundland. His National Policy and the building of the CPR were equally indicative of his determination to resist the north-south pull of geography and to create and preserve a strong country politically free and commercially autonomous.

*Location:* 110 & 112 Rideau Street, Kingston
*Type:* Bronze plaques on wall
*Sponsor:* Historic Sites and Monuments Board of Canada
*Date Erected:* 1927 (uniligual), 1983 (bilingual)
*Additional Information:* Because the 50th anniversary of Confederation fell in the midst of the First World War, the celebrations were limited. With the economic boom of the 1920s, Canada had a much more significant celebration in 1927 for the Diamond Jubilee of Confederation. The Rideau Street plaque for Sir John A. Macdonald, the first of the Macdonald plaques in Kingston, was erected as part of the commemoration for the architect of Confederation (top plaque text). With the implementation of the Canadian government's bilingualism policy, most of the pre-1960s federal plaques were replaced with new bilingual plaques in the 1970s and early 1980s. In a number of places across Canada, concern was expressed over the loss of the historic plaques that many saw as an important expression of Canada's culture and heritage of an earlier time period. At this site, a compromise was reached whereby the new bilingual plaque (bottom plaque text) was erected but the unilingual 1927 plaque was not removed, as was the usual procedure. This two-storey stone house, built in the early 19th-century, was owned by Macdonald's relatives, the Macphersons, at the time he lived in it as a young lawyer in the 1830s.
*Related Markers:* 36, 37, 123, 125, 126, 130, 157, 186, 187, 195, 201, 202, 203
*Readings:* Creighton 1952; Creighton 1955; Newman 1974; Angus 1984; Swainson 1979; Swainson 1989; DCB vol. 12.

*19th-century view of 110-112 Rideau Street.* National Archives of Canada

*1999 view of 110-112 Rideau Street.*
Queen's University Archives

# Mary (Molly) Brant (Tekonwatonti) c1736-1796

Map III – 13 &14

A Mohawk woman of great diplomatic skill, Molly Brant exerted an extraordinary influence on the powerful Iroquois confederacy. During the American Revolutionary War, she passed valuable information to British troops and in 1777 was forced by the rebels to flee her homeland in the colony of New York. Living at military posts, she emerged as a persuasive speaker, exhorting the Iroquois to maintain their traditional alliance with the British Crown. After the war this remarkable Loyalist settled near here. Molly Brant's tireless efforts helped preserve Canada from American conquest.

# Molly Brant (Konwatsi'tsaienni Degonwadonti)

Mohawk matriarch and British patriot, was settled here in 1783 by British Governor Haldimand, with a pension and a house overlooking the Great Cataraqui River. A respected Kingston pioneer and a founder of St. George's Cathedral, she lived here until her death in 1796. She is buried in St. Paul's churchyard.

*Location:* Rideaucrest Retirement Home, 175 Rideau Street, Kingston, in the back courtyard
*Type:* Bronze bust on stone cairn
*Sponsor:* Kingston Historical Society
*Date Erected:* 1996

*Location:* Rideaucrest Retirement Home, 175 Rideau Street, Kingston
*Type:* Trilingual bronze plaque on post
*Sponsor:* Historic Sites and Monuments Board of Canada
*Date Erected:* 1996
*Additional Information:* With the outbreak of the American Revolution, Molly Brant and her family remained loyal to the British crown. With the resettlement of the Loyalists at Cataraqui (Kingston) in 1784, Governor Haldimand provided a house for Molly Brant and her children. Historian Earle Thomas described it as 1½ storeys, with a frontage of 40 feet and a depth of 30 feet, situated on the high ground overlooking the Cataraqui River. As a result of archaeological work conducted in 1988 by the Cataraqui Archaeological Research Foundation, it is suggested that Molly Brant's home was located on what is now the Rideaucrest Home property. The federal plaque, the Kingston Historical Society's plaque and bust by sculptor John Boxtel were all unveiled as part of an extensive ceremony, which took place at St George's Cathedral, the cemetery at St Paul's Church, and at Rideaucrest on 25th August 1996, the 200th anniversary of her death.
*Related Markers:* 54, 55
*Readings:* Preston 1959; Wilson 1976; DCB vol. 4; Thomas 1989; Thomas 1996; Bazely 1997; Benedict 1997; Maracle 1997.

*Artist's rendition of Molly Brant.*

© Canada Post Corporation, 1986. Reproduced with permission.

# One Hundred Years of Daily Newspaper Publication in Kingston

Map III – 15

February 7, 1834: Dr. Edward Barker founded *The British Whig* as a semi-weekly organ of news and comment. January 1, 1849: *The British Whig* began daily publication. January 1, 1872: Dr. Barker retired and was succeeded by his grandson, Edward John Barker Pense, who continued as publisher until his death, May 7, 1910. April 1, 1925: William Rupert Davies purchased *The British Whig* from the Estate of E.J.B. Pense. December 1, 1926: *The British Whig* amalgamated with the *Kingston Daily Standard* to form *The Kingston Whig-Standard* under the joint ownership of Rupert Davies and Harry Basil Muir. January 25, 1939: Harry B. Muir died; Rupert Davies purchased his interest and became sole owner. December 31, 1948: *The British Whig* and its successor, *The Kingston Whig-Standard,* completed one hundred years of daily newspaper publication.

*Location:* Woollen Mill, 6 Cataraqui Street, Kingston, in the Whig-Standard lobby
*Type:* Brass plaque on wall
*Sponsor: Kingston Whig-Standard*
*Date Erected:* 1948
*Additional Information:* Both of the plaques (66, 67) were originally erected at the *Whig-Standard's* offices and printing plant located at 306-310 King Street East. This building had been the location for the *British Whig's* operations since 1894. The *Whig-Standard* remained in the Davies family until 1990 when it became part of the Southam chain of newspapers. In 1997 the *Whig-Standard* moved from King Street to its present location on Cataraqui Street, where it continues publication as the oldest continuous daily newspaper in Canada.
*Readings:* Edmison 1960; Fetherling 1993.

*British Whig press room, c1890. Kingston Whig-Standard,* 8 January 1949

Map III – 16

# The Canadian Press Association

*Location:* Woollen Mill,
6 Cataraqui Street, Kingston,
in Whig-Standard lobby
*Type:* Brass plaque on wall
*Sponsor:* Canadian Daily
Newspaper Publishers
Association
*Date Erected:* 1959

The first association of Canadian newspaper publishers was organized at Kingston, September 27, 1859. The first officers: W. Gillespy, *Hamilton Spectator;* J.G. Brown, *Toronto Globe;* Josiah Blackburn, *London Free Press;* D. McDougall, *Berlin Telegraph;* Thomas Sellar, *Montreal Echo;* George Sheppard, *Toronto Globe;* James Seymour, *St. Catharines Constitutional;* James Somerville, *Dundas Banner;* Thomas McIntosh, *Brantford Expositor;* John Jacques, *Milton Journal.* Other newspapers represented: *Kingston British Whig – Belleville Intelligencer – Picton Times – Brockville Recorder – Kingston News – Montreal Gazette – Cornwall Freeholder – Barrie Advance – Whitby Watchman – Napanee Standard – Belleville Independent – Kingston Herald – Milton New Era.*

This plaque erected in grateful remembrance.

*British Whig building, 306-310 King Street East, c1905.*
Queen's University Archives

*United Empire Loyalists, settled 1784, Kingston, Ontario.* See also p. 134.

Photo David Kasserra

*Founding Fort Frontenac at Cataraqui, July, 1673. Louis Henri Buade, Comte de Palluau et de Frontenac & Company with Algonquins meet Mohawks, Oneidas, Onondagas, Cayugas, Senecas & Hurons. Onontio Torontes'hati.* See also p. 31.

Photo David Kasserra

Presented to the City of Kingston in commemoration of its tercentennial in 1973, these large brass plaques in bas-relief are often used to make decorative paper rubbings. Located in the foyer of City Hall, 216 Ontario Street, they were created by E.H. (Ted) (1917-1990) Wakeling and donated by Du Pont Canada Inc.

# FORT FRONTENAC
## *and the*
# ROYAL MILITARY COLLEGE

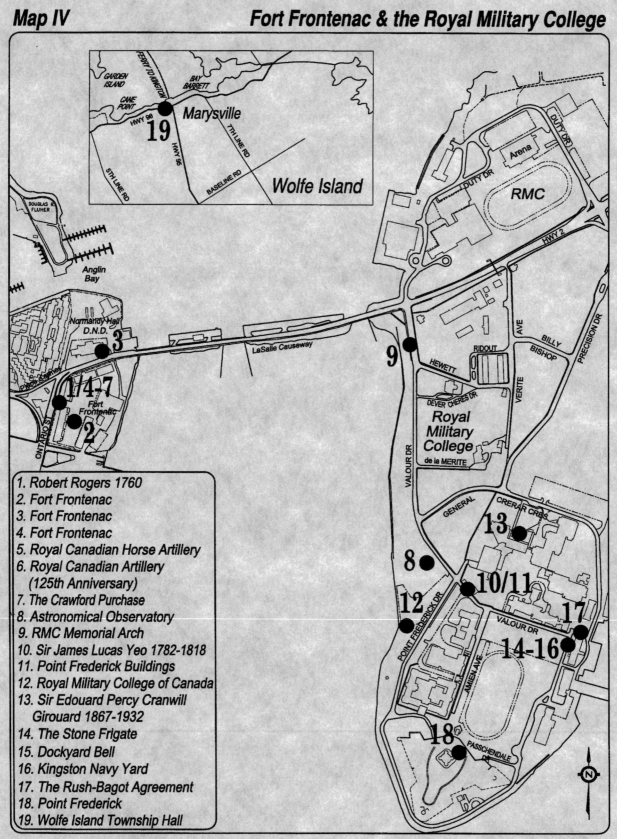

1. Robert Rogers 1760
2. Fort Frontenac
3. Fort Frontenac
4. Fort Frontenac
5. Royal Canadian Horse Artillery
6. Royal Canadian Artillery
   (125th Anniversary)
7. The Crawford Purchase
8. Astronomical Observatory
9. RMC Memorial Arch
10. Sir James Lucas Yeo 1782-1818
11. Point Frederick Buildings
12. Royal Military College of Canada
13. Sir Edouard Percy Cranwill
    Girouard 1867-1932
14. The Stone Frigate
15. Dockyard Bell
16. Kingston Navy Yard
17. The Rush-Bagot Agreement
18. Point Frederick
19. Wolfe Island Township Hall

*Strategic & Long-Range Planning - DJMartin*

Map IV – 1

**Location:** Fort Frontenac
(Canadian Land Forces Command and Staff College)
Ontario and Place d'Armes
Streets, Kingston, at the
entrance
**Type:** Brass plaque on wall
**Sponsor:** Kingston Historical
Society
**Date Erected:** 1961
**Additional Information:** Robert
Rogers was born in Metheun,
Massachusetts in 1731, and
died in London, England in
1795. Rogers led the colonial
Rangers during the Seven
Years' War, 1755-1763, as well
as during the War of Austrian
Succession, 1743-1748.
Rogers raised and led the
Loyalist Queen's (later
King's) Rangers during the
American Revolution. However, his most significant
achievements were not his
wartime exploits but his literary works. He published his
wartime journals, as well as *A
Concise Account of North America,* to name but a few.
**Related Markers:** 25
**Readings:** Rogers 1769;
Jackson 1953; Cuneo 1959;
DCB vol. 3.

# Robert Rogers 1760

Major Robert Rogers of Rogers Rangers camped
near here September 23-25, 1760, while on his
way to take over the western posts from the
French after capitulation of Montreal.

*Imaginary portrait c1776 of Robert Rogers.*
National Archives of Canada, C-6875

# Fort Frontenac

Map IV – 2

In 1673, Louis de Buade, Comte de Palluau et de Frontenac, Governor of New France, directed that a fortification be raised on this site. The Fort consisted of earthworks and log palisades. Between the years 1675-1685 Robert Cavelier, Sieur de la Salle, strengthened the Fort by adding stone bastions and a stone wall on the landward side. In Sep 1689 the fort was abandoned and partially destroyed by order of Jacques Rene de Brisay, Marquis de Denonville, then Governor of New France. In Oct 1689, the Comte de Frontenac was re-appointed Governor and in 1695 he supervised the rebuilding of the Fort. It was completed in stone as in early French plan above. On 28 Jul 1758 the Fort was captured by a British Force under Lt Col Bradstreet.

*Location:* Fort Frontenac (Canadian Land Forces Command and Staff College) Ontario and Place d'Armes Streets, Kingston, on the excavated bastion inside (check with the Commissionaire at the Guard Room to the right of the entrance)
*Type:* Brass plaque
*Sponsor:* Department of National Defence
*Date Erected:* 1959
*Additional Information:* A reconstruction of one of the bastions is found on Ontario Street at Place d'Armes Street.
*Related Markers:* 73, 154, 183
*Readings:* Horsey 1937; Preston and Lamontagne 1958; Grimshaw 1993; Canadian 1995.

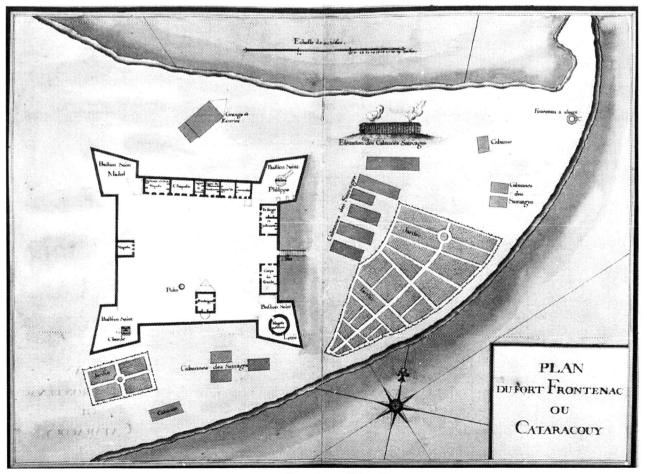

*Site plan of Fort Frontenac c1720.* Newberry Library, Chicago

Map IV – 3

*Location:* Fort Frontenac
(Canadian Land Forces
Command and Staff College),
Ontario Street, Kingston,
near Normandy Hall, west of
the La Salle Causeway
*Type:* Aluminum plaque on
post
*Sponsor:* Kingston Historical
Society
*Date Erected:* 1957

# Fort Frontenac

Count Frontenac erected a fort here in 1673 with La Salle as Commandant. It was partially destroyed in 1758. In 1783 Major Ross built barracks (later called Tête de Pont) on the site. The original name was restored to the building opposite in 1938.

Map IV – 4

*Location:* Fort Frontenac
(Canadian Land Forces
Command and Staff College)
Ontario and Place d'Armes
Streets, Kingston, at entrance
*Type:* Bronze plaque on wall
*Sponsor:* Historic Sites and
Monuments Board of Canada
*Date Erected:* 1926
*Related Markers:* 72, 154, 183
*Readings:* Horsey 1937;
Preston and Lamontagne
1958; Grimshaw 1993;
Canadian 1995.

# Fort Frontenac

Here stood Fort Cataraqui or Frontenac built by Count de Frontenac in July, 1673, and rebuilt by La Salle in 1675. For many years the key to the West, the base of La Salle's explorations and a French outpost against the Iroquois and English. Abandoned 1689, rebuilt 1696, captured by British troops under Colonel John Bradstreet, 27th August, 1758.

*Modern drawing showing buildings at Fort Frontenac c1670. Buildings from left: habitations of French and Senecas, Recollet Mission, fort with stone wall and bastions at rear, shipyard, lime kilns, barns and stables.*
By R.F. Fleming. National Archives of Canada, C-22007

# Royal Canadian Horse Artillery Memorial

Map IV – 5

This tablet is erected to commemorate the formation in Tete de Pont Barracks of "A" Battery Garrison Artillery, first unit of the Permanent Force of Canada, 20th October 1871, and to recall the continuous occupation of these barracks and of Artillery Park by the Royal Canadian Horse Artillery and the Royal Canadian Artillery until 1st September 1939, and in proud memorial to the officers and other ranks of these units who served in North-West Canada, 1885, The Yukon, 1898, The South African War, 1899-1902, The First World War, 1914-1918, The Second World War, 1939-1945.

*Location:* Fort Frontenac (Canadian Land Forces Command and Staff College) Ontario and Place d'Armes Streets, Kingston, at the entrance
*Type:* Bronze plaque on wall
*Sponsor:* Royal Canadian Horse Artillery
*Date Erected:* c1971
*Additional Information:* The efforts of the Canadian Artillery in the Riel Rebellion of 1885 were recognized in 1893 with the title "Royal." "A" and "B" Batteries were now known as the Royal Canadian Field Artillery. In 1905 the role was changed to that of support of the cavalry and the title changed to Royal Canadian Horse Artillery (RCHA). As such the regiment went into the line in the First World War in September 1915 as part of the 2nd Canadian Division. Because of the flexibility of the artillery, many of the battles in which the RCHA participated (and listed on their memorial in City Park) were in support of the British Army. In the Second World War the unit became the 1st Field Regiment RCHA (cavalry were long gone but the title remained) and fought in support of the 3rd Canadian Infantry Brigade, part of the 1st Canadian Division, in Sicily, Italy, and Northwest Europe. After 1945 the title became the 1st Regiment RCHA. In 1950-1951 the Canadian regular artillery was increased to four regiments because of the war in Korea and the formation of the Canadian NATO brigade. In 1970 the 4th Regiment was disbanded and today the RCHA consists of three regiments.
*Related Markers:* 75, 145
*Readings:* Nicholson 1967; Mitchell 1986.

*The Royal Canadian Horse Artillery at the Tête de Pont Barracks.*
Queen's University Archives

Map IV – 6

# Royal Canadian Artillery
# 125th Anniversary

**Location:** Fort Frontenac (Canadian Land Forces Command and Staff College) Ontario and Place d'Armes Streets, Kingston, at the entrance
**Type:** Brass plaque on wall
**Sponsor:** Royal Canadian Horse Artillery
**Date Erected:** 1996
**Related Markers:** 74, 145
**Readings:** Nicholson 1967; Mitchell 1986.

Fort Frontenac – 20 October 1996
In commemoration of the 125th Anniversary of the formation of A and B Batteries, Royal Canadian Artillery, the first units of the Permanent Active Militia as authorized by Militia General Order Number 24, 20 October 1871

*The Canadian Artillery (CA) entering Fort Frontenac, June 1891. The gate is draped with black cloth and decorated as a mark of respect for Sir John A. Macdonald who died in Ottawa on 6 June and was buried at Cataraqui Cemetery (Kingston) 11 June 1891.*
Queen's University Archives

# The Crawford Purchase

Map IV – 7

In October 1783, at Carleton Island near here, Captain William Redford Crawford of the King's Royal Regiment of New York met with the local Mississauga Indians led by the elderly Mynass. Crawford, acting for the British government, purchased from the Mississaugas for some clothing, ammunition and coloured cloth a large tract of land east of the Bay of Quinte. The land was subsequently settled by United Empire Loyalists and Britain's Indian allies who had been forced to leave their homes in the new United States.

*Location:* Fort Frontenac (Canadian Land Forces Command and Staff College) Ontario and Place d'Armes Streets, Kingston, at the entrance
*Type:* Bronze plaque on wall
*Sponsor:* Historic Sites and Monuments Board of Canada
*Date Erected:* 1934
*Additional Information:* The Mississauga, considered part of the Ojibwa culture, once lived a traditional nomadic life that respected the seasons, particularly as they affected food sources. Around 1700 Mississauga bands migrated to south-eastern Ontario where they participated in the fur trade with both the English and the French. After the British conquest, formalized in 1763, native bands faced increasing stresses, as the fur trade declined and the supply of alcohol increased. British guns, ammunition, and iron products were highly prized. The Crawford Purchase of vast tracts of Mississauga land for a token payment may have been misunderstood by natives not accustomed to British land dealings. Further the presence of Loyalist and Mohawk settlers may have appealed to the bands as protection from potentially encroaching American settlement (Osborne and Ripmeester, 93). Kingston Mississauga faced increasing hardships in the 19th century. In the late 1820s a number converted to Methodism and moved to farm on Grape Island in the Bay of Quinte, while others lived a more traditional lifestyle in Bedford Township on lands surveyed in 1832. The latter site was taken back by the Crown in 1836, and land in Alnwick Township near Rice Lake was given to the Mississauga.
*Related Markers:* 25, 134, 136, 158
*Readings:* Mika 1987; Smith 1987; Osborne and Swainson 1988; Osborne and Ripmeester 1995.

*Crawford Purchase, 9 October 1783*
National Archives of Canada

Map IV – 8

# Astronomical Observatory

*Location:* Royal Military College, Valour Drive Kingston, near the original Guard House building
*Type:* Brass plaque on a stone pier
*Sponsor:* Royal Military College of Canada
*Date Erected:* 1951
*Related Markers:* 82, 146
*Readings:* Preston 1969; Canada 1992; Uffen 1982.

This is the "Upper Pillar" of a small astronomical observatory which stood on this site between 1886 and 1951. The observatory was used in teaching astronomy and surveying to Gentlemen Cadets of the Royal Military College of Canada. In 1905 the Dominion Geodetic Survey determined the exact location of this site to be: Latitude North 44° 13' 52", Longitude West 76° 28' 13"

Photo David Kasserra

# Royal Military College Memorial Arch

Map IV – 9

## NORTH VIEW

**Top front:** To the glorious memory of the ex-cadets of the Royal Military College of Canada who gave their lives for the Empire. Erected *Anno Domini* – MCMXXIII.

**Bottom front right:** This stone was laid by His Excellency The Rt Hon. General Lord Byng of Vimy G.C.B. K.C.M.G. M.V.O. Governor General and Commander in Chief 25th June 1923.

**Outside left face:** [Remainder of First World War battles:] Kut el Amara, Gallipoli, Hill 70, Passchendaele, Cambrai, Amiens, Arras, Drocourt-Queant, Canal du Nord.

**Inside left face:** *Pro Deo et Patrio.* Erected by the Royal Military College Club of Canada, *Anno Domini,* 1923, [followed by a list of dead under the following headings:] The Emin Pasha Relief Expedition 1887-1890, West Africa 1892, South Africa 1899-1901, Great War 1914-1918.

**Inside top right face:** *Hark now the drums beat up again for all true Soldiers Gentlemen.* [Followed by the remainder of the list of dead from WWI.]

**Inside bottom right face:** On the 15th June 1924 this Memorial Arch was unveiled by Mrs. Joshua Wright, mother of two cadets who gave their lives in the First World War, and was dedicated by the Rt. Rev. Dr. Bidwell, Lord Bishop of Ontario.

**Outside top right face:** South Africa, [List of First World War battles:] Mons, Marne, Aisne, Ypres, Festubert, Loos, Somme, Vimy.

**Outside bottom right face:** *Je me souviens.*

**Left wing front face:** [List of dead beginning with India, 1926 and continuing with the Second World War beginning with the Navy and then the Army.]

**Left wing west face:** Battle of the Atlantic, Battle of Britain, Burma, Dieppe, Hong Kong, Lombardy Plain, Normandy.

**Right wing front face top:** [List of Army dead continuing from East Wing, then Air Force dead.]

**Right wing front face bottom:** The plaques and carvings commemorating the ex-cadets who gave their lives on active service 1926-1945 were unveiled on the 25th September 1949 by His Excellency Field Marshal, The Viscount Alexander of Tunis, K.G. Governor-General and Commander-in-Chief of Canada.

*Location:* Royal Military College, Kingston, east side of the La Salle Causeway

*Type:* Stone monument

*Sponsor:* Royal Military College Club of Canada

*Date Erected:* 1923

*Additional Information:* The Memorial Arch was designed by John M. Lyle (1872-1945), an important Canadian architect who attended L'École des Beaux-Arts, Paris in 1892. Lyle won the design competition, held by the Royal Military College, on the advice of architect and historian Ramsay Traquair (1874-1952). The cornerstone was laid by Lord Byng, governor general of Canada, on 25 June 1923. The arch was designed to serve both as a memorial monument and as a gateway to the college. It is in the classical tradition of triumphal arches originating in the Roman Empire to celebrate military triumphs of the Emperors.

*Related Markers:* 82

*Readings:* Preston 1969; Canada 1992; Uffen 1982.

**Right wing east face:** North Africa, North West Germany, The Pacific, Pas de Calais, The Rhine, Sicily, Southern Italy.

**Right wing west face:** [List of dead from the Second World War omitted from other lists.]

**SOUTH VIEW**

**Top front:** Truth Duty Valour

*Blow out your bugles over the rich dead. There's none of these so lonely and poor of old but dying has made us rarer gifts than gold.*

*Cadets march through the Memorial Arch on Copper Sunday.*

Massey Library, Royal Military College of Canada

# Sir James Lucas Yeo 1782-1818

Map IV – 10

Born at Southampton, England, Yeo entered the British Navy, served throughout the Napoleonic Wars and won rapid promotion by his ability. In 1813, already a Commodore, he came to Canada to command British forces on the Great Lakes. Yeo successfully blockaded the American fleet in Sackett's Harbour for some months and subsequently commanded the naval forces at the capture of Oswego in 1814. Returning to England after the war he was posted to the West African Coast and died at sea while returning from that tour of duty.

*Location:* Royal Military College, Valour Drive, Kingston, on stone pillar near original Guard House Building
*Type:* Bronze plaque
*Sponsor:* Historic Sites and Monuments Board of Canada
*Date Erected:* 1936
*Related Markers:* 86
*Readings:* Stanley 1950; Brock 1968; Spurr 1982; DCB vol. 5; Stewart and Wilson 1973: Malcomson 1998.

*Sir James Lucas Yeo and his coat of arms engraved by H.R. Cook in 1810.*
National Portrait Library, London, England

Map IV – 11

# Point Frederick Buildings

*Location:* Royal Military College, Valour Drive, Kingston, on stone pillar near original Guard House Building
*Type:* Bronze plaque
*Sponsor:* Historic Sites and Monuments Board of Canada
*Date Erected:* 1979
*Additional Information:* Architect Archibald Fraser supervised the building of the Stone Frigate in 1819. The Liberals under Prime Minister Alexander Mackenzie were in power when architect Robert Gage signed the drawings for the Empire style Educational Block (Mackenzie Building) of the Royal Military College in 1876.
*Related Markers:* 82, 84, 86, 88, 93
*Readings:* Stanley 1950; Brock 1968; Parks Canada 1976; Malcomson 1998.

This peninsula, headquarters of the Provincial Marine (c.1790-1813), and of the Royal Navy (1813-1853), was the major British naval base on Lake Ontario during the War of 1812. Buildings surviving from this period include the Naval Hospital, the Guard House complex, and the Stone Frigate. On the southern part of the peninsula stands Fort Frederick, erected 1812-13 but completely rebuilt in 1846. In 1875 the Point was chosen as the site of the Royal Military College of Canada which admitted its first class in June 1876.

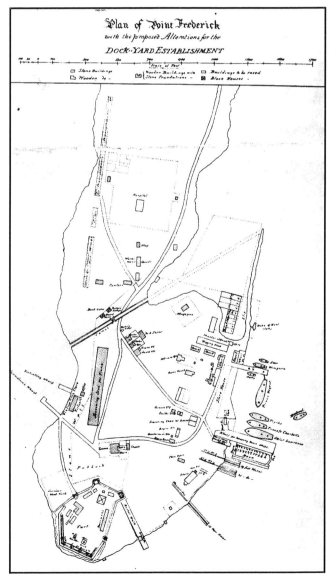

*Naval Dockyard, Point Frederick 1816.*
National Archives of Canada, C-51576

# Royal Military College of Canada

Map IV – 12

Following the withdrawal of British forces from Canada in 1870-71, the federal government recognized the need for an officer training college in Canada. In 1874, during the administration of the Hon. Alexander Mackenzie, enabling legislation was passed. Located on Point Frederick, the site of the former Royal Naval Dockyard, the new college opened on June 1, 1876, with 18 cadets under Lt.-Col. Edward O. Hewitt, R.E. Named the Royal Military College of Canada in 1878, it offered academic and military training courses designed to prepare cadets for both military and civil careers. The college was reorganized in 1948 as a tri-service institution and, in 1959, it became the first military college in the British Commonwealth to achieve degree-granting status.

*Location:* Royal Military College, Kingston, Point Frederick Drive gateway
*Type:* Aluminum plaque on pillar
*Sponsor:* Ontario Heritage Foundation
*Date Erected:* 1964
*Additional Information:* The Royal Military College (RMC) became once again the sole military college in Canada on the closing of its two sister colleges, Royal Roads Military College and Collège Militaire Royal de St Jean in 1995. All degree programs in Arts, Science, and Engineering are selected for their value to future officers in the military. It has been suggested that the RMC flag which was adopted in the immediate post war period became the stimulas for the design of the National flag of Canada in 1964. Readers are recommended to visit the Currie and Mackenzie buildings (a single structure), in which are located the names of graduated cadets and photographs of cadets killed on active service. There are also busts of Air Marshal W.A. Bishop and Lieutenant Colonel C.C.I. Merritt (Victoria Cross Winners), Air Commodore A. D. Ross (George Cross Winner), General Sir A. Currie (commander of the Canadian Corps in the First World War), and General H.D.G. Crerar (commander of the 1st Canadian Army in World War Two). The College Chapel, numerous stained glass windows, and various museum displays are also found in this location. The Educational Block, now Mackenzie Building, is a fine example of the Empire style, by architect Robert Gage.
*Related Markers:* 77, 78-79, 81, 82, 88
*Readings:* Preston 1969; Uffen 1982; Canada 1992; McKendry 1995.

*RMC from Fort Henry hill. In the centre is the Stone Frigate, on the right is the Mackenzie Building.*
National Archives of Canada

**Map IV – 13**

# Sir Edouard Percy Cranwill Girouard, 1867-1932

*Location:* Royal Military College, Girouard Building, Kingston
*Type:* Bronze plaque on wall
*Sponsor:* Historic Sites and Monuments Board of Canada
*Date Erected:* 1983
*Readings:* Preston 1969; Uffen 1982; Canada 1992.

Born in Montréal, Girouard was educated at Royal Military College, Kingston, commissioned in the Royal Engineers in 1888, and appointed to the Royal Arsenal Railways at Woolwich. Charged in 1896 with construction of the Wadi Halfa-Khartoum Railway, he was later director of railways in South Africa and as high commissioner in Northern Nigeria superintended the building of the line to Kano. Governor of Northern Nigeria (1908-9), of East Africa (1909-12), and director general of munitions supply in the British government (1915-16), he also wrote several books on the strategic importance of railways.

*Sir Edouard Percy Cranwill Girouard c1920.*
Massey Library, Royal Military College of Canada

# The Stone Frigate

Map IV – 14

Once part of a large and active naval dockyard, this substantial stone building was erected as a warehouse for naval stores. Although initially planned in 1816, it was not completed until four years later when the need for storage facilities to hold gear and rigging from British warships dismantled in compliance with the Rush-Bagot Agreement had become acute. After the Rebellion of 1837 the building briefly functioned as a barracks for the naval detachment charged with patrolling the lakes. It was then apparently used as a storehouse again. By 1876 the structure, now known as the Stone Frigate, had been refitted to house the newly-established Royal Military College of Canada, an institution it continues to serve.

*Location:* Royal Military College, Kingston, east side of the parade square, on the front of the Stone Frigate

*Type:* Aluminum plaque on wall

*Sponsor:* Ontario Heritage Foundation

*Date Erected:* 1957

*Additional Information:* The Stone Frigate, built under the supervision of architect Archibald Fraser, has been used as a student dormitory since 1876. See also p. 90.

*Related Markers:* 81, 82, 86, 87

*Readings:* Stanley 1950; Brock 1968; Preston 1969; Uffen 1982; Malcomson 1998.

*Stone Frigate in 1924.* National Archives of Canada

Map IV – 15

# The Dockyard Bell

*Location:* Royal Military College, Kingston, east side of the parade square in front of the Stone Frigate
*Type:* Bell and bronze plaque
*Sponsor:* Royal Military College Class of 1931
*Date Erected:* 1976
*Additional Information:* The bell (its inscription translates: Our Lady of Immaculate Conception) has an interesting history. The Royal Military College, at the time of its centenary in 1976, requested the return of the old Royal Navy Dockyard bell from St Mark's Church, Barriefield, where it had been mounted in its church tower since 1874. At that time it was lying on the Dockyard ground and the church vestry petitioned one of its parishioners, the Hon. Richard Cartwright, Minister of Finance, for "a grant of the bell." By 1976 the bell had inherited a more interesting history: it was said to have come from a castle in Spain owned by a friend of John Marks, custodian of the dockyard at the time of his retirement in 1843. Marks, who was also a founder of St Mark's that same year, was supposed to have taken the bell with him but since he died in 1872, he had no part in its acquisition. See also pp. 106, 112.
*Related Markers:* 82, 113
*Readings:* Patterson 1993.

The bell of the Spanish ship *Nuestra Senora De La Concepcion*, cast in 1806, regulated the routines of the R.N. Dockyard, Kingston at least as early as 1822. After the closing of the yard in 1853, it was acquired by St. Mark's Church, Barriefield in 1874, and presented to the R.M.C. on 17 October 1976 to commemorate a century of fruitful association between Church and College. The Class of 1931 generously provided for the restoration of the bell and its installation on this site.

Photo David Kasserra

# Kingston Navy Yard

Map IV – 16

The Navy Yard was established in 1789 as a transshipment point for the Great Lakes, and as the Provincial Marine's Lake Ontario base was administered by the Admiralty after 1813. During the War of 1812 Commodore James Yeo, R.N., commanded a considerable squadron built in these yards, including the 112-gun *St. Lawrence.* This base posed a constant threat to the Americans, who never felt strong enough to risk a direct attack. The Rush-Bagot agreement of 1817, which limited armaments on the lakes, brought about a decline in activity, and by mid-century the yards were closed.

*Location:* Royal Military College, Kingston, east side of the parade square, in front of the Stone Frigate
*Type:* Bronze plaque on wall
*Sponsor:* Historic Sites and Monuments Board of Canada
*Date Erected:* 1935
*Additional Information:* The squadron's ships were laid up "in reserve" following the Rush-Bagot Agreement, resulting in their eventual deterioration. Many of the ships were sunk in Navy Bay, Deadman's Bay or the nearby waters of Lake Ontario.
*Related Markers:* 80, 81, 87
*Readings:* Stanley 1950; Brock 1968; Preston 1969; Uffen 1982; Malcomson 1998.

*Launching of HMS St. Lawrence, 112 guns, 1814.* Anonymous. Royal Ontario Museum

**Map IV – 17**

# The Rush-Bagot Agreement

**Location:** Royal Military College, Kingston, north of the Stone Frigate, on the east side of the parade square
**Type:** Aluminum plaque on post
**Sponsor:** Ontario Heritage Foundation
**Date Erected:** 1967
**Additional Information:** The agreement allowed for one vessel, each no greater than 100 tons and armed with a single 18-pounder gun, on Lakes Ontario and Champlain and two on Lakes Erie and Huron. Although the terms were breached on several occasions, the agreement is still in effect. The plaque was unveiled on the 150th anniversary of the signing of the Rush-Bagot Agreement. It was placed here because the Royal Military College is located on the site of the Royal Naval Dockyard built during the War of 1812, and where the British fleet on Lake Ontario was located. The Stone Frigate (84) was built in 1819 to house the naval stores for the fleet which was mothballed because of the agreement. Although the agreement was often cited as an example of the "undefended border" between Canada and the United States, both countries continued to build fortifications for 50 years following the War of 1812.
**Related Markers:** 84, 86, 164
**Readings:** Scammell 1914; Stanley 1968.

A naval arms limitation agreement negotiated to demilitarize the Great Lakes and Lake Champlain after the War of 1812, this convention was concluded between the United States and Britain, represented respectively by Richard Rush and Charles Bagot, in 1817. Under its terms each country agreed to dismantle all armed vessels on the lakes with the exception of four retained for policing purposes and to construct no new warships. During the 19th century there were occasional infractions of the terms and during the Second World War they were somewhat modified, but the spirit of the convention has, in general, never been violated. Still technically in force, the Rush-Bagot Agreement has become a symbol of the long-standing, peaceful relations between Canada and the United States.

*Kingston and the Navy Yard from Fort Henry in 1828. The ships are laid up as a result of the Rush-Bagot Agreement.* By James Gray. Royal Ontario Museum, 960 276 26

# Point Frederick

Map IV – 18

A strategic location for the defence of the Loyalist settlement at Cataraqui (Kingston), this point was reserved in 1788 and named after Sir Frederick Haldimand, Governor of Quebec (1778-86). In 1790-91 a guardhouse and storehouse were built. By 1792 a dockyard was in operation and during the War of 1812 this vital naval base was fortified. On November 10, 1812, the Fort Frederick battery took part in repulsing an American naval squadron under Commodore Issac Chauncey. This structure, one of four massive stone Martello towers built to strengthen Kingston's defences, was erected in 1846-47 during the Oregon boundary crisis between the United States and Britain. In 1852 the dockyard was closed and in 1870 Fort Frederick was abandoned.

*Location:* Royal Military College, Kingston, beside Fort Frederick's main entrance
*Type:* Aluminum plaque on post
*Sponsor:* Ontario Heritage Foundation
*Date Erected:* 1980
*Related Markers:* 27, 28, 29, 81, 86, 94, 95, 142
*Readings:* Parks Canada 1976; Patterson 1981; Osborne and Swainson 1988

*Fort Frederick c1905 with the Educational Block (now the Mackenzie Building) in the centre background.*
Queen's University Archives

Map IV – 19

# Wolfe Island Township Hall

*Location:* Wolfe Island, Main Street, Marysville, just west of the ferry dock
*Type:* Bronze plaque on post
*Sponsor:* Historic Sites and Monuments Board of Canada
*Date Erected:* 1992
*Additional Information:* Edward Horsey was born in 1809 in Devonshire, England, emigrated to Kingston in 1832, and was buried in Cataraqui Cemetery in 1869.
*Readings:* Spankie 1914; Hawkins 1967.

The township hall, erected in 1859, survives as a symbol of the development of self-government in rural Ontario. Following the passing of the Municipal Act in 1849, many small communities erected simple, one-room structures as places of assembly for newly formed municipal councils and for the community at large. Edward Horsey, a noted Kingston architect, was chosen to design this hall. Its fine, hammer-dressed limestone construction and handsome Italianate detailing make it an unusually sophisticated example of its type.

Photo David Kasserra

On 3 November 1957, a historical plaque commemorating the Stone Frigate was unveiled on the grounds of the Royal Military College, Kingston. From left to right, Major the Reverend J.M. Anderson, Protestant Chaplain of RMC; Dr G.F.G. Stanley, a member of the Historic Sites Board; Commodore D.W. Piers, Commandant of RMC; the Hon. William M. Nickle, Q.C., Ontario Minister of Planning and Development; His Worship Frank P. Boyce, Mayor of Kingston; and Brigadier T.E. Snow, Commander, Eastern Ontario Area, Kingston. See also p. 84. Ontario Heritage Foundation

# FORT HENRY

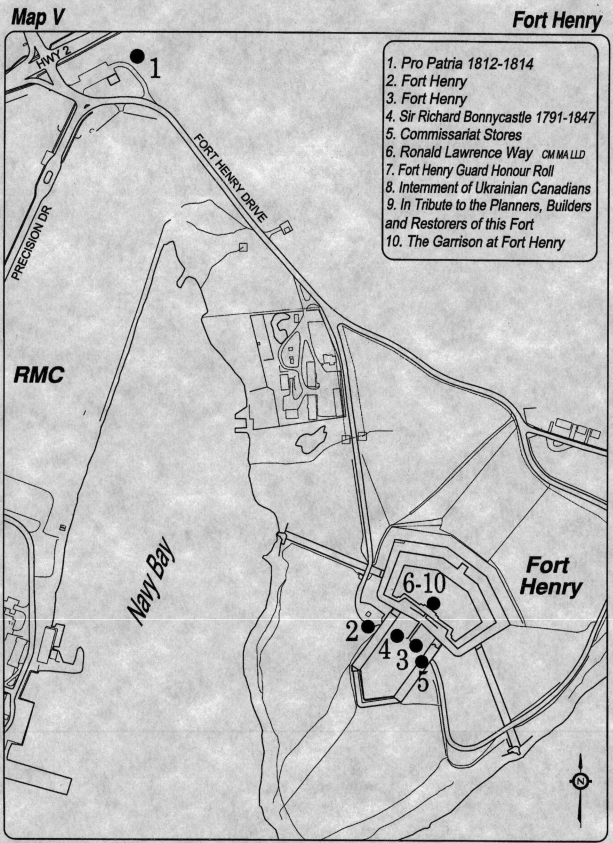

**Map V**

**Fort Henry**

HWY 2

PRECISION DR

FORT HENRY DRIVE

1

1. Pro Patria 1812-1814
2. Fort Henry
3. Fort Henry
4. Sir Richard Bonnycastle 1791-1847
5. Commissariat Stores
6. Ronald Lawrence Way   CM MA LLD
7. Fort Henry Guard Honour Roll
8. Internment of Ukrainian Canadians
9. In Tribute to the Planners, Builders
and Restorers of this Fort
10. The Garrison at Fort Henry

**RMC**

Navy Bay

6-10

2

4   3

5

**Fort Henry**

N

Strategic & Long-Range Planning - DJMartin

Map V – 1

# *Pro Patria* 1812-1814

*Location:* Tourist Information Centre, Fort Henry, Highway #2, Kingston
*Type:* Bronze plaque on stone cairn with anchor
*Sponsor:* Historic Sites and Monuments Board of Canada
*Date Erected:* 1937
*Additional Information:* The present site of this plaque may not make much sense today, but in 1937 it stood alone at the end of a large and commodious bay (now extensively filled-in to make playing fields for the Royal Military College). The bay was the base for the British fleet on Lake Ontario. In 1788 the Provincial Marine, a naval reserve force for British North America, established its Lake Ontario base here in Haldimand Cove, later to be known as Navy Bay. When the War of 1812 began, the Provincial

In memory of the officers and seamen of the Royal Navy and Provincial Marine, and of the officers and soldiers of the Royal Marines, Royal Newfoundland, King's (8th) and 100th Regiments, who served on Lake Ontario in defence of Canada in 1812-14.

Marine with its five ships was the dominant force on Lake Ontario and was a major reason for the British successes in the first year of the war. In 1813 when the presence of an American fleet on Lake Ontario threatened the control of water communications for supply of men and material vital to the defence of Upper Canada, the Royal Navy made Kingston its headquarters and a vast ship-building program was begun. By the end of the war, *HMS St Lawrence*, the largest ship afloat in the Royal Navy, was built here and the base was manned by thousands of sailors and marines. Because of a shortage of Royal Marines, infantry were used and the services of three line regiments are thus acknowledged on the plaque

*Related Markers:* 141, 219
*Readings:* Anonymous 1812; Morang 1902; Hitsman 1967; Malcomson 1998.

Photo David Kasserra

# Fort Henry

Map V – 2

An earlier fort was built here on Point Henry during the War of 1812 primarily to defend the nearby naval dockyard. When the Rideau Canal was built as part of a military route connecting Kingston with Montreal, the strategic importance of this site increased. The old fort was therefore replaced by the present structure of stronger and more advanced design which was completed in 1836 at a cost of over £70,000. Garrisoned by units of the British and then the Canadian army until 1890, the fort never saw action, although it was used as a prison for rebels captured during the Rebellions of 1837-38.

*Location:* Fort Henry, Kingston, main visitor entrance
*Type:* Bronze plaque on stone cairn
*Sponsor:* Historic Sites and Monuments Board of Canada
*Date Erected:* 1982
*Related Markers:* 96, 97, 98, 99, 100, 101, 102- 103, 104-105
*Readings:* Walkem 1897a; Walkem 1897b; Kirkconnell 1920; Lavell 1936; Patterson 1981; Bradford 1988; Mecredy 1989; Fort Henry.

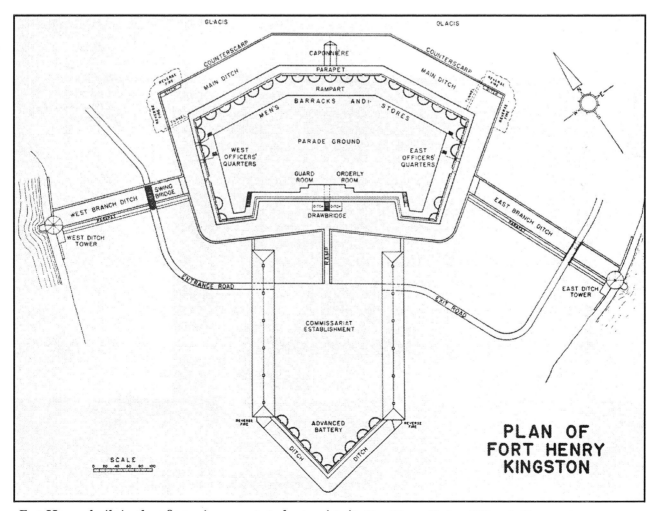

*Fort Henry, built in the 1830s, is now a popular tourist site.* Fort Henry National Historic Site

Map V – 3

# Fort Henry

*Location:* Fort Henry, Kingston, in the advanced battery
*Type:* Aluminum plaque on post
*Sponsor:* Ontario Heritage Foundation
*Date Erected:* 1957

*Additional Information:* In November 1812, when the American navy drove the *Royal George* into the Kingston harbour, the defence on Point Henry included only a small block-house and two guns. Over the next two years, building on the point in timber and earth resulted in an extensive fortification. The importance of Kingston and the Point Henry site in the post-War of 1812 period was recognized by the Duke of Wellington who in his capacity as Master-General of the Ordnance, wrote in 1819, "Kingston … is the connecting link between the Upper and Lower Province. It contains the Dockyard on Lake Ontario... there must be a good fort on Point Henry." Although Lieutenant Colonel Ross Wright was dispatched in 1826 to begin work on the new Fort, approval to begin construction was only given after the Rideau Canal was completed in 1832.

*Related Markers:* 96, 97, 98-99 100, 101, 102-103, 104-105

*Readings:* Walkem 1897a; Walkem 1897b; Kirkconnell 1920; Lavell 1936; Patterson 1981; Bradford 1988; Mecredy 1989; Fort Henry.

The first Fort Henry was built during the War of 1812 to protect the British dockyards in Navy Bay. The present limestone citadel, constructed between 1832 and 1837, replaced the old fort as part of a larger plan for the defence of the recently completed Rideau Canal. Commissariat stores were built to join the advanced battery with the main fort in 1841-42. Fort Henry was garrisoned by British troops until 1871, when Canadian Gunnery Schools (forerunner of the Royal Canadian Artillery) took over. Abandoned by the military in 1891, the fort fell into disrepair. Restoration work began in 1936, and two years later Fort Henry opened as a historical museum.

*A view of Fort Henry in 1839.* By H.F. Ainslie.
National Archives of Canada, C-510

# Sir Richard Bonnycastle
## 1791-1847

Map V – 4

As an officer in the Corps of Royal Engineers, Bonnycastle was trained in engineering, mapmaking, geology and painting. He served in Europe and Nova Scotia before coming to Upper Canada in 1826. The military surveys and related scientific work that he produced while posted at Niagara, Kingston and York contributed to the economic development of the province. Bonnycastle was recalled here in 1837 to supervise completion of the new Fort Henry. His masterful defence of Kingston during the Rebellions of 1837-38 earned him a knighthood. An interested observer of human nature, Sir Richard wrote four books detailing the social life, history and physical features of British North America.

*Location:* Fort Henry, Kingston, in the advanced battery
*Type:* Aluminum plaque on post
*Sponsor:* Ontario Heritage Foundation
*Date Erected:* 1957
*Additional Information:* Bonnycastle was in Kingston in 1837 as the commanding Royal Engineer for Kingston with the principal task of completing Fort Henry. However, soon after arriving, rebellion broke out in Lower Canada and the Lieutenant Governor for Upper Canada, Sir Francis Bond Head, sent most of the regular British troops to Montreal. Early in December 1837, Bonnycastle received a message that rebellion had broken out in Toronto and because there were no regular troops available, he should assume command of the militia to "preserve intact the great military depot of Kingston and its nearly finished fortress." It was because of Bonnycastle's organization and leadership of the militia and the protection of Kingston from rebel forces that he was knighted in March 1840. Bonnycastle died in Kingston on 3 November 1847 and was buried in the cemetery at St. Paul's Church. Bonnycastle's Canadian experiences were published in London (Colburn & Co.) in a number of books: *The Canadas in 1841* (1842); *Newfoundland in 1842: A Sequel to "The Canadas in 1841"* (1842); *Canada and the Canadians, in 1846* (1846); and *Canada as It Was, Is and May Be* (1852).
*Related Markers:* 94, 95, 97, 98, 102, 104, 153
*Readings:* Patterson 1981; Grenville 1988; Fort Henry; DCB vol. 7.

*Sir Richard Bonnycastle.*
Fort Henry National Historic Site

**Map V – 5**

# Commissariat Stores

**Location:** Fort Henry, Kingston, inside the gift shop in the advanced battery,
**Type:** Brass plaque on wall
**Sponsor:** Royal Engineers
**Date Erected:** c1844
**Additional Information:** This plaque is probably one of the earliest in Kingston. Erected apparently to commemorate the auspicious occasion of completing the commissariat stores within budget, it also recognizes the three officers who were responsible for the work. The Royal Engineers may still have been smarting from the problems of completing the Rideau Canal. It was estimated in 1826 at £169,000 for a modest barge canal and was completed in 1832 at almost five times the estimate – at the time the most expensive ordnance project in the empire. It appears that the plaque was first erected over the entrance archway on the west side of the Commissariat Stores. Kirkconnell makes reference to the plaque in a 1920 article in *Queen's Quarterly* but in 1936 Lavell notes that it had disappeared since the First World War. It is now located securely inside one of the Commissariat Stores casemates – first casemate south of the east archway.
**Related Markers:** 94, 95, 96, 98, 102, 104
**Readings:** Walkem 1897a; Walkem 1897b; Kirkconnell 1920; Lavell 1936; Patterson 1981; Bradford 1988; Mecredy 1989; Fort Henry.

These Commissariat Stores 22 in number, each being 30 feet long and 18 feet broad and 6 feet from the floor to the Springing of the Arch.
Estimated at £12,527 – 18 – 6 Sterling
Cost £10,632 – 5 – 2 ½ Sterling
Commenced 24 June 1841, Completed 12 November 1843. Colonel Oldfield, K.H., A.D.C. to the Queen, Colonel on the Staff being Commanding Royal Engineers. Lieut.-Colonel Ward and Captain Whitmore Royal Engineers, Executive Officers.

*"A" Battery in front of the Commissariat Stores, Fort Henry, 25 May 1890.*
Queen's University Archives

# Ronald Lawrence Way CM MA LLD

Map V – 6

Founder of the Fort Henry Guard in 1938, he pioneered the creation of historical military interpretive units. First Director of Fort Henry and Upper Canada Village, he was an innovative genius in the field of historical interpretation in outdoor museums. Restorer of Fort Henry, Fort Erie, Fort George, Upper Canada Village and Fortress Louisbourg, he was an acknowledged expert in the field of historical restoration in Canada.

*Si monumentum requiris, circumspice*

*Fort Henry opening day, 1 August 1938. From left to right: W.Y. Mills, Chairman Opening Ceremonies; Hon. Norman Rogers, MP (Kingston), Minister of Labour; Rt. Hon. W.L. Mackenzie King, Prime Minister; and Ronald Way.* Fort Henry National Historic Site

*Location:* Fort Henry, Kingston, at the entrance to the parade square
*Type:* Bronze plaque on wall
*Sponsor:* The Fort Henry Guard Club of Canada
*Date Erected:* 1988
*Additional Information:* R.L. Way (1908-1978) was born in Kingston and graduated from Queen's University in 1936 with an MA in History and English. Although he had spent a great amount of time studying the ruins of Fort Henry and its history, his thesis was written on the fortifications in the Niagara Peninsula. Nevertheless, when the restoration of Fort Henry began in August 1936 as a federal-provincial works project to relieve unemployment during the Great Depression, Way was picked to be the Director. For two years he worked night and day, living most of the time in the fort, while researching, planning, and directing a vast array of artisans, tradesmen, and labourers in the largest historical restoration to date in Canada. What is more remarkable he was able to put his dreams of animating the fort into reality by creating and training a "Guard" of university and high school students to carry out the routine of the British garrison of the nineteenth century. On parade for the first time on 1 August 1938 for W.L. Mackenzie King, the Prime Minister of Canada, the Fort Henry Guard began a tradition of excellence in historical military interpretation that continues to the present, unequalled anywhere in the world. Next he restored Forts George and Erie and then wrote the definitive history of the Niagara Parks Commission during the Second World War (Fort Henry was used as a Prisoner-of-War camp during the war). Way reopened Fort Henry in 1948 and soon made it the premier military museum in Canada, based largely on the excellence of the Fort Henry Guard as an authentic re-creation of the British army of 1867. In 1958 he was appointed Director of Historic Sites for the St. Lawrence Parks Commission and put in charge of the creation of Upper Canada Village. Opened in 1961, the Village instantly became a significant model for subsequent living history outdoor museums world-wide. At the same time he continued to manage Fort Henry where the Guard continued to make history as the only Canadian unit to perform twice at the prestigious Royal Tournament in London, England. From 1962 to 1967 Ronald Way was "loaned" to the federal government to direct the reconstruction of the Fortress of Louisburg, while at the same time carrying out his responsibilities at Fort Henry and Upper Canada Village. After making nearly 100 trips to Cape Breton Island and with the pressure of work, he was forced to retire by reason of ill-health from the Ontario Public Service in 1965. For his work in historical restoration (in his own words) "Selling Canada to Canadians by making them take a sugar-coated pill of history," Ronald Way was made a Member of the Order of Canada and given the honourary degree of Doctor of Laws by Queen's University.
*Related Markers:* 94, 95, 97, 100, 102, 104
*Readings:* Walkem 1897a; Walkem 1897b; Kirkconnell 1920; Lavell 1936; Snell 1964; Patterson 1981; Bradford 1988; Mecredy 1989; Fort Henry.

*Ronald Way, 28 July 1973.* George Lilley, Fort Henry National Historic Site

# Fort Henry Guard
# Honour Roll

Map V – 7

Members of the Fort Henry Guard 1938-40 who served in the Canadian Armed Forces during the Second World War.
J.R. Barker, J.H. Brais, D.G. Brown, P.G. Carr-Harris, K.S. Clarke, F.L. Cliff, S.M. Clow, W.G. Coffey, C.P. Dark, H.J. Dick, E.B. Forde, A Gunn*, D.R. Hackett*, H.P. Hackett, L.J. Hyslop, E.L. Johnston*, E.O. Johnston, W.R. King*, G.T. Lake, W.O. Macnee, F. Metcalfe, G.M. Patrick, J.H. Reid, W.A. Reid, J.R. Salisbury, G.C. Scott, J.D. Scott, G.S. Sims, A.B. Smith, G.F. Weatherall.
*Died on active service.
*Merentur etiam*

*Location:* Fort Henry, Kingston, at the entrance to parade square
*Type:* Bronze plaque on wall
*Sponsor:* St Lawrence Parks Commission
*Date Erected:* 1968
*Additional Information:* "When the time came in 1938 to plan the interpretation of Fort Henry to those who would come to visit it following its restoration, it was the genius of Ronald Way, the restorer, to come up with the idea of a 'Guard' to represent the garrisons of former days. Simple as it may sound, it was a pioneering step designed to breathe life into the presentation of history." (Fort Henry, 39) When the Second World War began, practically all of the student civilians of the Guard of 1938-39 enlisted for military service. The Guard resumed its duties at the Fort in 1948 and has interpreted the Fort to millions of visitors since then. "At home and abroad members of the Guard have brought honour and distinction to Canada, helping not only to explain something of its past, but also giving an example of Canadian present and future capabilities." (Fort Henry, 48)
*Related Markers:* 94, 95, 96, 97, 98, 101, 102, 104
*Readings:* Bradford 1988; Mecredy 1989; Fort Henry.

*Prime Minister the Rt. Hon. W.L. Mackenzie King (right centre) inspecting the Fort Henry Guard, 1 August 1938, at the opening of Fort Henry, accompanied by the Hon. Norman Rogers.*
Fort Henry National Historic Site

**Map V – 8**

# Internment of Ukrainian Canadians

*Location:* Fort Henry, Kingston, on the south wall of the parade square
*Type:* Bronze plaque on wall
*Sponsor:* Ukrainian Canadian Civil Liberties Association
*Date Erected:* 1994
*Additional Information:* Within weeks of the declaration of war by Britain on Austria-Hungary and Germany, Fort Henry was officially opened on 18 August 1914 as an internment camp for enemy aliens of many nationalities – Ukrainians, Turks, Slovaks, Czechs, Poles and Bulgarians. A month after opening, the Fort held about 200 prisoners and continued in use as a prison for almost three years. A few managed to get away from the fort: for example, three prisoners who were repairing a small boat, escaped to the United States. On 4 May 1917 the Fort Henry prisoners were taken by train to other internment camps.
*Related Markers:* 94, 95, 104
*Readings:* Luciuk 1980; Luciuk 1988; Gregorovich 1994.

Over 5,000 Ukrainian Canadians were unjustly interned as "enemy aliens" during Canada's first national internment operations, which lasted from 1914 to 1920. This plaque is in memory of those who were interned in Canada's first permanent internment camp, Fort Henry, 1914-1917.

*Prisoners at Fort Henry during World War One.* Queen's University Archives

Map V – 9

# In Tribute to the Planners, Builders and Restorers of this Fort

Strategic Planning 1819-1828:
Field Marshal, His Grace, The Duke of Wellington, Master General of the Ordnance; General Gother Mann, Inspector General of Fortifications; Lieutenant-General Sir James Kempt, Governor of Lower Canada; Major-General Sir James Carmichael Smyth, Bt., President, Canadian Defence Commission; Lieutenant-Colonel Edward Fanshawe, Royal Engineers; Lieutenant-Colonel Griffith Lewis, Royal Engineers.
Design Committee 1829:
Major-General Sir Alexander Bryce, President; Colonel John T. Jones, Royal Engineers; Lieutenant-Colonel William Gosset, Royal Engineers; Lieutenant-Colonel Edward Fanshawe, Royal Engineers.
Construction 1832-1842:
Colonel Elias W. Durnford, Commanding Royal Engineers, Canada; Lieutenant-Colonel John Ross Wright, Commanding Royal Engineers, Upper Canada; Lieutenant-Colonel Sir Richard Bonnycastle, Royal Engineers; Colonel John Oldfield, Commanding Royal Engineers, Canada; Lieutenant-Colonel William Ward, Royal Engineers; Captain George Whitmore, Royal Engineers.
Preservation and Restoration 1936-1938:
Hon. Norman McLeod Rogers, M.P. Minister of Labour, Canada; Hon. T.B. McQuesten, M.L.A., Minister of Highways, Ontario; R.M. Smith, Deputy Minister of Highways, Ontario.

*Location:* Fort Henry, Kingston, on the south wall of the parade square
*Type:* Bronze plaque
*Sponsor:* St Lawrence Parks Commission
*Date Erected:* 1968
*Additional Information:* Fort Henry was an active military installation for a relatively brief period of time from the hastily built fortification of the War of 1812 until the British army left Canada in 1870. In that year the present stone fortification was turned over to the fledgling Canadian army. For the next 60 years the Fort deteriorated badly with concerns being expressed in the mid-1930s by the Kingston Historical Society and others about the loss of Canada's heritage. "Dramatically, it was saved by a combination of interested local citizens and the desire of the federal and provincial governments to put men to work during the great Depression. From 1936 to 1938 a work force of nearly one thousand men laboured to restore the mighty fortress." (Fort Henry, 18) The Fort was opened by Prime Minister Mackenzie King on 1st August 1938.
*Related Markers:* 94, 95, 96, 97, 98, 99, 100, 104
*Readings:* Walkem 1897a; Walkem 1897b; Kirkconnell 1920; Lavell 1936; Patterson 1981; Bradford 1988; Mecredy 1989; Fort Henry.

*Reconstruction of the west officers' quarters at Fort Henry c1936.* Fort Henry National Historic Site

*An example of the deterioration at Fort Henry c1936.* Queen's University Archives

Commemorating the services of the British and Canadian Forces in garrison at Fort Henry, 1812-1940.

THE BRITISH ARMY

ARTILLERY – The Royal Regiment of Artillery 1812-1870

ENGINEERS – The Corps of Royal Engineers 1812-1870

INFANTRY – The 9th Regiment of Foot, now The Royal Norfolk Regiment 1856-1857; The 15th Regiment of Foot, now The East Yorkshire Regiment, (The Duke of York's Own) 1827-1828, 1833-1834; The 20th Regiment of Foot, now The Lancashire Fusiliers 1849-1850; The 23rd Regiment of Foot, now The Royal Welch Fusiliers 1842-1843; The 24th Regiment of Foot, now The South Wales Borderers 1835-1837; The 34th Regiment of Foot, now The Border Regiment 1840-1841; The 37th Regiment of Foot, now The Royal Hampshire Regiment 1817-1818, 1824-1825; The 43rd Regiment of Foot, now The Oxfordshire & Buckinghamshire Light Infantry 1841-1842; The 54th Regiment of Foot, now The Dorset Regiment 1853; The 58th Regiment of Foot, now The Northamptonshire Regiment 1815; The 60th Regiment of Foot, now The King's Royal Rifle Corps 1823-1824, 1870; The 62nd Regiment of Foot, now The Wiltshire Regiment (Duke of Edinburgh's) 1862-1863; The 65th Regiment of Foot, now The York and Lancaster Regiment 1839-1840; The 66th Regiment of Foot, now The Royal Berkshire Regiment (Princess Charlotte of Wales's) 1831-1833, 1834-1835; The 68th Regiment of Foot, now The Durham Light Infantry 1822-1823, 1825-1827; The 70th Regiment of Foot, now The East Surrey Regiment 1815-1817, 1819-1821; The 71st Regiment of Foot, now The Highland Light Infantry (City of Glasgow Regiment) 1828-1829, 1838, 1852-1853; The 73rd Regiment of Foot, now The Black Watch (Royal Highland Regiment) 1838; The 76th Regiment of Foot, now The Duke of Wellington's Regiment, (West Riding) 1818-1819, 1821-1822; The 79th Regiment of Foot, now The Queen's Own Cameron Highlanders 1829-1831; The 81st Regiment of Foot, now The Loyal Regiment (North Lancashire) 1846-1847; The 82nd Regiment of Foot, now The South Lancashire Regiment (The Prince of Wales's Volunteers) 1844-1846; The 83rd Regiment of Foot, now The Royal Ulster Rifles 1838; The 85th Regiment of Foot, now The King's Shropshire Light Infantry 1838; The 93rd Regiment of Foot, now The Argyll and Sutherland Highlanders (Princess Louise's) 1838, 1843-1844; The Rifle Brigade, now The Rifle Brigade (Prince Consort's Own) 1847-1849, 1850-1852; The 104th Regiment of Foot – (disbanded in 1817) 1813;

Canadian Fencible Regiment – (disbanded in 1816) 1814; Regiment de Watteville-(disbanded in 1816) 1813; 10th Royal Veteran Battalion-(disbanded in 1817) 1812; Royal Canadian Rifle Regiment – (disbanded in 1870)1854-1856, 1857-1862, 1863-1870.

## THE CANADIAN MILITIA

ARTILLERY – The Perth Artillery Company 1837-1838; "A" Battery of Garrison Artillery (School of Gunnery) 1871-1880; "B" Battery of Garrison Artillery (School of Gunnery) 1880-1883; The Regiment of Canadian Artillery, "B" Battery 1883-1885, "A" Battery 1885-1891

INFANTRY – Provincial Corps of Light Infantry (Canadian Voltigeurs) 1813; The 8th Battalion of Incorporated Militia (disbanded in 1839)1838-1839; 1st Regiment of Frontenac Militia 1837-1838; 14th Battalion, "The Princess of Wales' Own Rifles" 1870, 1885-1887; The Princess of Wales' Own Regiment 1914-1918, 1939-1940.

*Merentur Etiam Qui Stent Parati.*

**Location:** Fort Henry, Kingston, on the south wall of the parade square
**Type:** Bronze plaque

**Sponsor:** Department of Highways, Ontario
**Date Erected:** 1953
**Related Markers:** 94, 95, 96, 97, 98, 99, 100, 101, 102

**Readings:** Walkem 1897a; Walkem 1897b; Kirkconnell 1920; Lavell 1936; Patterson 1981; Bradford 1988; Mecredy 1989; Fort Henry.

*Members of the Royal Regiment of Artillery in front of the west officers' quarters c1867.* Royal Artillery Museum, Woolwich, England

*The Dockyard Bell being presented to RMC by the Rector of St Mark's Church, Barriefield, the Reverend F.C.*
*Bell, 17 October 1976.* See also pp. 85, 112. St Mark's Church

# EAST *of the* GREAT CATARAQUI RIVER

# Map VI

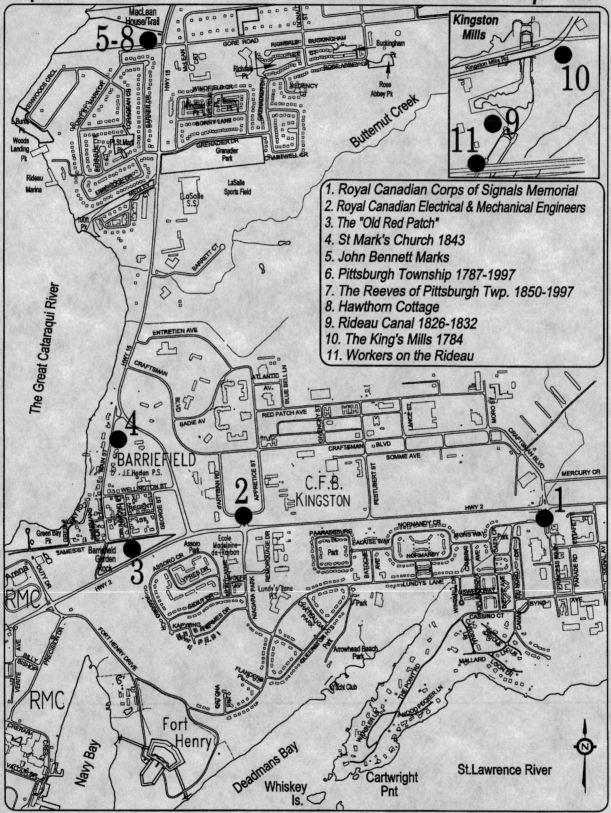

1. Royal Canadian Corps of Signals Memorial
2. Royal Canadian Electrical & Mechanical Engineers
3. The "Old Red Patch"
4. St Mark's Church 1843
5. John Bennett Marks
6. Pittsburgh Township 1787-1997
7. The Reeves of Pittsburgh Twp. 1850-1997
8. Hawthorn Cottage
9. Rideau Canal 1826-1832
10. The King's Mills 1784
11. Workers on the Rideau

*Strategic & Long-Range Planning - DJMartin*

Map VI – 1

# Royal Canadian Corps of Signals Memorial

*Location:* Princess Mary Avenue, south entrance to Vimy Barracks, Canadian Forces Base, Kingston, on Highway 2
*Type:* Bronze statue on wall, brass plaques on stone cairn and on stone flanking walls
*Sponsor:* Royal Canadian Corps of Signals
*Date Erected:* 1962
*Additional Information:* 1. At the entrance to Vimy Barracks; 2. On the right flanking wall; 3. On the left flanking wall; 4. In the rear of the guard house. In 1903 the Canadian Signalling Corps was founded under the leadership of Captain Bruce Carruthers, a Kingstonian, who was a veteran of the South African War. Beginning as a training establishment, the Corps taught signalling, using flags and telephones, to the entire Canadian Militia. Its value providing communications was proven in the First World War and rewarded by being given the title "Royal Canadian Corps of Signals" in 1921. By the increasing use of radio the Corps proved invaluable providing rapid communications in the Second World War. With the unification of the Canadian Forces on 1 February 1968, the Corps ceased to exist, its work being the responsibility of the Communications and Electronics Branch. The school for communicators established here in 1938 continues to the present as the Canadian Forces School of Communications and Electronics.
*Readings:* Moir 1962

[1.] To those in The Royal Canadian Corps of Signals who gave their lives for their country.

[2.] Ground broken by Her Royal Highness, The Princess Royal C.I., G.C.V.O., G.B.E., R.R.C., T.D., C.D., Colonel-in-Chief 19 June 1962

[3.] Unveiled and dedicated by His Excellency, Major-General Georges P. Vanier, D.S.O., M.C., C.D., Governor-General of Canada. 6 October 1962

[4.] Princess Mary Avenue named in commemoration of H.R.H., The Princess Royal, Colonel-in-Chief, The Royal Canadian Corps of Signals, 1940-1965

Photo David Kasserra

Map VI – 2

# Royal Canadian Electrical and Mechanical Engineers Memorial

This entrance is dedicated to the memory of all ranks of the Corps of Royal Canadian Electrical and Mechanical Engineers who have died in the service of Canada.

For many years this gun was used in the training of Craftsmen at the RCEME School here in Barriefield, Ontario. 25-Pounder guns were the standard field artillery guns when RCEME was formed on May 15, 1944. It wears the tactical signs of the 13th Field Regiment RCA which used 25-Pounder guns during World War Two.

*Location:* Highway 2 entrance to McNaughton Barracks, Canadian Forces Base, Kingston
*Type:* Bronze plaques on stone walls, a Sherman tank and a 25-Pounder Gun
*Sponsor:* Royal Canadian Electrical and Mechanical Engineers
*Date Erected:* 1961
*Additional Information:* The Corps was founded on 1 February 1944 by transferring technicians from the Engineering branch of the Royal Canadian Ordnance Corps. Formed to repair and maintain all equipment in the Canadian Army, the Corps took part in the remaining campaigns of the Second World War. It continued in existence until 1 February 1968 when it was superseded by Land Ordnance Engineering, which was renamed in 1985 Land Electrical and Mechanical Engineering. In 1994 the title "Land" was dropped as the branch was assigned the task of providing engineering and maintenance support for all ground equipment in the Canadian Forces. The Corps School for craftsmen was in this location from 1939 until 1970.
*Readings:* Johnson

Photo David Kasserra

**Map VI – 3**

*Location:* Barriefield Rock Garden, James Street, Barriefield
*Type:* Bronze plaque on stone cairn
*Sponsor:* Barriefield Rock Garden Committee & 1st Divisional Headquarters
*Date Erected:* 1994

*Additional Information:* The 1st Canadian Division was the first Canadian formation into battle in the First World War. After only a month in the line the Division was subjected to the first gas attack in the history of warfare. The fact that it stood firm in spite of over 5,000 casualties established the reputation of the Canadian soldier as a tenacious and courageous fighter. After the Somme the Canadian Corps adopted in 1916 distinctive formation shoulder badges and the 1st Division was assigned a red rectangular 'patch,' which became its historical symbol. The Division took part in all the remaining significant battles of the war: Vimy Ridge, Passchendaele, Amiens, the Drocourt-Queant line, and the Canal du Nord. In total it suffered over 52,000 casualties. Again in the Second World War the 1st Division was the first to be formed, proceeding overseas in 1939. The Division went into action in July 1943 participating in the invasion of Sicily, a campaign that cost it over 2,000 casualties. In September 1943 the Division invaded Italy and for the next 18 months fought in some of the most severe battles of the Italian campaign: the Moro River, Ortona, and the Hitler and Gustav lines. In February 1945 the 1st Division joined the rest of the Canadian Army in Northwest Europe. In total the Division suffered 14,000 casualties. In 1954 Canada organized its first peacetime regular division when the 1st Division was reactivated. Once again the "old red patch" was worn by more than 12,000 Canadian soldiers, but only for four years as once more the Division was disbanded. In 1988 it was reactivated although with a much smaller establishment. In 1999 the Division was once again removed from the Order of Battle. The memorial is constructed of local limestone to which is affixed a stone cross carved by inmates of Kingston Penitentiary over a century ago.

*Readings:* Nicholson 1962; Morton 1981

# The "Old Red Patch"

Dedicated to the memory of the men and women of the Canadian Forces who proudly served with the 1st Canadian Division at home and abroad in the pursuit of peace, and to those who will continue to serve in the future. Since its activation on 26 January 1915, the Division has established and maintained a distinguished tradition of courage, discipline and endurance. This heritage will be carried on by those who wear the "Old Red Patch" on the right shoulder of their uniform.

Photo David Kasserra

# St Mark's Church 1843

Map VI – 4

This church, a fine example of the early style of Gothic Revival architecture, was built with the aid of funds subscribed by the British Admiralty and by settlers at Barriefield, many of whom had been employees of the Royal Naval dockyard at Navy Bay. John Bennett Marks, a naval paymaster, donated the land for a site. The corner-stone was laid by Bishop John Strachan, July 10, 1843, and the church, designed by Alfred Brunel, was opened by Archdeacon George Okill Stuart, July 7, 1844. The first rector, the Rev. John Pope, served from 1844-1846. The church was consecrated by the Rt Rev. John Travers Lewis, first Bishop of Ontario, September 25, 1862.

*Location:* 268 Main Street, Barriefield, near the entrance to the churchyard
*Type:* Aluminum plaque on post
*Sponsor:* Ontario Heritage Foundation
*Date Erected:* 1962
*Additional Information:* The cornerstone was not laid by Bishop Strachan but by "John B. Marks, Esq., President of the District." (*British Whig*, 15 July 1843). In 1897 the one and only significant change to the original structure was made when the existing small sanctuary was demolished and replaced by a large chancel, complete with choir stalls, sanctuary, organ chamber, and adjoining vestry. The chancel included a large stained glass east window and was completely furnished by its donor, Edward Barker Pense, publisher of the *British Whig* and grandson of the paper's founder, Edward Barker who was also a founder of St Mark's. On the occasion of its sesquicentennial, the parish was presented with armorial bearings by the Canadian Heraldic Authority. See also pp. 85, 106.
*Related Markers:* 113
*Readings:* Anderson 1963; Patterson 1993; McKendry 1995.

*From its elevated height, St Mark's looks down over Barriefield, the Cataraqui River, and Kingston.*
Photo David Kasserra

Map VI – 5

# John Bennett Marks

**Location:** Pittsburgh Library, northwest corner of Highway 15 and 80 Gore Road, Kingston
*Type:* Bronze plaque on a stone cairn
*Sponsor:* Pittsburgh Township Historical Society
*Date Erected:* 2000
*Related Markers:* 85, 112
*Readings:* Patterson 1989; Patterson 1993

Pittsburgh's most important resident was born in 1777 in Devonshire, England. Enlisting in the Royal Navy in 1793, Marks served until wounded at the Battle of Copenhagen, 1801, then transferred to the Civil Service Afloat. Sent to Kingston in 1813 he became paymaster on the HMS *St. Lawrence.* After the War of 1812 Marks was secretary to the commandant of the Naval Dockyard, and when it became a naval depot he was custodian until it closed in 1844. In 1824 Marks purchased a farm north of Barriefield, where he became a successful farmer and community leader. A Justice of the Peace he was appointed Colonel of the 3rd Frontenac Militia in 1838, and was active in local politics and business. Marks served as treasurer of the Midland District and warden of its council; was elected MPP for Frontenac, 1836-40, and the first reeve of Pittsburgh Township in 1850. He was director and treasurer of the Cataraqui Bridge Company, the Kingston, Pittsburgh, and Gananoque Road Company, and the Commercial Bank of Upper Canada. He was a founder and president of the Frontenac Agricultural Society, and the Kingston Turf Club. Marks was a founder and benefactor of St. Mark's Church, Barriefield, under which he was buried in 1872.

*John Bennett Marks in his later years.*
St Mark's Church, Barriefield

# Pittsburgh Township
## 1787-1997

Map VI – 6

Surveyed as a rectangular township, it became by 1853 a triangle of 50,000 acres situated with Rideau Canal on the west, the St Lawrence River on the south, and Leeds County to the east. Named for Prime Minister William Pitt, it was designated a Loyalist township with a large military reserve opposite Kingston. Although Loyalists were granted two-thirds of the 301 farm lots, few took up land; the majority of the settlers were Protestant Scots-Irish immigrants who arrived before Confederation. For the next 80 years Pittsburgh was a typical Ontario rural township with strong agricultural roots based on a stable homogenous population of 2,000. An exception was the Military Reserve which contained the Royal Naval Dockyard and Fort Frederick, now the Royal Military College, Fort Henry, and Barriefield Camp, now Canadian Forces Base Kingston. After the Second World War, Pittsburgh's population rose with the growth of a permanent military community, and the formation of subdivisions, suburbs of an expanding Kingston. By 1987 the township had 10,000 residents, equally distributed among farming descendents of the original settlers, military personnel, and suburbanites. It was amalgamated with the City of Kingston on 1 January 1998.

*Location:* Pittsburgh Library, northwest corner of Highway 15 and 80 Gore Road, Kingston
*Type:* Bronze plaque on a stone cairn
*Sponsor:* Pittsburgh Township Historical Society
*Date Erected:* 2000
*Additional Information:* In 1785 Kingston Township was enlarged to include either side of the Great Cataraqui River. The eastern area consisted of the Military Reserve including Points Frederick, Point Henry, and 21 lots from the Military Reserve north to the Mill Reserve at Kingston Mills. Pittsburgh was one of a second group of townships established to provide additional land for the Loyalists. The first survey in 1787-1788 laid out five concessions. To fill a gap between the Military Reserve and the lots East of the Great Cataraqui River (EGCR) and Pittsburgh, five lots were inserted adjoining the Military Reserve (AMR) along the St Lawrence River, and one in the "Gore" behind the lots AMR and EGCR. By 1790 this area, together with Howe Island, was joined to Pittsburgh. In 1807 the remainder of Pittsburgh, 10 more concessions, was surveyed extending the township north to a depth of 20 miles. In 1845 all land northwest of the Rideau Canal was split from Pittsburgh, while in 1853 six lots east of the Rideau at Kingston Mills were added, leaving the township its present size and shape. Settlement was extremely slow, the population in 1821 was only 518. During the period 1820-1867 heavy immigration increased the population to over 4,000, but with the loss of Howe Island in 1871, the lack of unoccupied good land, and the move to urban areas, the population slowly fell to near 2,000 by 1945. Throughout its history Pittsburgh remained a good dairy farming area, attracting little industry or commerce beyond a few small mills and cheese factories. Barriefield, the township's largest hamlet, became a Heritage Conservation District in 1980 based on its collection of early 19th century buildings.
*Related Markers:* 116
*Readings:* Patterson 1989.

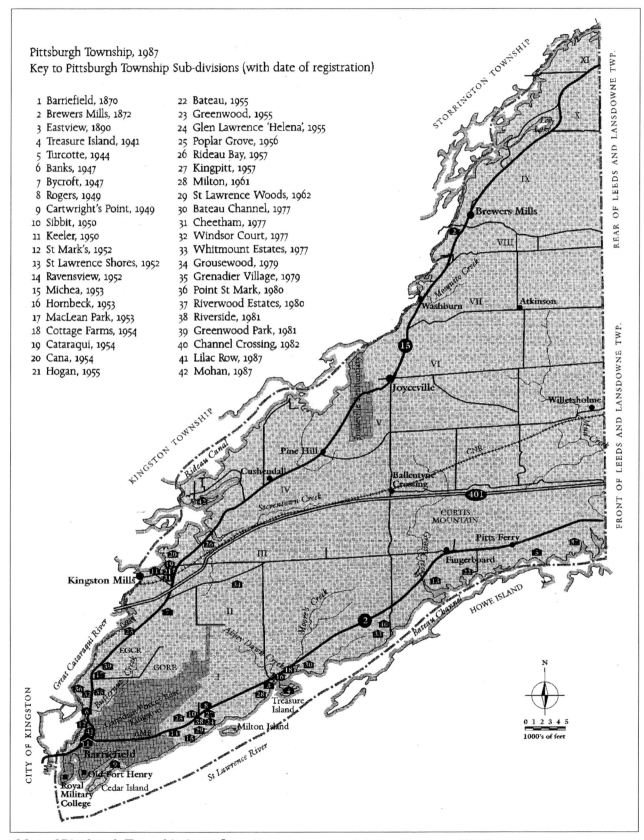

Pittsburgh Township, 1987
Key to Pittsburgh Township Sub-divisions (with date of registration)

 1 Barriefield, 1870
 2 Brewers Mills, 1872
 3 Eastview, 1890
 4 Treasure Island, 1941
 5 Turcotte, 1944
 6 Banks, 1947
 7 Bycroft, 1947
 8 Rogers, 1949
 9 Cartwright's Point, 1949
10 Sibbit, 1950
11 Keeler, 1950
12 St Mark's, 1952
13 St Lawrence Shores, 1952
14 Ravensview, 1952
15 Michea, 1953
16 Hornbeck, 1953
17 MacLean Park, 1953
18 Cottage Farms, 1954
19 Cataraqui, 1954
20 Cana, 1954
21 Hogan, 1955

22 Bateau, 1955
23 Greenwood, 1955
24 Glen Lawrence 'Helena', 1955
25 Poplar Grove, 1956
26 Rideau Bay, 1957
27 Kingpitt, 1957
28 Milton, 1961
29 St Lawrence Woods, 1962
30 Bateau Channel, 1977
31 Cheetham, 1977
32 Windsor Court, 1977
33 Whitmount Estates, 1977
34 Grousewood, 1979
35 Grenadier Village, 1979
36 Point St Mark, 1980
37 Riverwood Estates, 1980
38 Riverside, 1981
39 Greenwood Park, 1981
40 Channel Crossing, 1982
41 Lilac Row, 1987
42 Mohan, 1987

*Map of Pittsburgh Township in 1987.* William J. Patterson. *Lilacs and Limestone.* (1989) p. xxx

115

# The Reeves of Pittsburgh Township 1850-1997

Map VI – 7

John Marks 1850-1854, Samuel Rees 1855-1857, John Ruttan 1858, Alexander McArthur 1859-1860, Hugh McCaugherty 1861-1862, James Hutton 1863, William Ferguson Jr 1864, Martin Strachan 1865-1870, 1876-1879, Peter Graham (W) 1871-1875, Thomas Stark 1880-1881, Richard Patterson 1882-1884, Richard Anglin 1885, Michael Graves 1886, William Hutton 1887-1888, 1890, David Trotter 1889, Thompson Whitney 1891-1893, William Toner 1894, John Kane 1895-1896, John Bennett 1897-1898, Robert McAlpin 1899, Daniel C. McLean 1900, Daniel McLean 1901-1902, Thomas Maxwell 1903, James Greenlee 1904, John McFarlane 1905-1906, William Franklin (W) 1907-1908, 1912-1917, Thomas Spence 1909, James Gordon 1910, David Rogers 1911, George Maitland 1918-1920, John Sibbit (W) 1921-1926, 1932-1938, Alfred Franklin 1927-1928, 1931, William Atkinson 1929-1930, John McMaster (W) 1939-1943, Wilson Franklin 1944-1945, Colin Woods (W) 1946-1950, Robert Wilson 1951-1953, Earl Shepherd (W) 1954-1958, Eric Pearson (W) 1959-1966, Hugh Wilson 1967-1968, Wilmer Nuttal (W) 1969-1971, Donald Hunter 1972, Edward Swayne (W) 1973-1980, Hans Westenberg 1981-1982, Vincent Maloney 1983-1985, Cameron English (W) 1986-1988, Barry Gordon 1989-1994, Carl Holmberg 1995-1997.

*Location:* Pittsburgh Library, northwest corner of Highway 15 and 80 Gore Road, Kingston
*Type:* Bronze plaque on a stone cairn
*Sponsor:* Pittsburgh Township Historical Society
*Date Erected:* 2000
*Additional Information:* The reeves marked with a (W) were chosen as Wardens of Frontenac County for a single year. With the amalgamation on 1 January 1998, the position of Reeve of Pittsburgh Township and Warden of Frontenac County disappeared.
*Related Markers:* 114
*Readings:* Patterson 1989.

*Pittsburgh Township Hall, built 1886.*
R. Cardwell

Map VI – 8

# Hawthorn Cottage

*Location:* Pittsburgh Library, northwest corner of Highway 15 and 80 Gore Road, Kingston

*Type:* Bronze plaque on a stone cairn

*Sponsor:* Pittsburgh Township Historical Society

*Date Erected:* 2000

*Additional Information:* The style of Hawthorn Cottage (also known as MacLean House) is conservative for the 1860s. It is based on the traditional one-and-a-half storey 'Ontario Cottage,' which evolved in the 1840s with the gable pediment permitting illumination to the upper floor levels. By the 1860s the upper front window was often round-arched and tall. Hawthorn Cottage, a well proportioned stone building, has particularly handsome detailing in its fenestration with modified Venetian windows, one to each side of the front door with its intricate fanlight.

*Related Markers:* 114

*Readings:* Patterson 1989.

Situated on farm lot 10, East of the Great Cataraqui River, Pittsburgh Township, this house was built in 1866 by John Canniff and Sarah Baillie Ruttan. They purchased the lot, unoccupied, in 1839 from Mary Hamilton, who had received it as a Loyalist grant which she patented in 1798. John and Sarah, who were married in 1838 in Pittsburgh Township, had Loyalist antecedents. John was the son of Joseph Brant and Alley Canniff Ruttan who were among the first children born in Adolphustown Township settled by their Loyalist parents in 1784. Sarah was the daughter of John and Ann Parlow Baillie, one of the first settlers in Pittsburgh Township in 1794. Ann was the daughter of Lawrence Parlow, a Loyalist, stationed on Carleton Island. The building, erected by the Hay brothers, Scottish stone-masons, living on the Middle Road, Pittsburgh Township, is a typical, rather fine, mid-nineteenth century Ontario one and a half storey farm house. It and its surrounding land between Highway 15 and the Great Cataraqui River was purchased by Pittsburgh Township for municipal purposes. In 1997 it was declared to be the site for a new Pittsburgh Branch of the Kingston Frontenac Public Library.

*On the left is an addition designed by Shoalts and Zaback. The library was officially opened on 22 January 2000.* Photo David Kasserra

# Rideau Canal 1826-1832

Map VI – 9

Financed by the British government, on the Duke of Wellington's advice, it was built to provide a secure military route between Upper and Lower Canada. Work was supervised by military engineers commanded by Lieut. Colonel John By whose technical ability and perseverance overcame many obstacles. Many of his Irish emigrant labourers died of a virulent fever. Traversing 126 miles of largely unsettled country between Kingston and Bytown (now Ottawa), and including 47 locks, the canal was opened May 24, 1832.

*Location:* Kingston Mills, County Road 21, off Highway 15, beside the turning basin
*Type:* Aluminum plaque on post
*Sponsor:* Ontario Heritage Foundation
*Date Erected:* 1957
*Related Markers:* 119, 120
*Readings:* Gray 1951; Sneyd 1962; Tulloch 1981; Passfield 1982; Turner 1992; Turner 1995.

*Early view of Kingston Mills, Rideau Canal.* Queen's University Archives

Map VI – 10

# The King's Mills 1784

**Location:** Kingston Mills, County Road 21, off Highway 15, by the blockhouse
**Type:** Bronze plaque on stone cairn
**Sponsor:** Pittsburgh Township Historical Society
**Date Erected:** 1996
**Additional Information:** The last grist mill was destroyed by a flood in 1905.
**Related Markers:** 118, 120
**Readings:** MacKay 1977; Patterson 1989

In July 1783 the commanding officer of the British garrison at Cataraqui (Kingston) was directed to construct a saw mill and a grist mill to provide boards and flour for the Loyalist settlers arriving the following year. This site at the falls of the Great Cataraqui River was chosen and the "King's Mills" built in 1784. This was one of the earliest mill sites in Ontario. A succession of mills was located here, and in 1914 the present electric generating station was constructed to harness the power of the falls.

*A view of the last grist mill.* Queen's University Archives

# Workers on the Rideau

Map VI – 11

Between 1826 and 1832 thousands of French Canadians and recently arrived immigrants, notably Irish, Scottish and British, were recruited to work on the Rideau Canal. Working with only simple tools, they toiled 14 to 16 hours a day, six days a week, excavating, quarrying, and clearing the land to construct the locks and the dams. Many died from dangerous working conditions, malaria and other diseases at sites such as Kingston Mills and in the shantytowns where their families lived. Workers protested their predicament upon occasion but the deployment of soldiers along the canal served to inhibit such unrest. The canal was a project of the British Army but it could never have succeeded without the efforts of the civilian workers and their families. This plaque is dedicated to their memory.

*Location:* Kingston Mills, County Road 21, off Highway 15, under the railway bridge
*Type:* Aluminum plaque on post
*Sponsor:* Kingston and District Labour Council and Ontario Heritage Foundation
*Date Erected:* 1993
*Additional Information:* A related marker and painting titled *Pulling Together – The Builders on the Rideau* is in the lobby of the Hotel Dieu Hospital, 166 Brock Street. The mural, is the work of Laurie Swim and was installed in 1995.
*Related Markers:* 118, 119
*Readings:* Gray 1951; Sneyd 1962; Passfield 1982; Turner 1992; Turner 1995.

*View of workers in 1831-2 constructing the lock at Brewer's Lower Mill.* By Thomas Burrowes. Archives of Ontario

# VII

# THE OLD SYDENHAM WARD

**Map VII**                    **The Old Sydenham Ward**

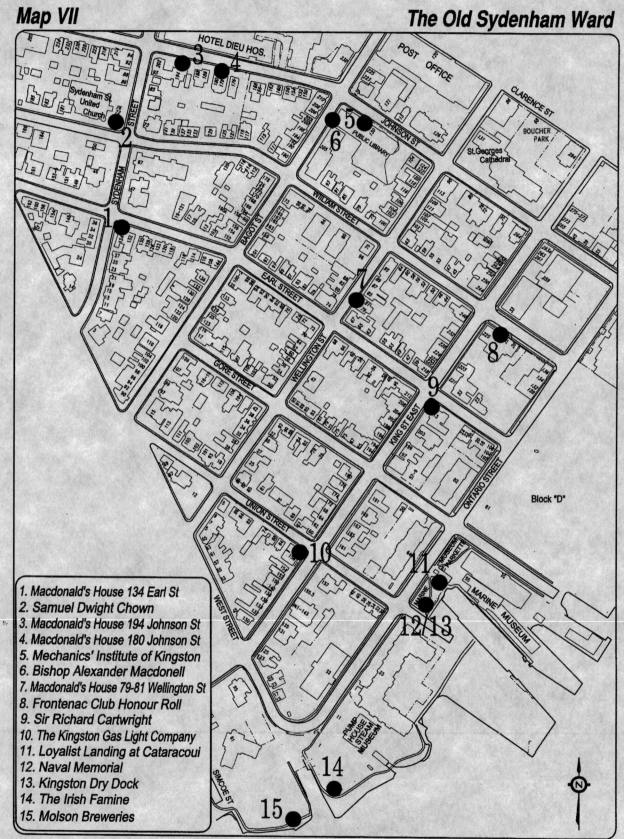

1. Macdonald's House 134 Earl St
2. Samuel Dwight Chown
3. Macdonald's House 194 Johnson St
4. Macdonald's House 180 Johnson St
5. Mechanics' Institute of Kingston
6. Bishop Alexander Macdonell
7. Macdonald's House 79-81 Wellington St
8. Frontenac Club Honour Roll
9. Sir Richard Cartwright
10. The Kingston Gas Light Company
11. Loyalist Landing at Cataracoui
12. Naval Memorial
13. Kingston Dry Dock
14. The Irish Famine
15. Molson Breweries

*Strategic & Long-Range Planning - DJMartin*

**Map VII – 1**

# Macdonald's House
# 134 Earl Street

*Location:* 134 Earl Street, Kingston
*Type:* Bronze plaque on post
*Sponsor:* Parks Canada
*Date Erected:* 1992
*Additional Information:* Macdonald's sister, Louisa, always seeming to be dissatisfied with her accommodation, continued her moves – but this one was to be her last. Macdonald was still officially recorded as the tenant for the house although living in Ottawa and by 1883 with a permanent home at Earnscliffe. The move to the corner of Earl and Sydenham Streets placed Louisa closer to a number of her Macpherson relatives. Professor Williamson still resided with Louisa until she passed away on 18 November 1888, after a series of strokes.
*Related Markers:* 36, 37, 62, 125, 126, 130, 157, 186, 187, 195, 201, 202, 203
*Readings:* Creighton 1952; Creighton 1955; Newman 1974; Angus 1984; Swainson 1979; Swainson 1989; DCB vol. 12.

Sir John A. Macdonald: Father of Confederation, Prime Minister of Canada
134 Earl Street, built 1866.
In 1878 Sir John A. Macdonald rented this house for his widowed brother-in-law Professor James Williamson and his sister Louisa Macdonald. Louisa died here in 1888. While he was member of Parliament for Kingston, this was Macdonald's legal residence until 1889.

Photo David Kasserra

# The Reverend
# Samuel Dwight Chown

Map VII – 2

In memory of The Reverend Samuel Dwight Chown D.D., LL.D., distinguished son of this Church, 1853-1933; Methodist Circuit Minister, 1874-1902; Secretary Temperance Board, 1902-1910; General Superintendent Methodist Church, 1910-1925; Christian, Patriot, Evangelist, Administrator
*Servant of God, Well Done!*

*Location:* Sydenham Street United Church, 82 Sydenham Street, Kingston, inside the church
*Type:* Brass plaque on wall
*Sponsor:* Sydenham Street United Church
*Date Erected:* c1934
*Additional Information:* As the General Superintendent of the Methodist Church, Chown (1853-1933) successfully led all the congregations across Canada into church union in 1925. The United Church of Canada is composed of Methodist, Presbyterian and Congregationalist churches. Chown was an advocate for world peace and supported the League of Nations.
*Readings:* Canadian Encyclopaedia 1985; Cossar 2000.

Photo David Kasserra

Map VII – 3

# Macdonald's House
# 194 Johnson Street

*Location:* 194 Johnson Street, Kingston
*Type:* Bronze plaque on post
*Sponsor:* Parks Canada
*Date Erected:* 1992
*Additional Information:* In 1855 Macdonald had decided that it would be best to move his wife, Isabella, and his son, Hugh John, with him wherever Parliament met and so they moved to Toronto. However, Macdonald's name remained on the Kingston assessment rolls and this house was his legal residence. When Isabella became too ill to look after her son early in 1857, Hugh John came to live here with his grandmother, two aunts and his uncle. A few months later Isabella also came to Kingston when Macdonald went on a government mission to London. She remained in Kingston when she became too ill to return to Toronto, and died in this house.
*Related Markers:* 36, 37, 62, 123, 126, 130, 157, 186, 187, 195, 201, 202, 203
*Readings:* Creighton 1952; Creighton 1955; Newman 1974; Angus 1984; Swainson 1979; Swainson 1989; DCB, vol. 12.

Sir John A. Macdonald: Father of Confederation, First Prime Minister of Canada
194 Johnson Street, built 1842.
John A. Macdonald rented this house from 1856 to 1860 as a residence for his mother, his sisters Louisa and Margaret, and Margaret's husband Professor James Williamson. Isabella, Macdonald's first wife, died here December 28, 1857. This was Macdonald's legal residence as a member of the Legislative Assembly for Kingston.

Photo David Kasserra

# Macdonald's House
# 180 Johnson Street

Map VII – 4

Sir John A Macdonald: Father of Confederation, First Prime Minister of Canada
180 Johnson Street, built 1843.
John A. Macdonald and his wife Isabella lived in this house from 1849 to 1852. Their second son Hugh John was born here in 1850.

*Location:* 180 Johnson Street, Kingston
*Type:* Bronze plaque on wall
*Sponsor:* Parks Canada
*Date Erected:* 1992
*Additional Information:* After giving up Bellevue House, Macdonald and his wife moved to what is now 180 Johnson Street. This house, designed by William Coverdale, had been built a few years earlier in 1843-44 for Thomas Askew, a Kingston merchant. According to Margaret Angus, it was a "modest house compared to Bellevue, but comfortable, adequate, less expensive to rent, to heat and to care for," (Angus 1984, 21) important considerations for Macdonald, given his responsibilities for the house in which his mother and sisters lived, on Brock near Barrie Street. Macdonald remained in this house until the fall of 1852 when he made some alterations to his Brock Street house and moved his family there.
*Related Markers:* 36, 37, 62, 123, 125, 130, 157, 186, 187, 195, 201, 202, 203
*Readings:* Creighton 1952; Creighton 1955; Newman 1974; Angus 1984; Swainson 1979; Swainson 1989; DCB, vol. 12.

Photo David Kasserra

Map VII – 5

# Mechanics' Institute of Kingston

**Location:** Kingston Public Library, 130 Johnson Street, Kingston, next to elevator
**Type:** marble wall plaque inscribed and carved in high relief
**Sponsor:** Mechanics' Institute of Kingston
**Date Erected:** c1834
**Additional Information:** Mechanics, constituting the vast majority of male workers in 19th century Kingston, learned their trades as apprentices to carpenters, painters, plasterers, sailors, etc.. They could also be manufacturers and the Mechanics' Institute, originating in Scotland and organized in Kingston in 1834, provided literature and lectures to improve their understanding of their trades and to upgrade their education. With the passage of the Public Libraries Act in 1895, the Mechanics' Institute's collection of books was transferred to a public library association, which has evolved into the Kingston Public Library.
**Readings:** Cohoe 1984; Cohoe 1985; Mika 1987; Osborne and Swainson 1988.

Mechanics Institute of Kingston
*Labore et Scientia*

Photo David Kasserra

Map VII – 6

# Bishop Alexander Macdonell 1762-1840

Patriot, colonizer and priest, he was born in the Highlands of Scotland. In 1804 he came to Canada as chaplain of the disbanded Glengarry Fencibles and later became Auxiliary Bishop of Quebec. As the first Bishop of the Roman Catholic diocese of Kingston, formed in 1826, he lived in this building and in 1831 was appointed to the Legislative Council of Upper Canada. In 1837 he founded Regiopolis College in Kingston and is buried in St. Mary's Cathedral in this city.

*Location:* Kingston Public Library, Johnson Street and Bagot Street corner, Kingston
*Type:* Aluminum plaque on post
*Sponsor:* Ontario Heritage Foundation
*Date Erected:* 1957
*Additional Information:* The Reverend Alexander Macdonell, 1762-1840, as priest to a large number of poor, landless Glengarry Highlanders living in the area of Glasgow, was largely responsible for the British government authorizing the raising of a fencible regiment, The Glengarry Fencibles, as means of relieving their distress. The Regiment with the Rev. Macdonell as Roman Catholic chaplain, the first in the history of the British Army, served from 1794 until 1802, during which it did much to reduce the element of unrest in Ireland. When it was disbanded following the Peace of Amiens, Macdonell was instrumental in securing government assistance to bring members of the Regiment and their families to Glengarry County, Upper Canada. He became pastor of St. Raphael's parish, where he established the Iona Seminary for the training of priests. In 1807 he was appointed Vicar General of Upper Canada and, as well carried out missionary work throughout the province. With the threat of impending war with the United States, he promoted the raising of a

*Bishop Alexander Macdonell in 1825. Reminiscences of the Late Honourable and Right Reverend Alexander Macdonell*

fencible regiment for Upper Canada, resulting in the Glengarry Light Infantry Fencibles in 1812. Macdonell was appointed chaplain and was an active recruiter for the Regiment until its disbandment in 1816 after illustrious service during the War of 1812. In 1820 he was consecrated Bishop of Rhesina and Auxiliary Bishop of Upper Canada, and in 1822 was responsible for the building of a parish house at the corner of Bagot and Johnson Streets, next to St Joseph's Roman Catholic Church

(demolished 1891). As the first Bishop of Kingston he used this house as his headquarters but lived mostly at St Raphael's. The parish house, a fine limestone building in the neoclassical style, forms the lower two storeys of the Kingston Public Library. A third storey and mansard roof were added in 1877 while it was the Notre Dame Academy, a girls' high school.

**Related Markers:** 46

**Readings:** Stanley 1972; Stewart and Wilson 1973; Rea 1974; Flynn 1973; Flynn 1976; DCB vol. 7. Reid 1983.

*Conjectural drawing of the Parish House in 1822.* By Jennifer McKendry

*Late 19th-century view of the Parish House in use as Notre Dame Academy with St Joseph's Church (Cathedral after 1826) in use as a school (on the right). St Joseph's, built in 1808, was closed as a church when St Mary's Cathedral opened in 1846. In 1859 the old stone building at the corner of Bagot and William Streets was converted into a school.* Louis Flynn. *At School in Kingston 1850-1973* (1973), 35

# Macdonald's House
# 79-81 Wellington Street

Map VII – 7

Sir John A. Macdonald: Father of Confederation, First Prime Minister of Canada
79-81 Wellington Street.
Sir John A. Macdonald rented half of this double house from 1876 to 1878 as a home for his sister Louisa Macdonald and his widowed brother-in-law Professor James Williamson.

*Location:* 79-81 Wellington Street, Kingston
*Type:* Bronze plaque on post
*Sponsor:* Parks Canada
*Date Erected:* 1992
*Additional Information:* Although by 1865 Macdonald was living in Ottawa, the capital of the United Province of Canada (Ontario and Quebec) and in 1867 married to Susan Agnes Bernard, he continued to maintain a presence in Kingston, which he represented in Parliament. After Macdonald's sister, Margaret Williamson, had died at Heathfield in 1876, Sir John A. leased half this Wellington Street building as a home for his sister Louisa and Professor Williamson, as well as Louisa's maid-companion and a servant. This house was built in the mid-1860s by carpenter and builder, Robert Waddington, and provided income as a rental property.
*Related Markers:* 36, 37, 62, 123, 125, 126, 157, 186, 187, 195, 201, 202, 203
*Readings:* Creighton 1952; Creighton 1955; Newman 1974; Angus 1984; Swainson 1979; Swainson 1989; DCB vol. 12.

Photo David Kasserra

**Map VII – 8**

# Frontenac Club Honour Roll

*Location:* 30 William Street at King Street East, Kingston

*Type:* Bronze plaque on William Street wall

*Sponsor:* Frontenac Club

*Date Erected:* c1918

*Additional Information:* The Frontenac Club was a gentlemen's club that had its origins in the 14th Battalion (Princess of Wales' Own Rifles) Officers' Club, formed in the nineteenth century before the Kingston Armouries, complete with an officers' mess, was built in 1900. A number of leading Kingstonians, garrison officers, faculty of Queen's University and the Royal Military College, and some officers of the PWOR, established a new club in 1908 in the old Bank of Montreal, a very fine stone structure built in 1845-1846. Three of the officers listed were serving in the PWOR in 1914, including George T. Richardson, brother of James A. Richardson who financed the building of Queen's first football stadium in memory of his brother. By 1931 the club was closed due to a lack of interest, as well as being a victim of the Great Depression.

*Related Markers:* 58, 59, 173

*Readings:* Mackenzie-Naughton 1946; Nicholson 1962; Wilson 1977; Morton 1981; McKendry 1995.

In memory of the members of this Club who fell in the Great War, 1914-1918.
Lt.-Col. Frank Strange,
Major J. McD. Mowat,
Lt.-Col. H.R. Duff,
Capt. G.T. Richardson,
Lt.-Col. D.I.V. Eaton,
Capt. J.M. Lanos,
Lt.- Col. B. McLennan, D.S.O.,
Capt. G.E. Francklyn,
Major S.L. Cunningham, M.C.,
Major W.E. Steacy, M.C.

*Frontenac Club in 1959.* George Lilley, Queen's University Archives

# Sir Richard Cartwright

Map VII – 9

Canadian Minister of Finance and Minister of Trade and Commerce, advocate of unrestricted reciprocity with the United States, was born in this house December 24, 1835. His father was the Rev. [Robert] David Cartwright, Chaplain to the Forces and Curate of St. George's.

*Location:* 191 King Street East at Gore Street, Kingston
*Type:* Aluminum plaque on wall of house
*Sponsor:* Kingston Historical Society
*Date Erected:* 1956
*Additional Information:* Sir Richard was named after his grandfather, the Honourable Richard Cartwright (1759-1815), United Empire Loyalist and merchant who married Magdalen Secord (sister-in-law of Laura Secord). They had eight children, including twin sons John Solomon and Robert David, born in 1804. The Reverend Robert Cartwright who married Harriet Dobbs, built the two-storey stone house at 191 King Street East in 1832. Three years later Richard (1835-1912) was born here. He brought his bride Francis Lawe to his family home in 1860. They lived here with their eight children until 1875, when the house was sold. In 1976 this handsome classically styled house became one of the heritage properties owned by the Ontario Heritage Foundation, but recently it has returned to private ownership. The Foundation maintains, however, an easement to protect its heritage features.
*Related Markers:* 24
*Readings:* Cartwright 1912; Angus 1966; Swainson 1968; DCB vol. 14. McKendry 1995.

Photo David Kasserra

Map VII – 10

# The Kingston Gas Light Company

Last Gas Lamp 1847-1947

*Location:* 156 King Street East, Kingston
**Type:** Gas lamp
*Sponsor:* Kingston Historical Society
***Date Erected:*** Re-dedicated 1959
***Additional Information:*** The Last Gas Lamp was re-dedicated by the Kingston Historical Society c1960 to commemorate the Kingston Gas Light Company incorporated in March 1848. This private company under the guidance of its first president, John Counter, built a plant on Queen Street to convert coal into gas to light Kingston's streets and major buildings. The company was taken over by the City in 1904.

Photo David Kasserra

# Loyalist Landing at Cataracoui 1784

Map VII – 11

Following the end of the American Revolution in 1783, Frederick Haldimand, Governor of Quebec, approved the resettlement of loyalist refugees in what is now southern Ontario. Favourable reports on the Cataracoui area led to its occupation by British forces in the spring of 1783 and to the commencement of surveys the following October. In June 1784 a party of Associated Loyalists from New York State under the command of Captain Michael Grass, part of a loyalist flotilla travelling from Montreal, established a camp here on Mississauga Point. Grass later recalled: "I led the loyal band, I pointed out to them the site of their future metropolis and gained for persecuted principles a sanctuary, for myself and followers a home."

*Location:* Marine Museum of the Great Lakes at Kingston, 55 Ontario Street at Lower Union Street, Kingston
*Type:* Aluminum plaque on post
*Sponsor:* Ontario Heritage Foundation
*Date Erected:* 1984
*Additional Information:* Grass had picked out Cataracoui (Cataraqui) as a place of settlement before his party left New York City in July 1783. Although unproven, it is recorded that Grass had taken part in the Seven Year's War, had been captured by the French, and imprisoned at Fort Frontenac. In any case, in the fall of 1783 he led a small group to Cataraqui where he left 17 men to help prepare for the arrival of his party of 106 men, women, and children the following year. The site had been occupied already, in the spring of 1783, by a force of 25 officers and 422 men of four different regular British regiments and the 2nd Battalion, King's Royal Regiment of New York, including women and children. Some years later when his claim to have been the founder of Kingston was challenged, Grass recanted saying, "he did not want to take the claim as founder...."
*Related Markers:* 68, 158
*Readings:* Preston 1959; Waltman 1981; MCC 1985

*A southeast view of Cataraqui (Kingston), August 1783.*
By James Peachy. National Archives of Canada, C-1511

Map VII – 12

# Naval Memorial

*Location:* Marine Museum of the Great Lakes, 55 Ontario Street at Lower Union Street, Kingston
*Type:* Bronze plaque on stone cairn
*Sponsor:* HMCS Cataraqui Association
*Date Erected:* 1994
*Additional Information:* This memorial, consisting of a pedestal surmounted by an anchor, was unveiled 1 May 1994, on Battle of the Atlantic Sunday. Cobblestones from Ontario Street surround the pedestal, which is made from limestone taken from St Mary's Cathedral, Kingston. Although barely in existence in the First World War and nearly financially starved out of existence during the 1930s, the Royal Canadian Navy with 306 ships had become the third largest navy in the world by 1945. During the Second World War over 100,000 men and women served in every theatre of war, but primarily on North Atlantic convoy duty. The RCN lost 23 ships and had 2,204 fatal casualties. The Canadian Merchant Marine lost 1,148 men. The Kingston Naval Veteran's Association erected a plaque in the Kingston Memorial Centre's entrance foyer in remembrance of those from Kingston and District who gave their lives while serving with the Canadian Naval Forces in the Second World War.
*Related Markers:* 20, 35
*Readings:* German 1990; Halford 1994; Crickard 1996.

In memory of the men and women of the Royal Canadian Navy and the Merchant Navy who served their country in War and Peace.
*We will remember them.*

*The Naval Memorial with Lake Ontario in the background, the Marine Museum (left), and the retired Canadian Coast Guard Ship Alexander Henry (right).*
Photo David Kasserra

# Kingston Dry Dock

Map VII – 13

Mississauga Point was for over 150 years the site of major shipyards when Kingston was one of the important ports and ship building centres on the Great Lakes. The significance of this industry led the federal government to construct this dry dock in 1890. Initially operated by the Department of Public Works as a repair facility for lake vessels, it was enlarged and leased in 1910 to the Kingston Shipbuilding Company, the first of a series of private concerns which operated the shipyards until 1968. During the Second World War naval vessels, notably corvettes, were built in this shipyard.

*Location:* Marine Museum of the Great Lakes at Kingston, 55 Ontario Street at Lower Union Street, Kingston
*Type:* Bronze plaque on post
*Sponsor:* Historic Sites and Monuments Board of Canada
*Date Erected:* 1986
*Additional Information:*
Mississauga Point was named after the Mississauga natives who had once lived in this region. They relinquished their claims to the land in the 1780s after the arrival of the United Empire Loyalists.
*Related Markers:* 76
*Readings:* Perley 1896; Rushbrook 1977.

*Kingston Dry Dock c1905.* Queen's University Archives

136

**Map VII – 14**

# The Irish Famine

*Location:* An Gorta Mór (The Great Hunger) Park, West and Ontario Streets, Kingston
*Type:* Trilingual carved stone cross
*Sponsor:* The Kingston Irish Famine Commemoration Association
*Date Erected:* 1998
*Additional Information:* "Several thousand Irish, sick with typhus, were crammed into hastily erected fever sheds on waterfront land at Lower Emily Street (near Murney Tower in Macdonald Park) and at Kingston General Hospital. They had survived a perilous journey across the Atlantic in the hold of a coffin ship, survived the horrors of Grosse Ile, and endured the slow trip on an overcrowded barge only to die painfully in a Kingston fever shed. Hundreds of Kingstonians of many denominations, stricken while helping the Irish immigrants in their hour of need, also died of typhus" (Tony O'Loughlin of the Irish Famine Commemoration Association).
More than 1,500 people died of typhus in Kingston, and were buried in a mass grave outside of Kingston General Hospital. In 1894 the Angel of the Resurrection (also known as the Angel of Mercy) was placed on that site. In 1966 the statue and some of the remains of the typhus victims were moved to St. Mary's Cemetery, 718 Division Street. The Celtic Cross monument, designed by Kim A. Whalen, was constructed by the Campbell Monument Company Limited, Belleville, Ontario.
*Related Markers:* 205, 206
*Readings:* Flynn 1976; MacKay 1990; Towns 1990; Deslauriers 1995; O'Gallagher 1995.

On this shore, more than 1500 Irish, fleeing The Great Hunger, along with compassionate citizens of many faiths, who cared for them, died of typhus in the fever sheds of Kingston. 1847-1848
*We Hold Their Memory Sacred*
*In Memory of An Gorta Mór 1847-1848*

*Celtic dancers honour the victims of the famine at the unveiling of the Cross in 1998.* Irish Famine Commemoration Association

# Molson Breweries

Map VII – 15

In 1824, Thomas Molson, brewer and distiller, purchased a residence and brewery at this location from Captain Henry Murney. A new and enlarged brewery was built, producing a product that became known for its fair price and excellent quality. In 1831, a second brewery was purchased on lot 23 of the then Kingston Township. Both breweries were sold in 1835 when Thomas Molson returned to Montreal.

*Location:* Between West and Simcoe Streets, Kingston, on the lakeshore
*Type:* Aluminum plaque on post
*Sponsor:* Kingston Historical Society
*Date Erected:* 1984
*Additional Information:* Loyalist Kingston was the birthplace of Ontario's brewing industry. As one of his first duties, John Graves Simcoe, Upper Canada's first Lieutenant Governor, offered a bonus to anyone who would grow barley for malt. He also instructed the Loyalists to brew, not only as a healthy 'British' alternative to American whiskey, but also to fight off the evils of Republicanism. The Finkle Brothers, as obedient subjects, obliged their governor and opened Upper Canada's first brewery and tavern in the Village of Bath before 1793. Less than a decade later, merchant Joseph Forsyth began Upper Canada's first commercial brewery, later the Bajus Brewery. To service a huge thirst for beer, Thomas Molson (1791-1863), as well as Scottish, English and German brewers, established breweries in town. Some early stone breweries have survived: the remains of Fisher's Brewery is across from the Portsmouth Olympic harbour, while the brew tower at Morton's Brewery now forms part of the home for the Cataraqui Archaeological Foundation at 370 King Street West.
*Readings:* Denison 1955; Molson's 1972; Patterson 1985; Bowering 1991.

*Thomas Molson.* Molson Breweries Canada

# CITY PARK
## *and*
# MACDONALD PARK

# Map VIII

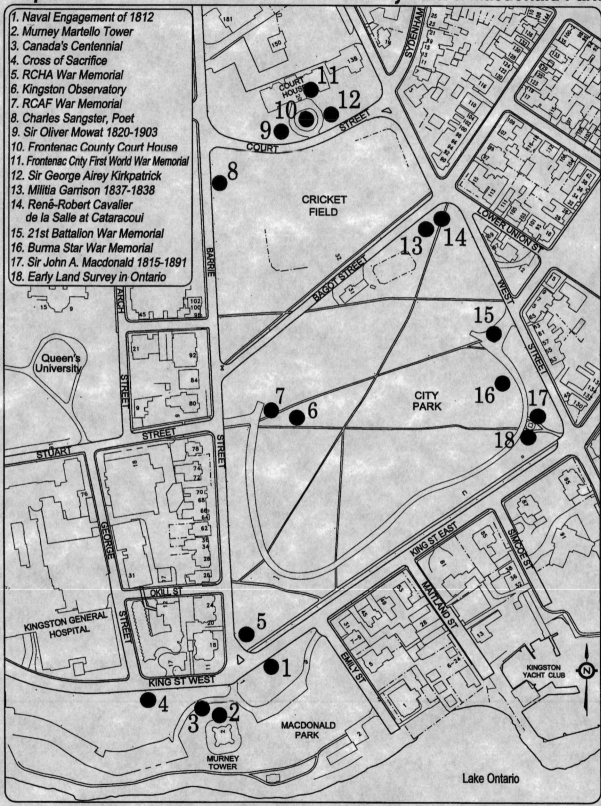

1. Naval Engagement of 1812
2. Murney Martello Tower
3. Canada's Centennial
4. Cross of Sacrifice
5. RCHA War Memorial
6. Kingston Observatory
7. RCAF War Memorial
8. Charles Sangster, Poet
9. Sir Oliver Mowat 1820-1903
10. Frontenac County Court House
11. Frontenac Cnty First World War Memorial
12. Sir George Airey Kirkpatrick
13. Militia Garrison 1837-1838
14. Renê-Robert Cavalier
    de la Salle at Cataracoui
15. 21st Battalion War Memorial
16. Burma Star War Memorial
17. Sir John A. Macdonald 1815-1891
18. Early Land Survey in Ontario

*Strategic & Long-Range Planning - DJMartin*

**Map VIII – 1**

# Naval Engagement of 1812

*Location:* Macdonald Park, King Street East between Emily and Barrie Streets, Kingston
*Type:* Aluminum plaque on post
*Sponsor:* Kingston Historical Society
*Date Erected:* 1953
*Additional Information:* At the outset of the War of 1812, the British enjoyed a decided advantage on the Great Lakes as the result of a naval force known as the Provincial Marine of Upper Canada. The chief supply route in the Lake Ontario region was via water from Kingston to Fort George situated at the mouth of the Niagara River. On 8 November 1812 Commodore Isaac Chauncey, commander of the newly built American squadron on the lake, set sail. The following day, the American fleet fell upon the 22-gun corvette *Royal George* commanded by Commodore Hugh Earl. Chauncey chased the *Royal George* that day, throughout the night and the following morning, until the *Royal George* sought refuge in Kingston harbour. The American fleet sailed into Kingston harbour, but came under heavy fire not only from the *Royal George,* but from the

On Nov. 10 a naval engagement was fought at the entrance to Kingston harbour between *H.M.S. Royal George* and *U.S.S. Oneida* supported by American schooners.

shore batteries whose protection Earl had sought. The engagement continued for almost two hours. The Americans withdrew at sundown. The engagement was a small affair but of strategic significance. The importance of the control of the waterways as the main supply route, for both British and Americans alike, led to a shipbuilding race for the rest for the war. Control of Lake Ontario depended on which fleet was the strongest at the moment.
*Related Marker:* 93, 219
*Readings:* Anonymous 1812; Hitsman 1967; Malcomson 1998.

*Naval warfare near Kingston harbour.* National Archives of Canada, C-40593

# Murney Martello Tower

Map VIII – 2

This tower was constructed in 1846 as a part of the new naval defences authorized for Kingston Harbour by the Imperial government during the Oregon Crisis of 1845-46. It was one of the last British works of defence commenced in the Canadian interior and one of the most sophisticated of the Martello Towers built in British North America. Although in regular use as a barracks after 1849 it was not fully armed until 1862, when it had already become obsolete because of rapid advance in offensive military technology.

*Location:* Macdonald Park, Barrie Street and King Street West, Kingston
*Type:* Bronze plaque on stone base
*Sponsor:* Historic Sites and Monuments Board of Canada
*Date Erected:* 1950
*Additional Information:* The land on which Murney Tower was built was acquired from Captain Henry Murney (died 1835). It was part of Farm Lot 25, the first lot west of the town of Kingston, which had been granted to Loyalist Michael Grass in 1784. When the tower was constructed in 1846, the British government decided to name the fortification Murray Redoubt after Sir George Murray, Master General of the Ordnance, a senior military officer who died that year. Although 'Murray Redoubt' was carved in stone above the entrance, local residents continued to associate the site with Captain Murney. *Heritage Kingston* states that "by 1850, the similarity of the names and the difficulty of changing the habits of Kingstonians, had doomed the new name to oblivion and continued the old." (Stewart and Wilson 1973, 83) At some point the second stone 'R' in Murray's name was replaced by a metal 'N' to create a hybrid name - Murnay Redoubt - as it remains today. In 1925 the tower was opened as a museum by the Kingston Historical Society. Visitors are welcome to tour this National Historic Site during the summer season.
*Related Markers:* 27, 28, 29, 88, 94, 95
*Readings:* Walkem 1897b; Lavell 1936; Preston and Lavell 1963; Angus 1966; Stewart and Wilson 1973; Parks Canada 1976; Davidson 1981; Moorehead 1987.

Queen's University Archives

**Map VIII – 3**

# Canada's Centennial

**Location:** Macdonald Park, Barrie Street and King Street West, Kingston
**Type:** Flat concrete and stone monument
**Sponsor:** Girl Guides of Canada, Boy Scouts of Canada & the Parks and Recreation Committee for the City of Kingston
**Date Erected:** 1967
**Additional Information:** This was one of thousands of markers celebrating Canada's one hundredth birthday in a spirit of nationalism and patriotism. A stylized maple leaf composed of coloured stones and flanked by the dates 1867 and 1967 lies on a round concrete bed.

**Related Markers:** 26

This emblem commemorating Canada's centennial year is constructed with stone collected and placed here by members of the Girl Guide and Boy Scout movement of the Kingston area in co-operation with the Parks and Recreation Committee. June 3, 1967.

Photo David Kasserra

# Cross of Sacrifice

Map VIII – 4

To the Glory of God and in proud and loving memory of those Kingston men and women who gave their lives in the Great War.
*Their name liveth for evermore.*
1914-1918, WW II 1939-1945, Korea 1950-1953

*Location:* Macdonald Park, King Street West at George Street, Kingston
**Type:** Stone cross
*Sponsor:* Kingston Chapters of the Imperial Order of the Daughters of the Empire (IODE)
*Date Erected:* 1925
*Additional Information:* Since its construction the Cross of Sacrifice has been the main focus of Remembrance Day ceremonies in the City of Kingston. Erected on the north shore of Lake Ontario its site is a usually chilly place on 11 November; still, the personal discomfort helps to serve as a reminder of the 110,000 Canadians, who, in this century, made the supreme sacrifice. When the Cross was unveiled on 17 May 1925, more than 3,000 people attended the ceremony. When the first chapter of the IODE first met in Fredericton, NB, on 13 February 1900, the women gathered to knit items for Canadian soldiers fighting the Boers in South Africa. There were various Kingston IODE chapters of this charitable organization from 1905 to 1996 (*Kingston Whig-Standard,* 26 February 2000).
*Readings:* IODE 1950, 1954; Nicholson 1962; Wilson 1977; Morton 1981.

Photo David Kasserra

**Map VIII – 5**

# Royal Canadian Horse Artillery War Memorial

*Location:* City Park, corner of Barrie Street and King Street East, Kingston

*Type:* Stone monument

*Sponsor:* Royal Canadian Horse Artillery Officers and Men

*Date Erected:* 1930

*Additional Information:* The names of the members of the RCHA who were killed in both World Wars are listed on the memorial. In 1996, on occasion of the 125th Anniversary of the Royal Regiment of Canadian Artillery 1871-1996, a 25 Pounder Gun used by the Canadian Artillery from 1943-1955 was erected by the Royal Canadian Horse Artillery Brigade Association and Kingston Gunners as a memorial to Fallen Gunners. (The McCallum Granite Co. Ltd. Monument Builders of Kingston and Canadian Wm. A. Rogers Limited Bronze Founders of Toronto built this monument.)

*Related Markers:* 74, 75

*Readings:* Nicholson 1962; Nicholson 1967; Wilson 1977; Morton 1981; Mitchell 1986.

Erected by the Officers, N.C.O.'s and men of the Royal Canadian Horse Artillery in glorious memory of their comrades who fell in the Great War.

*Their name liveth for evermore.*

1914-1918 – Somme 1916-1918, Guillemont, Ginchy, Transloy, Hill 70, Cambrai 1917-1918, France & Flanders 1915-1918, St. Quentin, Rosières, Avre, Amiens, Hamel, Pursuit to the Selle

In the glorious memory of those who gave their lives in the Second World War.

1939-1945 – Sicily, Moro River, Ortona, Liri Valley, Gothic Lines, San Fortunato, Lamone River, Northwest Europe 1945

Photo David Kasserra

# Kingston Observatory

Map VIII – 6

The first optical astronomical observatory in the province, the Kingston Observatory was established in 1855 after a solar eclipse aroused public interest in astronomical studies. Under the auspices of a committee of British military officers and "gentlemen amateurs" a frame observatory was built here. It was transferred to the control of Queen's College in 1861 and within a year a new brick structure had been erected on the site. Staffed by Nathan Fellowes Dupuis, an able mathematician, the observatory, in addition to making conventional astronomical observations, produced barometric and thermal readings, fixed meridians for surveying and provided a time service. In 1881 it was moved to Queen's and today four cylindrical stones, former supports for the telescope, are all that remain of the old observatory building.

*Location:* City Park, Stuart and Barrie Streets, Kingston [Not presently in place]
*Type:* Aluminum plaque on post
*Sponsor:* Ontario Heritage Foundation
*Date Erected:* 1985
*Additional Information:* Four stones (resembling mill stones) from the pillar on which the telescope was mounted can still be found in the park near King Street. In addition to his involvement with the Kingston Observatory, Nathan Fellowes Dupuis (1835-1917) designed the clock in Grant Hall, Queen's University. He was also the first Dean of Applied Science from 1894 to 1911 at Queen's University.
*Related Markers:* 77, 172
*Readings:* Cohoe 1979; Hughes 1986.

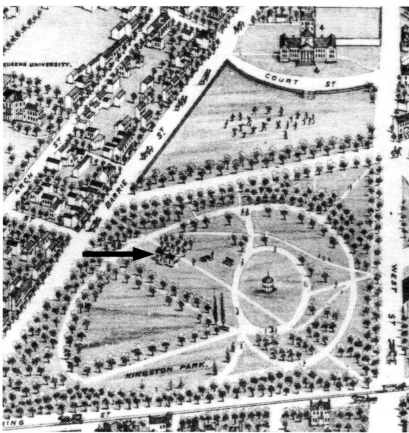

*Detail of Brosius's bird's eye map showing the Kingston Observatory in 1875.*
Queen's University Archives

Map VIII – 7

# Royal Canadian Air Force War Memorial

**Location:** City Park, facing Stuart Street, Kingston
**Type:** Stone monument
**Sponsor:** 416 Wing Royal Canadian Air Force Association
**Date Erected:** c1967
**Additional Information:** In 1916 the Canadian Aviation Corps was formed. Canadians, however, fought during the First World War in the Royal Flying Corps or the Royal Naval Air Service, where they had a magnificent record as fighter aces. On 1 April 1924 the Royal Canadian Air Force was established. It became, by 1945, the world's fourth largest air force, with a strength of over 230,000. Canadian men and women served during the Second World War in every theatre of war, but especially in Bomber Command in the United Kingdom. Over 18,000 lost their lives. This marker was built by Kingston Memorials of Cataraqui, Ontario.
**Readings:** Wilson 1977; Canada 1980a, 1980b, 1986, 1994; Morton 1981.

To the glory of God and in loving memory of all who gave their lives and served with the Royal Canadian Air Force and Commonwealth Air Forces.

1914-1918, 1939-1945
*They have slipped the surly bonds of earth.*

Photo David Kasserra

# Charles Sangster, Poet

Map VIII – 8

Sangster, one of the most significant Canadian poets of the pre-confederation period was born at the naval yard, Point Frederick. In 1849 he edited the *Courier* at Amherstburg but the following year returned to Kingston to work for the *British Whig* and subsequently the *Daily News*. In this community he did his best literary work, including two books, *The St. Lawrence and Saguenay and Other Poems* (1856) and *Hesperus and Other Poems and Lyrics* (1860). Sangster's writings are imbued with a love for Canada, its scenery, its history and its traditions. Following employment with the Post Office Department at Ottawa, 1868-1886, he spent the remainder of his life in retirement here in Kingston.

*Location:* City Park, across from 144 Barrie Street, Kingston
*Type:* Aluminum plaque on post
*Sponsor:* Ontario Heritage Foundation
*Date Erected:* 1964
*Additional Information:*

*A warm light permeates the sky,*
*A silvery mist is lingering nigh,*
*And floating up the trees near by.*
*A slumberous silence fills the air,*
*Silence upon the Lake, and where*
*The pine drops pearls from out their hair.*
*The birdlings have no voice to sing,*
*There's not a bird upon the wing,*
*Nature, herself, is slumbering.*

From "Rideau Lake," 1856,
Charles Sangster (1822-1893)

*Readings:* Robb 1963; Hamilton 1971; Hamilton 1988; DCB vol 12; Downie 1993.

*Charles Sangster.*
Kingston Historical Society

**Map VIII – 9**

# Sir Oliver Mowat 1820-1903

*Location:* Frontenac County Court House, Court Street, Kingston
*Type:* Aluminum plaque on post
*Sponsor:* Ontario Heritage Foundation
*Date Erected:* 1962
*Readings: Anonymous* 1962; Swainson 1972; DCB vol. 12; Evans 1992.

Born in Kingston, Mowat studied law under John A. Macdonald. After moving to Toronto in 1840 he was elected a Liberal member of the legislature of the Province of Canada in 1857 and served as provincial secretary in 1858 and postmaster general, 1863-64. He took part in the Quebec Conference of 1864, which led to Confederation in 1867. Mowat became Ontario's third Prime Minister in 1872, succeeding the Honourable Edward Blake, and retained that post for almost 24 years. Resigning in 1896, he accepted a seat in the Senate, and became minister of justice, 1896-97 in the cabinet of Sir Wilfrid Laurier. Mowat served as lieutenant-governor of Ontario from 1897 until his death.

*Oliver Mowat at the end of his premiership.*
Archives of Ontario, Acc. 1750-5315

# Frontenac County Court House

Map VIII – 10

This grand Neo-classical building has served the courts of Frontenac County since its opening in 1858. Designed by the Dorset-born architect, Edward Horsey, it is superbly sited on land originally acquired in 1840 for a house of parliament, at a time when Kingston was one of several possible sites for the capital of Canada. Constructed of stone quarried on site, it features many of the traditional exterior elements of large-scale mid-19th century court houses: the use of classical detailing, the balanced three-part composition of centre pavilion and side wings, and a bold portico and dome.

*Location:* Frontenac County Court House, Court Street, Kingston, directly in front of the fountain
*Type:* Bronze plaque on post
*Sponsor:* Historic Sites and Monuments Board of Canada
*Date Erected:* 1986
*Additional Information:* The court house suffered a severe fire in 1875, and was rebuilt with a new elevated dome by J. Power and Son. They also designed the adjacent Registry Office at this time. The jailer's house of 1858 survives behind the court house, but the jail walls and jail were demolished in 1974. The last hanging was in 1949. This complex of buildings served three functions for the United Counties of Frontenac, Lennox and Addington from 1858 to 1864, and for the County of Frontenac from 1865 to 1997: judicial, penal and administrative.
*Readings:* Angus 1966; Carter 1983; MacRae 1983; McKendry 1995.

*Frontenac County Court House c1905.* Queen's University Archives

**Map VIII – 11**

# Frontenac County
# First World War Memorial

**Location:** Frontenac County Court House, Court Street, Kingston, on the stairway landing

**Type:** Bronze plaque and stained-glass windows

**Sponsor:** Frontenac County

**Date Erected:** 1921

**Additional Information:** A list of 125 Frontenac County residents killed in action is inscribed on a bronze plaque below the window. The Frontenac County Court House, once the administrative offices for Frontenac County, was a logical location for this memorial. The stained-glass windows were designed by N.T. Lyon Company of Toronto in 1921.

**Related Markers:** 20, 21

**Readings:** Rollason 1982.

Call to arms, victory, triumphant return.
County of Frontenac Honour Roll. The heroic dead who gave their lives in the Great War 1914-1918.

Photo David Kasserra

# Sir George Airey Kirkpatrick

Map VIII – 12

This fountain was erected in 1903, in honour of Lieutenant Colonel Sir George Airey Kirkpatrick 1841-1899, a son of Thomas Kirkpatrick, Esq., first mayor of the Town of Kingston 1838, Member of Parliament for Frontenac 1870-1892, Speaker of the House of Commons 1883-1887, Lieutenant Governor of Ontario 1892-1897. It was renovated in 1958.

*Location:* Frontenac County Court House, Court Street, Kingston, plaque is just east of the fountain
*Type:* Cast-iron fountain, aluminum plaque on post
*Sponsor:* Committee for Kirkpatrick Memorial Fountain, Kingston Historical Society (plaque)
*Date Erected:* 1903 (fountain), 1958 (plaque)
*Additional Information:* In 1903 a fountain designed by J. Power and Son was dedicated to the memory of Sir George Airey Kirkpatrick. After the zinc statue at the top of fountain was vandalized in 1996, it was replaced by a bronze replica sculpted by John Boxtel. On the base of the fountain the following text can be found: "Kirkpatrick: Sir George Airey Kirkpatrick, K.C.M.G., Member for Frontenac, Speaker House of Commons, Lieutenant-Governor of Ontario. 1841-1899."
*Readings:* Gundy 1958; Swainson 1971; DCB vol.12.

*The fountain dedicated to Sir George Airey Kirkpatrick.*
Photo David Kasserra

Map VIII – 13

# Militia Garrison 1837-1838

*Location:* City Park, Bagot and West Streets, Kingston

*Type:* Aluminum plaque on post

*Sponsor:* Ontario Heritage Foundation

*Date Erected:* 1958

*Additional Information:* "The day was passed in reviewing, organizing, drilling and disciplining the Militia; in ordering great guns and little guns, bedding, cartridges, powder, flints and firelocks; in strengthening the batteries and Fort Henry, bringing old sand-bags into use, which had rotted in oblivion of war. In mounting traversing platforms and drying damp casements, building ovens, and preparing safe places for the specie of the Commissariat and the Public Banks; in meeting the wishes of the rich inhabitants by providing bomb proof vaults to put their plate and deeds in, and in arranging secure places in the event of the worst; in palisading, picketting, drawbridging, and in short, in all the pomp and circumstances of war..." Taken from Richard Bonnycastle's book *Canada As It Was, Is, and May Be* (London: Colburn & Co., 1852), in which he describes the preparations for the defence of Kingston against the militant insurgents in December 1837.

*Related Markers:* 96

*Readings:* MGO 1838; Dent 1885; Fryer 1987;

Commemorating the services of the first permanent Militia Garrison of Kingston, assembled by Lieutenant-Colonel R.H. Bonnycastle to defend this city during the Upper Canadian Rebellion. The mobilization saved Kingston from invasion since the regular forces had been sent to Lower Canada. The troops used this area as their drill ground: Queen's Marine Artillery, Perth Artillery, Frontenac Light Dragoons, 1st Hastings Light Dragoons, 1st and 2nd Addington Light Dragoons, 1st and 2nd Frontenac, 2nd and 3rd Prince Edward, 1st and 2nd Addington, 2nd Lennox, Belleville Rifles, Independent Companies, Tyendinaga Mohawks.

*Unveiling of the plaque in 1958, from left to right: The Reverend J. Minto Swan; D. Rankin, MPP; Brigadier R. Rowley; Professor T.F. McIlwraith; and Bogart W. Trumpour representing the Kingston Historical Society.*

Photo courtesy Bogart Trumpour

# René-Robert Cavelier de La Salle at Cataracoui

Map VIII – 14

Early in his celebrated career the explorer La Salle played a principal role in the expansion of the French fur trade into the Lake Ontario region. In 1673 he arranged a meeting between Governor-General Frontenac, who wanted to shift the centre of the fur trade away from Montreal, and representatives of the Iroquois at Cataracoui, the site of present-day Kingston. Placed in command of Fort Frontenac, the post the governor ordered built here, La Salle soon gained control over trade in the area by acquiring ownership of the establishment as a seigneurial grant. Using the fort as a base, he then undertook expeditions to the west and southwest in an attempt to expand his Cataracoui operation into a vast fur-trading empire.

*Location:* City Park, West and Lower Union Streets, Kingston
*Type:* Aluminum plaque on post
*Sponsor:* Ontario Heritage Foundation
*Date Erected:* 1957
*Additional Information:* René-Robert Cavelier de La Salle, born at Rouen, France in 1643, was assassinated in 1687 in the area now known as Texas.
*Related Markers:* 31, 72, 73, 211
*Readings:* Preston and Lamontagne 1958; Preston 1959; DCB vol. 1; Breck 1993; Grimshaw 1993.

*A modern painting depicting La Salle overseeing the construction of Fort Frontenac in 1676.* National Archives of Canada

**Map VIII – 15**

# 21st Battalion War Memorial

*Location:* City Park, across from 65 West Street, Kingston
*Type:* Bronze statue on stone base
*Sponsor:* 21st Battalion Association
*Date Erected:* 1931
*Additional Information:* The 21st Battalion memorial was unveiled on 11 November 1931 by mothers of sons killed with the battalion. The 21st Battalion "Colours" that had been presented prior to the unit's departure for overseas were paraded by ex-members of the battalion. The memorial was dedicated Lt Col J. Stewart, DSO. The pipe band of the Princess of Wales' Own Regiment played "Flowers of the Forest" and former buglers of the 21st Battalion sounded the Last Post and Reveille. (Osborne and Swainson 1988, 295)
*Related Markers:* 56, 57
*Readings:* Mackenzie-Naughton 1946; Osborne and Swainson 1988.

To the memory of our valiant comrades of the Twenty-First Canadian Infantry Battalion, C.E.F. who in the Great War made the supreme sacrifice, 1914-1918.
*To the end, to the end, they remain.*
Amiens, Arras 1917, 1918, Mount Sorrel, Ancre Heights, Drocourt-Quéant, Scarpe 1918, Vimy Ridge, Somme 1916, 1918, Ypres 1917, Hindenburg Line, Hill 70, Cambrai 1918, Flers Courcelette, Passchendaele, Canal du Nord, Thiepval, Pursuit to Mons, France and Flanders 1915-1918.

Photo David Kasserra

# Burma Star War Memorial

Map VIII – 16

Dedicated to the memory of those who served in the Far East and Pacific Theatres of War 1941-1945. Through this stone we touch the souls of those who died for our freedom.

*When you go home tell them of us, and say for your tomorrow we gave our today.* (Kohima Epitaph)

*Location:* City Park, across from 55 West Street, Kingston
*Type:* Stone monument
*Sponsor:* Eastern Ontario Branch of The Burma Star Association
*Date Erected:* 1995
*Additional Information:* This memorial was dedicated on 15 August 1995, recognizing Victory over Japan, 15 August 1945. Each year on this day there is a commemoration ceremony remembering Canada's contribution to the Pacific and Far East theatres of war.
*Readings:* Slim 1972.

*The monument is decorated for the Victory over Japan Day ceremony, 15 August 1999.* Photo David Kasserra

**Map VIII – 17**

# Sir John A. Macdonald 1815-1891

**Location:** City Park, corner of King Street East and West Street, Kingston
**Type:** Bronze statue; bronze plaque
**Sponsor:** City of Kingston (statue), Historic Sites and Monuments Board of Canada (plaque)
**Date Erected:** 1895 (statue), 1952 (plaque)
**Additional Information:** A week after Macdonald's funeral, the Kingston Board of Trade met "to discuss the erection of a monument to the late Sir John A. Macdonald." It was at this meeting that it was proposed that a statue should be erected near Murney Tower and that the area should be called Macdonald Park. Although a proposal to have an illuminated statue of Macdonald on top of Murney Tower was not implemented, a statue sculpted by George Wade was unveiled at the corner of West and King Streets in 1895. Cohoe notes that funds for the statue were limited and there was an appeal for further subscriptions at the unveiling to provide for the curbing stones and to buy a metal plaque. The lack of a plaque was not rectified until 1952 when the federal tablet was erected. In 1977 it was replaced by the current bilingual marker. See also frontispiece and covers.
**Related Markers:** 36, 37, 62, 123, 125, 126, 130, 186, 187, 195, 201, 202, 203
**Readings:**
Anonymous 1950; Creighton 1952; Newman 1974; Cohoe 1978; Angus 1984; Swainson 1979; Swainson 1989; Grenville 1992; DCB vol. 12.

First elected from Kingston to the Legislative Assembly of the Province of Canada in 1844, he was for forty-seven years a leading figure in the public life of his country. One of the Fathers of Confederation, he became the first Prime Minister of Canada and held the office 1867-73; 1878-91. Under his leadership the new Dominion was extended from sea to sea by incorporation of the territories of the Hudson's Bay Company, British Columbia and Prince Edward Island; and linked together by construction of the Intercolonial and Canadian Pacific Railways.

*The unveiling of Sir John A. Macdonald's statue in 1895.* Queen's University Archives

# Early Land Survey in Ontario

Map VIII – 18

In September 1783, Deputy Surveyor-General John Collins was dispatched to Cataraqui by Governor Haldimand to lay out townships for loyalist settlers. The necessary land was purchased from Mississauga Indians, and on 27 October the first survey marker was planted. By the year's end the front concessions of four townships, stretching from Cataraqui to the Bay of Quinte, had been surveyed. A fifth was laid out the following summer. Collins thus completed the first major survey made under civil authority in what is now Ontario.

*Location:* City Park, King Street East near West Street, Kingston
*Type:* Bronze plaque on stone cairn
*Sponsor:* Historic Sites and Monuments Board of Canada
*Date Erected:* 1938
*Additional Information:* The original plan for the Loyalist settlement at Cataraqui (now Kingston) was to lay out the town on the east side of the Cataraqui River, in the area later known as Pittsburgh Township. However, before the survey began, a decision was made to place both the town and the first township on the west side of the river, partly because of the "stoney and barren" land on the east side. However, as Preston points out, there were probably other reasons – to make it easier for those Loyalists who would draw both town lots as well as farm lots and secondly, the beginnings of a town were already developing close to the old French fort (Preston 1959, xlv).
The Early Land Survey plaque was erected near the dividing line (West Street) between the western limits of the town and the first farm lot in Kingston Township. In addition to laying out the town of Kingston, Collins was responsible for surveying the townships of Kingston, Ernestown, Fredericksburg, Adolphustown and Marysburg – named after George III and his sons and daughter. The survey and settlement of the land east of the Cataraqui River (Pittsburgh Township), was not done until 1788.
*Related Markers:* 76, 134
*Readings:* Preston 1959; MCC 1985; Allen 1992.

Photo David Kasserra

# QUEEN'S UNIVERSITY *and the* KINGSTON GENERAL HOSPITAL

# Map IX

## Queen's University & Kingston General Hospital

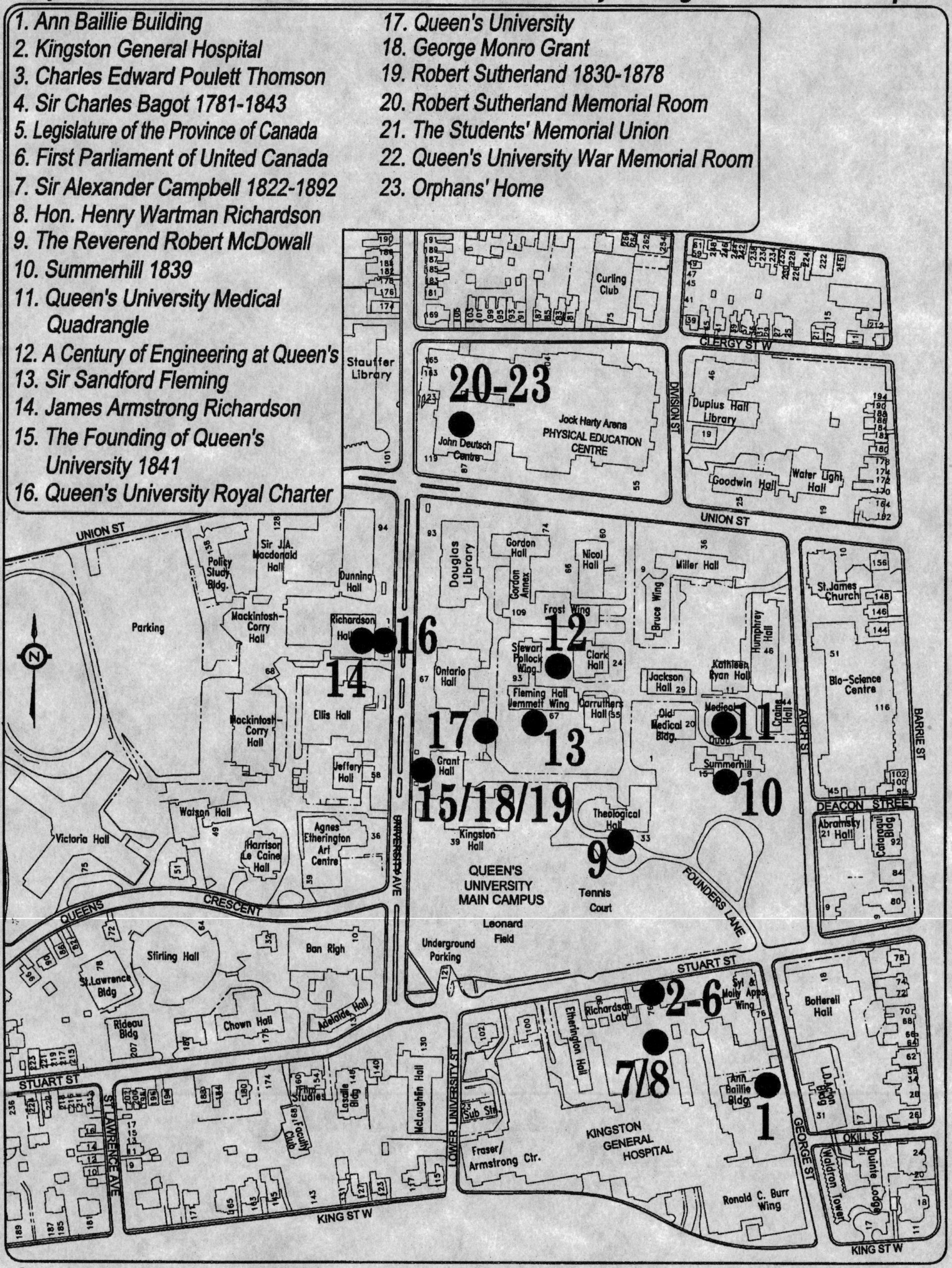

1. Ann Baillie Building
2. Kingston General Hospital
3. Charles Edward Poulett Thomson
4. Sir Charles Bagot 1781-1843
5. Legislature of the Province of Canada
6. First Parliament of United Canada
7. Sir Alexander Campbell 1822-1892
8. Hon. Henry Wartman Richardson
9. The Reverend Robert McDowall
10. Summerhill 1839
11. Queen's University Medical Quadrangle
12. A Century of Engineering at Queen's
13. Sir Sandford Fleming
14. James Armstrong Richardson
15. The Founding of Queen's University 1841
16. Queen's University Royal Charter
17. Queen's University
18. George Monro Grant
19. Robert Sutherland 1830-1878
20. Robert Sutherland Memorial Room
21. The Students' Memorial Union
22. Queen's University War Memorial Room
23. Orphans' Home

Map IX – 1

# Ann Baillie Building

*Location:* George Street, between King Street West and Stuart Street, Kingston
*Type:* Bronze plaque on stone base
*Sponsor:* Historic Sites and Monuments Board of Canada
*Date Erected:* 1999
*Additional Information:* The nurses' training program at the Kingston General Hospital traces its beginnings to 1886 when the Hospital accepted applications from young women seeking training as nurses. The nursing graduates residing in the Kingston area formed the Kingston Nurses' Alumnae in 1896 and began raising money for the construction of a nurses' home so that the nurses being trained could live outside the hospital. These efforts resulted in the laying of the cornerstone on 11 August 1903 for the new residence. When the home was finished in 1904, it provided accommodation for 26. The stone building in the Ionic Order was designed by William Newlands. A second residence was opened in 1927 providing space for 150 students, with a third nurses' residence completed in 1969 for 306 students. In 1974 the Ontario Government transferred responsibility for training of nurses to the community college system thereby closing KGH's Nursing School.
*Related Markers:* 18, 19, 162
*Readings:* Angus 1973a; Crothers 1973; Hill 1991; Wishart 1997.

One of the earliest nurses' residences in Canada, this stately building symbolizes the development and recognition of nursing as a profession. The home was completed in 1904 for students at the Kingston General Hospital's nursing school, who cared for patients in the wards and operating rooms as part of their training. The building was later named in honour of Ann Baillie, a graduate of the school and its superintendent from 1924 to 1942. Here as elsewhere, a place of their own helped nurses shape a professional role indispensable to health care within the hospital and in the community.

*Ann Baillie* Queen's University Archives

*The Nurses' Home c1904 (now the Ann Baillie Building).* Queen's University Archives

# Kingston General Hospital

Map IX – 2

An enduring witness to the evolution of public health care, Kingston General is one of Canada's oldest functioning hospitals. Most of its early buildings have survived, notably the Main Building and the Watkins Wing which date to a time when hospitals were places for the care of the poor. Expansion in the late-19th and early-20th centuries marked the transformation of this charitable hospital into a centre of scientific medicine. The Nickle Wing for patients with infectious diseases, the Doran Building for the care of women and children, and the Fenwick Operating Theatre all date to the 1890s. They show the gradual shift away from treatment in the home in favour of the hospital, which offered new surgical techniques and an antiseptic environment. The new nurses' home, completed in 1904, acknowledged the advance of nursing as a profession critical to the institution. Opened in 1914, the Empire Wing with its private and semi-private rooms demonstrates the hospital's acceptance by the well-to-do. These early buildings form an integral part of a larger hospital complex that continues to reflect new approaches to medical treatment.

*Location:* Kingston General Hospital, 76 Stuart Street, Kingston, in front of the old entrance
*Type:* Bronze plaques on stone base
*Sponsor:* Historic Sites and Monuments Board of Canada
*Date Erected:* 1997
*Additional Information:* The Kingston General Hospital was built in 1833-1835 under the supervision of architect Thomas Rogers (c1780-1853) with plans influenced by Wells and Thompson of Montreal. Located on the western outskirts of Kingston, the stone building had two equally formal facades, one facing north towards Archdeacon George Stuart's Summerhill and one south towards Lake Ontario (nearby streets Arch, Deacon, George, Okill and Stuart are named after him). Three storeys high, it had sheltered balconies for patients wishing to enjoy the lake breezes during the summer.
*Related Markers:* 161, 165, 169
*Readings:* Kennedy 1955; Angus 1973a; Angus 1994; McKendry 1995.

*Kingston General Hospital from the north, early 20th century, showing the Watkins Wing, the Main Building, and Nickle Wing.*
Queen's University Archives

Map IX – 3

# Charles Edward Poulett Thomson Baron Sydenham 1799-1841

**Location:** Kingston General Hospital, 76 Stuart Street, Kingston, in front of the old entrance
**Type:** Bronze plaque on stone base
**Sponsor:** Historic Sites and Monuments Board of Canada
**Date Erected:** 1931
**Additional Information:** Among the earliest plaques erected by the Kingston Historical Society in 1923 was one to Lord Sydenham. It was located on the gates of Alwington House (Government House), but the plaque's present status is unknown.
**Related Markers:** 42, 164, 165, 189
**Readings:** Scrope 1844; Shortt 1926; Angus 1967; Careless 1967; DCB vol. 7.

Thomson, a British businessman and politician, was sent to North America to implement the Union of the Canadas. Having won assent for the union in 1840, he was elevated to the peerage and served as the new province's Governor-General until his untimely death in Kingston. In establishing a system based on harmony between legislative and executive branches, yet one which fell short of responsible government, he succeeded in bringing together moderates in an administration designed to aid in recovery from the recent political, social and economic troubles that culminated in the Rebellions of 1837-38.

*Lord Sydenham in 1842.*
National Archives of Canada, C-178

# Sir Charles Bagot 1781-1843

Map IX – 4

Born in Staffordshire, Bagot commenced a distinguished career in the diplomatic service of Great Britain in 1807. As ambassador to the United States he signed the important Rush-Bagot Convention of 1818 limiting naval armaments on the Great Lakes. In 1842 he assumed the office of Governor General of Canada. Although the principle of responsible government had not yet been conceded, an executive council, which he believed to have the confidence of the assembly, was chosen under his administration.

*Location:* Kingston General Hospital, 76 Stuart Street, Kingston, in front of the old entrance

*Type:* Bronze plaque on stone base

*Sponsor:* Historic Sites and Monuments Board of Canada

*Date Erected:* 1931

*Additional Information:* Sir Charles Bagot died in Alwington House 18 May 1843, only a year and a half after Lord Sydenham, his predecessor as Governor General, died in the same residence. Bagot's successor was Sir Charles Metcalfe (1785-1846).

*Related Markers:* 42, 87, 163, 165, 189

*Readings:* Ryerson 1843; Glazebrook 1929; DCB, vol. 7.

*Sir Charles Bagot.*
Queen's University Archives

Map IX – 5

*Location:* Kingston General Hospital, 76 Stuart Street, Kingston, in front of the old entrance
*Type:* Bronze plaque on stone base
*Sponsor:* Historic Sites and Monuments Board of Canada
*Date Erected:* 1973
*Related Markers:* 42, 162, 163, 164
*Readings:* Angus 1966; Careless 1967; Stanley 1976; Dale 1993; Osborne and Swainson 1988.

# Legislature of the Province of Canada 1841-1844

Following the union of Upper and Lower Canada in 1841, Kingston was chosen as the capital of the United Province. The new municipal hospital was hurriedly modified to provide temporary legislative chambers and here the three sessions of the first Parliament were held between June 1841 and December 1843. Political pressures and inadequate accommodations led to the decision in 1843 to transfer the seat of Government to Montreal, where the second Parliament met for the first time in November 1844.

Map IX – 6

*Location:* Kingston General Hospital, 76 Stuart Street, Kingston, on left wall outside the old entrance
*Type:* Bronze tablet
*Sponsor:* Kingston Historical Society
*Date Erected:* 1923
*Additional Information:* In 1923 the Kingston Historical Society erected five plaques; however, only two survive – this one and the one for the First Location Queen's College at 67 Colborne Street (60). They are very good examples of the brevity of plaque texts in an early context.
*Related Markers:* 42, 162, 163, 164
*Readings:* Angus 1966; Careless 1967; Stanley 1976; Dale 1993; Osborne and Swainson 1988.

# First Parliament of United Canada

The first parliament of United Canada assembled in this building June 1841.

*Kingston General Hospital in 1857.* Kingston General Hospital

# Sir Alexander Campbell
# 1822-1892

Map IX – 7

The Honourable Sir Alexander Campbell, K.C.M.G. Lieutenant Governor of Ontario from 1887 until 1892 and a subscription governor of this hospital, although deeply interested in its welfare regretted often his inability to aid it as he desired. His son Charles Sandwith Campbell, K.C. who died in 1923 in pious remembrance of his father's wish greatly extended the usefulness of the hospital by a most generous bequest. This tablet gratefully acknowledges his loyalty to a parent and to his native city.

*Location:* Kingston General Hospital, 76 Stuart Street, Kingston, in the lobby of the old main entrance
*Type:* Bronze plaque on wall
*Sponsor:* Kingston General Hospital
*Date Erected:* 1931
*Additional Information:* In June 1923, Charles S. Campbell, eldest son of Sir Alexander Campbell of Kingston, died in Montreal. He left one fifth of his considerable estate to the Kingston General Hospital. It was the largest single gift to the Hospital, amounting in the end to well over $350,000. The estate was finally settled after the death, from old age, of Mr. Campbell's favourite horse, Kodiak who had been provided for under the will. (Angus 1973a, 109)
*Related Markers:* 188, 204
*Readings:* Anonymous 1892; Christie 1950; Swainson 1969; DCB vol. 12.

*The Honourable Sir Alexander Campbell.* Queen's University Archives

**Map IX – 8**

# The Honourable Henry Wartman Richardson

*Location:* Kingston General Hospital, 76 Stuart Street, Kingston, in the lobby of the old main entrance

*Type:* Bronze plaque on wall

*Sponsor:* Governors of the Kingston General Hospital

*Date Erected:* 1931

*Additional Information:* Henry Richardson was the son of James Richardson (1819/20-1892) who started the family firm of James Richardson and Sons grain merchants in Kingston in 1857. Henry was involved with a number of businesses as well as president of the family firm from 1906 until 1918. Henry and his wife, Alice Ford, were major benefactors of Kingston General Hospital. According to Margaret Angus, Richardson's wife provided the funding in 1922 for the Richardson Laboratories and the Douglas Wing of the hospital which opened in 1925 as well as funding to establish the Alice Ford Richardson Fellowships in Medicine and Surgery. Henry was the uncle of James Armstrong Richardson (1885-1939).

*Related Markers:* 162, 173

*Readings:* Angus 1973a; Swainson, 1990.

To the Honourable Henry Wartman Richardson, 1855 to 1918, member of the Senate of Canada, diligent and successful in business, fervent in spirit, serving God, his country and his fellow men and to his wife Alice Ford Richardson 1865 to 1931 who shared, enlarged and completed his interests and his undertakings. Their generous contributions and benefactions to this hospital made possible its restoration and continuance for the care of the sick and the education of nurses and physicians. In grateful remembrance this tablet is erected by the Governors of the Hospital in the year 1931.

*Senator Henry W. Richardson, c1900.*
Archives of James Richardson & Sons, Limited, Winnipeg

**Map IX – 9**

# The Reverend Robert McDowall

*In Memoriam.*

Rev. Robert McDowall. Ordained by the Dutch Reformed Church at Albany. Came to Upper Canada 1798 to minister to U.C. Loyalists. As pioneer missionary his labours were of pre-eminent importance in establishing the Church in this Province. He was elected first Moderator of the Synod of the Canadas in 1820. He was active in founding Queen's University. He organized this congregation in 1800, and remained its faithful pastor till his death August 3rd 1841. His remains are interred in this churchyard.

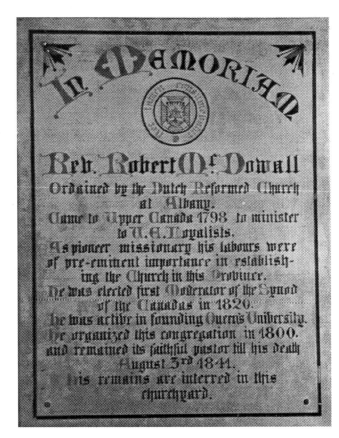

*Location:* Theological Hall, Queen's University, Kingston, inside on the main floor
*Type:* Brass plaque on wall
*Sponsor:* Jessie Currie Polson, Isabel Polson Davis, Hannah Washburn Polson
*Date Erected:* 1941
*Additional Information:* This plaque, erected on the 100th anniversary of McDowall's death, is a copy of an older one, now installed in St Andrew's Presbyterian Church (Princess and Clergy Streets, Kingston) after being rescued from the fire of 13 September 1921 that destroyed the McDowall Memorial Church at Sandhurst on Highway No. 33. The original brass plaque with red enamel detailing was made by William Grieg Jr of Montreal. McDowall, born in New York state in 1768, settled in the township of Ernestown, but traveled, often under harsh conditions, from Brockville to the head of the Bay of Quinte on his circuit preaching to Presbyterians. He was involved in the early history of the congregation of St Andrew's Presbyterian Church, which played a key role in founding Queen's College (now University), granted a Royal Charter in October 1841. McDowall was one of the first College trustees. Their initial meeting was in the church on 20 May 1840. The Reverend Robert McDowall helped to pave the way for development of Presbyterianism in Ontario. His headstone is in the McDowall Memorial Cemetery, Sandhurst.
*Related Markers:* 48, 60, 174, 175
*Readings:* DCB 7; Canadian Encyclopaedia 1985.

Photo David Kasserra

Map IX – 10

# Summerhill 1839

*Location:* Summerhill, Queen's University, west of Arch Street, north of Stuart Street, Kingston
*Type:* Aluminum plaque on post
*Sponsor:* Ontario Heritage Foundation
*Date Erected:* 1958
*Additional Information:* Summerhill, constructed in 1836-1839, is the oldest building on the Queen's University campus. It was built as a grand private villa in the Palladian style for Archdeacon George Stuart, rector of St George's Church (now Cathedral), on land granted to his Loyalist father, the Reverend John Stuart. After Queen's College bought the building, all of the classes were held here. However, the building was soon too small despite enlarging the wings in 1870. Principal William Snodgrass moved into Summerhill in 1867, and the east wing still functions as the Principal's Residence. Alumni Affairs, Advancement offices and the Department of Development presently occupy offices in the rest of the building.
*Related Markers:* 48, 60, 170, 174, 175
*Readings:* Angus 1966; Neatby 1978; Angus 1981; Gibson 1983; Queen's University Alumni Association 1990; McKendry 1995.

This house, built in 1839 by Archdeacon George Okill Stuart, was known as "Okill's Folly." When the Province of Canada's first parliament met in the nearby hospital, the members were housed in Summerhill. Leased for government offices 1842-44, it was later occupied by a school. In 1853 it was purchased by Queen's College and served for several years as the university's only building. During most of its history, it has been used in part as the principal's residence.

*Summerhill in 1865 (right and centre) and the Old Medical Building of 1858 (left).*
Queen's University Archives

# Queen's University Medical Quadrangle

Map IX – 11

The Board of Trustees of Queen's University established a Faculty of Medicine on 20 June 1855. In the four buildings surrounding this quadrangle generations of Queen's medical students began their study of medicine until 1986.

Medical Quadrangle plaques made possible through the Friend Trust. Three brothers from Wolfe Island graduated in Medicine, William (1929), Austin (1924) and Amos (1922).

*Location:* On a boulder in front of Kathleen Ryan Hall, Queen's University, Kingston
*Type:* Bronze plaque
*Sponsor:* Friend Trust
*Date Erected:* 1986
*Additional Information:* The Medical Quadrangle is so named because the four buildings surrounding the square once belonged to the Faculty of Medicine. These buildings are: Summerhill, Kathleen Ryan Hall, the Crane Building, and the Old Medical Building.
*Related Markers:* 48 169, 174, 175
*Readings:* Gundy 1955; Queen's University 1979.

*Kathleen Ryan Hall (on right, originally the New Medical Building of 1907), now houses the Queen's University Archives.* Queen's University Archives

Map IX – 12

# A Century of Engineering at Queen's 1893-1993

*Location:* Queen's University, Kingston, behind Clark Hall
*Type:* Aluminum plaque on post
*Sponsor:* Queen's University
*Date Erected:* 1993
*Related Markers:* 48, 172, 174, 175
*Readings:* Neatby 1978; Gibson 1983; Queen's University Alumni Association 1990; Richardson 1992.

This plaque was unveiled on 30 October 1993 in honour of the graduates, professors and staff who raised this Faculty from humble beginnings to become a leading school of engineering in North America. On this day, one hundred years ago, the School of Mining and Agriculture was inaugurated. In 1894 the Queen's Faculty of Applied Science was established to provide instruction in Civil, Electrical and Mechanical Engineering. Other programs were created in keeping with the needs of Canada's industries: Chemistry and Geology in 1895, followed by Chemical Engineering (1902), Metallurgical Engineering (1904), Engineering Physics (1919), and Mathematics and Engineering (1963). The School of Mining was incorporated into the Faculty in 1916. This plaque has been erected on the former site of the first engineering laboratory and a favoured recreation area for engineering students.

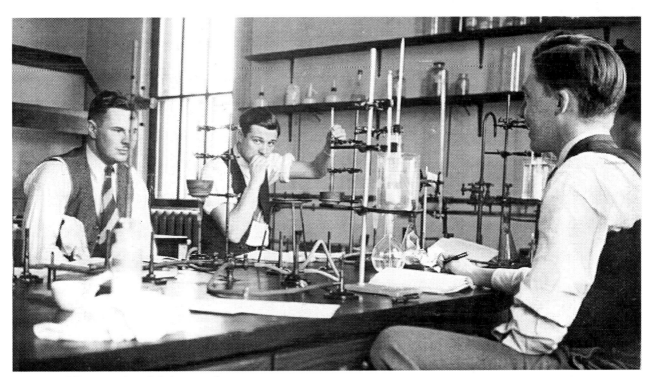

*Chemical Engineering lab in 1936.* Queen's University Archives

Map IX – 13

# Sir Sandford Fleming
# 1827-1915

This stone was laid by
Sir Sandford Fleming, K.C.M.G.,
Chancellor of Queen's University,
April 30th, 1902.

*Location:* Fleming Hall, Queen's University, Kingston, cornerstone next to south main doorway and bust in elevated walkway between Jemmett Wing and Stewart Pollack Wing
*Type:* Cornerstone and bust
*Sponsor:* Queen's University
*Date Erected:* 1902 (cornerstone); 1907 (bust)
*Additional Information:* George M. Grant (1835-1902), principal of Queen's College (now University) from 1877-1902, recruited Fleming as the first Chancellor from December 1879-1915. Grant who had accompanied Fleming on his expeditions across the Rockies in 1872 and 1883, wrote a record of the earlier trip, *Ocean to Ocean, Sandford Fleming's Expedition through Canada in 1872,* published in 1873. Fleming took an active interest in Queen's, especially as part of his vision of seeing science as the focus of university education. Due in large part to his efforts the school of Mining and Agriculture was established at Queen's in 1893 and, a year later, the Faculty of Applied Science under Nathan Fellowes Dupuis (1836-1917). Fleming supported Grant's efforts to separate Queen's from the Presbyterian church. He continued this goal after Grant's death in 1902 and, by his own death in 1915, Queen's was a secular institution. In 1908 he was granted an honourary doctorate from Queen's University. An emigrant from Scotland in 1845, he is well known in Canada for his many accomplishments. He was appointed in 1871 as the engineer of and surveyor for the new proposed railway from Montreal to the Pacific. He advocated for the Pacific Cable which was laid in 1902 and formed an important communication link from Canada to Australia. Fleming is perhaps best remembered for his work to establish standard time on an international basis in 1884. The bust of Fleming who is wearing his honourary decorations (CMG – 1877, Knighthood – 1897), was designed by sculptor Hamilton McCarthy RCA, (1846-1939) in 1907, and was cast by the Henry Bonnard Bronze Company of Mount Vernon, New York, in the same year.
*Related Markers:* 146, 171, 176
*Readings:* Canadian Encyclopaedia 1985; Angus 1991; DCB 14.

*Bronze bust of Sir Sandford Fleming.*
Photo David Kasserra

Map IX – 14

# James Armstrong Richardson

Richardson Hall. This hall of administration is named in honour of James Armstrong Richardson, 1885-1939. A man of far vision, strong to will and to do. A builder of Canada, graduate and trustee, and for ten years Chancellor. Wise, generous and devoted. A maker of Queen's.

*Location:* Richardson Hall, Queen's University, University Avenue, Kingston, in the front foyer
*Type:* Bronze plaque on wall
*Sponsor:* Queen's University at Kingston
*Date Erected:* 1954
*Additional Information:* James Armstrong Richardson who was born in Kingston and died in Winnipeg, was named after his grandfather, James Richardson (1819/20-1892) who was characterized by historian Donald Swainson as "the most important businessman produced in Kingston." His grain trading business, built between 1857 and 1892, "was strong enough to become the base for one of the twentieth-century Canada's most dynamic corporate instruments." James Armstrong Richardson who was educated at Queen's University, entered the family firm of James Richardson and Sons Ltd in 1906, became Vice-President in 1912, and President in 1919. The executive offices were moved to Winnipeg in 1922. In the 1920s Richardson Securities of Canada (now RBC Dominion Securities Inc.) was added to the firm. After James A. Richardson's death in 1939, his widow Muriel Sprague Richardson, became President until 1966. Richardson Hall at Queen's University was built in 1954. A plaque unveiled in 1989 at Lac du Bonnet on the shores of the Winnipeg River explains one of Richardson's many contributions: "In Memory of James A. Richardson 1885-1939. The Father of Canadian Aviation founded Western Canadian Airways Ltd on December 2, 1926 and its successor company Canadian Airways Ltd in 1930. These airlines eventually operated from coast to coast in Canada and north to the Arctic. In the spring of 1927, the first commercial air base in Manitoba was established at Lac du Bonnett by Western Canada Airways Ltd. Because of its proximity to Winnipeg, this site was chosen as the most suitable location from which to operate a commercial seaplane air service to the isolated central Manitoba mining areas."
*Related Markers:* 131, 167
*Readings:* Canadian Encyclopaedia 1985; Swainson 1990; Angus 1991.

*James Armstrong Richardson.*
Queen's University Archives

# The Founding of Queen's University 1841

Map IX – 15 & 16

In 1839 the Synod of the Presbyterian Church of Canada laid plans to establish a university at Kingston. In 1841 a royal charter was received and the principal, the Rev. Thomas Liddell, arrived from Edinburgh. Classes opened in 1842 in a rented house on Colborne Street and the first degrees were conferred five years later. "Summerhill," purchased in 1853, was the earliest university building on the present campus. Adjacent to it, the Old Medical Building was erected in 1858-59. Through the efforts of its principals and graduates Queen's overcame early financial difficulties and, under Principal George M. Grant, 1877-1902, emerged as one of Canada's leading universities.

*Location:* Queen's University, Kingston, in front of Grant Hall [Not presently in place]
*Type:* Aluminum plaque on post
*Sponsor:* Ontario Heritage Foundation
*Date Erected:* 1963
*Additional Information:*
Queen's University now offers undergraduate, graduate and professional degrees and diplomas in 15 faculties, schools and colleges. It draws its faculty and students from across Canada and around the world. The University has an overseas campus, the International Study Centre located in the historic Herstmonceaux Castle in East Sussex, U.K. In 1999 the number of students registered at Queen's was approximately 14,000.

## Queen's University Royal Charter

This plaque was unveiled by Her Majesty The Queen during the tercentenary celebration of the City of Kingston to commemorate the granting of Queen's University's Royal Charter by Queen Victoria on 16 October 1841.

*Location:* Queen's University, Richardson Hall, University Avenue, Kingston
*Type:* Metal plaque on wall
*Sponsor:* Queen's University
*Date Erected:* 1973

*Aerial view of Queen's University c1919 taken by Billy Bishop.*
Queen's University Archives

Map IX – 17

# Queen's University

*Location:* Queen's University, University Avenue, Kingston, between Grant and Ontario Halls
*Type:* Bronze plaque on stone base
*Sponsor:* Historic Sites and Monuments Board of Canada
*Date Erected:* 1991
*Related Markers:* 48, 60, 169, 170, 171, 172, 173, 174, 175, 176, 177, 178, 179, 190, 191
*Readings:* Neatby 1978; Gibson 1983; Queen's University Alumni Association 1990.

Queen's University was the earliest degree-granting liberal arts college established in the united Province of Canada, holding its first classes in March of 1842. Established by the Presbyterian Church, it evolved into a national institution under George Monro Grant, who was principal from 1877 to 1902. By the 20th century Queen's had emerged as one of Canada's major universities with a reputation for scholarship and social purpose. Many of the nation's notable political figures and public servants have been Queen's graduates.

*In October 1991 His Royal Highness Prince Charles (left of plaque) and Minister of the Environment, the Hon. Jean Charest (right) unveiled the Historic Sites and Monuments Board of Canada plaque commemorating Queen's University.*
Parks Canada

# George Monro Grant

Map IX – 18

In loving memory of George Monro Grant D.D. L.L.D. C.M.G. Born in Nova Scotia Dec. 22nd 1835. Principal of this university from Dec. 5th 1877 till his death May 10th 1902. Author, teacher, speaker and administrator, he was eminent alike in the educational world, in the church and in public affairs. His manly character, fearless love of the truth and untiring service to Queen's University were a constant inspiration to its students. Under his wise guidance the University prospered greatly having grown from one single building to the present six forming the quadrangle, and having increased three-fold its teaching staff and six-fold the number of students.

*Si monumentum requiris circumspice*

*Location:* Grant Hall, Queen's University, University Avenue, Kingston, over the stage
*Type:* Brass plaque on wall
*Sponsor:* Alma Mater Society
*Date Erected:* 1902
*Additional Information:* A.B. McKillop described Grant's contribution to Queen's University: "Grant inherited a small and financially unstable denominational college and spent much of his indomitable energy thereafter in raising an endowment fund and acquiring (and retaining) major scholars, especially in the humanities. He was also fully aware, however, of the necessity of strong faculties of science (pure and applied) if Queen's was to acquire a truly national stature. By the time of his death few denied that his goal had been realized (*The Canadian Encyclopaedia*)." He was a leader in the Presbyterian Church, the denomination that founded Queen's. His grandson, George Grant (1918-1988), was a noted Canadian philosopher who wrote *Lament for a Nation* in 1965. Another plaque, commemorating the opening of Grant Hall and honouring George Monro Grant, is in the main foyer of Grant Hall.
*Related Markers:* 174, 175
*Readings:* Neatby 1978; Gibson 1983; Canadian Encyclopaedia 1985; Queen's University Alumni Association 1990; Mack 1992; DCB vol. 13.

*George Monro Grant.*
Queen's University Archives

Map IX – 19

*Location:* Grant Hall, Queen's University, University Avenue, Kingston, main foyer
*Type:* Metal plaque on wall
*Sponsor:* City of Kingston
*Date Erected:* 1974

# Robert Sutherland 1830-1878

The City of Kingston, Ontario, commemorates Robert Sutherland, a generous benefactor of Queen's and the first Jamaican of African origin to graduate from the University in 1852. Mr. Sutherland bequeathed his lifetime savings to the young University, setting a fine example to many since then whose genuine concern and support have helped make Queen's an outstanding university.

Map IX – 20

*Location:* John Deutsch University Centre, Queen's University, Union Street and University Avenue, Kingston, second floor
*Type:* Metal plaque on wall
*Sponsor:* Queen's University
*Date Erected:* 1998
*Related Markers:* 174, 175
*Readings:* Hazelgrove 1974; Neatby 1978; Gibson 1983; Queen's University Alumni Association 1990.

# Robert Sutherland Memorial Room

Queen's University is honoured to dedicate this room in memory of Robert Sutherland B.A. (Queen's, 1852). Called to the bar of Canada West (1855). 1830-1878. Jamaican by birth, an outstanding scholar and citizen, the first person of African heritage to graduate from the University and its first major benefactor. His indomitable spirit continues to inspire all who come to know of his legacy.

*Robert Sutherland's Bachelor of Arts degree granted by Queen's University in 1852.*
Queen's University Archives

# The Students' Memorial Union

Map IX – 21

This building was erected in grateful memory of the Queen's men who gave their lives in The Great Wars of 1914-1918 and 1939-1945. It is a place for training in human relations. Where students, staff, graduates and guests may have recreation, companionship and good talk.

*Location:* John Deutsch University Centre, Queen's University, Union Street and University Avenue, Kingston, in the hallway on the main floor
*Type:* Stone plaque on wall
*Sponsor:* Queen's University
*Date Erected:* c1949
*Additional Information:* The first Students' Memorial Union was located on the same site partly in the Orphan's Home, built in 1862 and enlarged in 1877. The university purchased the building in 1927 and renovated it as a club for male students where they could relax and purchase meals. Although it was the university's official memorial to those who died in the First World War, it was not open to women until after the Second World War. It was destroyed by fire in September 1947, and replaced by a modern structure designed by Drever and Smith in 1949. This second building was added to in 1977, and renamed the John Deutsch University Centre after Queen's 14th principal who died in 1976.
*Related Markers:* 174, 175, 179, 180
*Readings:* Bindon 1978; Queen's University Alumni Association 1995.

*No 5 Stationary Hospital with Lt Col Etherington at extreme left, in front of Kingston Hall, 1915.*

Map IX – 22

# Queen's University War Memorial Room

*We must be free or die who speak the tongue that Shakespeare spake / The faith and morals hold which Milton held.*

**Location:** John Deutsch University Centre, Queen's University, Union Street and University Avenue, Kingston, on the main floor

**Type:** Decorated room and furnishings

**Sponsor:** Queen's University

**Date Erected:** 1949

**Additional Information:** The above quotation is taken from William Wordsworth (1770-1850), and is located on the upper perimeter of the room. This room memorializes the more than 350 Queen's students and alumni who died in the First and Second World Wars. There are two large bronze plaques inscribed with the names of the fallen, a stone altar, seven oil paintings of men and women from each branch of the armed forces, and stained glass windows. The two plaques containing the names of those who died in the two world wars were originally mounted in the Douglas Library and moved here after the Memorial Room was opened in 1949. The very ornate First World War plaque was first mounted in Grant Hall where it was dedicated by the Governor General, Lord Byng of Vimy, in 1921 and later moved to the Douglas Library. The seven oils, representing members of the armed forces, were painted by Marion Long, RCA, (1892-1970) and set in oak panels designed and arranged by sculptor Ted Watson. In the nearby Polson Room there are photographs of all the Queen's students and alumni who died in the Second World War.

**Related Markers:** 20, 21, 151, 174, 175

**Readings:** Bindon 1978; Queen's University Alumni Association 1995.

*Queen's War Memorial Room. Kingston Whig-Standard*

# Orphans' Home

Map IX – 23

On this site stood the Orphans' Home 1862-1927. To commemorate 125 years of service of the Orphans' Home and Widows' Friend Society.

*Location:* John Deutsch University Centre, Queen's University, Kingston, outside near the Union Street entrance
*Sponsor:* Orphans' Home and Widows' Friend Society
*Type:* Bronze plaque on wall
*Date Erected:* 1983
*Additional Information:* In response to the large numbers of deaths and hardships caused by the typhoid epidemic of 1846-1847, a House of Industry was established in December 1847 to house 183 destitute persons. Included were 44 widows and 63 children under the age of ten. Members of the Female Benevolent Society helped find employment for these disadvantaged inhabitants, as well as setting up a school for the children. The society came to be known as the Widows' Friend Society, when it was decided to found an orphans' home in 1856. Influential Kingston women organized this charity, and in the spring of 1861 acquired two acres of land on Union Street near the corner of University Avenue. Architect William Coverdale provided plans for a handsome two-storey stone building in the classical style. The original structure, topped by a dome lantern, was added to during the later decades of the 19th and early 20th centuries. It was acquired by Queen's University in 1927, and destroyed by fire in September 1947. A new Students' Memorial Union was then built and is incorporated today within the John Deutsch University Centre of 1977.
*Related Markers:* 137, 174, 175, 178, 179, 205, 206
*Readings:* Tulchinsky 1976; Errington 1988; Angus 1991; McKendry 1995.

*Original Orphans' Home of 1862.* Queen's University Archives

# KINGSTON VILLAS *and* PORTSMOUTH

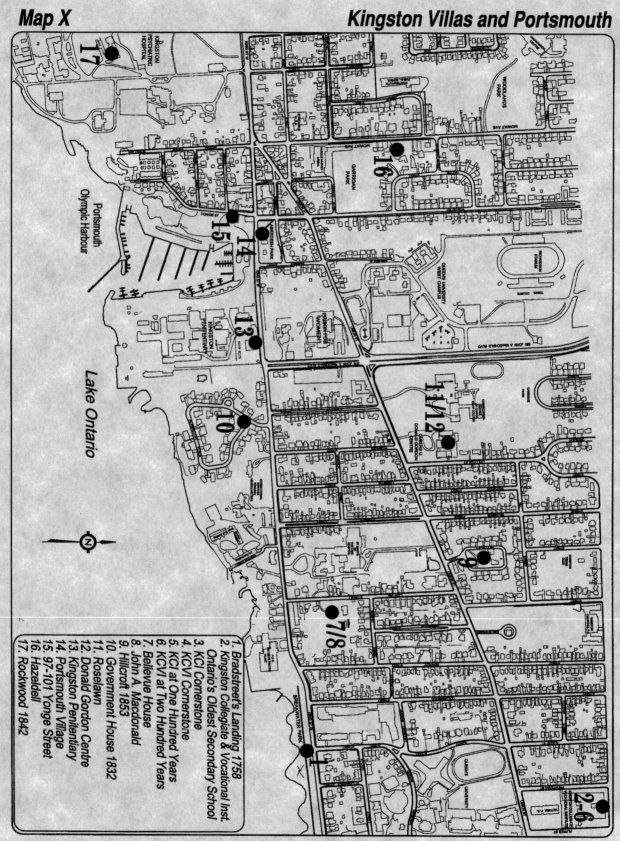

**Map X**

Portsmouth Olympic Harbour

Lake Ontario

N

1. Bradstreet's Landing 1758
2. Kingston Collegiate & Vocational Inst.
   Ontario's Oldest Secondary School
3. KCI Cornerstone
4. KCVI Cornerstone
5. KCI at One Hundred Years
6. KCVI at Two Hundred Years
7. Bellevue House
8. John A. Macdonald
9. Hillcroft 1853
10. Government House 1832
11. Roselawn
12. Donald Gordon Centre
13. Kingston Penitentiary
14. Portsmouth Village
15. 97-101 Yonge Street
16. Hazeldell
17. Rockwood 1842

*Strategic & Long-Range Planning - DJMartin*

182

**Map X – 1**

*Location:* Breakwater Park, King Street West and Lower Albert Street, Kingston, across from 189 King Street West
*Type:* Aluminum plaque on post
*Sponsor:* Kingston Historical Society
*Date Erected:* 1953
*Additional Information:* The Seven Year's War between France and Great Britain began in North America in May 1756. In August, Marquis de Montcalm led a French force from Fort Frontenac across Lake Ontario and captured the British post at Oswego – thereby gaining control of the Great Lakes waterway. In 1758 the British went on the offensive and plans were made to collect an army of 3,000 in the Mohawk Valley to move against Fort Frontenac. Under the command of Lieutenant Colonel John Bradstreet (1711-1774) a mixed force of regulars and militia left the Mohawk River on August 16th and by the 25th reached Kingston. By setting up his artillery on the

# Bradstreet's Landing 1758

On Aug. 25, Lt.-Col. Bradstreet and 3,000 men crossed from Garden Island and landed near this point. He captured Fort Frontenac from the French Commander, M. De Noyan, Aug. 27.

high ground overlooking Fort Frontenac, which was weakly manned, Bradstreet forced its surrender in two days. With the capture of the fort and its huge store of supplies the French control of all the country to the west was lost.
*Related Markers:* 72, 73
*Readings:* Bradstreet 1759; Preston and Lamontagne 1958; Rahmer 1973; Smith 1987.

*J. Walker's conjectural drawing of the destruction of Fort Frontenac after its capture from the French in 1758.*
Queen's University Archives

# Kingston Collegiate & Vocational Institute
# Ontario's Oldest Secondary School

Map X – 2, 3, 4, 5, 6

This school traces its origins to 1792 when Lt.-Governor Simcoe proposed government grants for grammar school education. The pioneer school started by the Reverend John Stuart in 1786 became the Kingston Grammar School. In 1807 it was renamed the Midland District Grammar School and remained in use until 1849. After four years at Summerhill on the Queen's University campus, students and staff moved into the new Kingston County Grammar School, now Sydenham Public School. In 1872 the Grammar School became the Kingston Collegiate Institute which, since 1892, has operated on this site. Upon expansion in 1931 the school acquired its present name, Kingston Collegiate and Vocational Institute. The module de langue française, providing French first language education to francophone students, was established at K.C.V.I. in 1980. Kingston Grammar School 1792; Midland District Grammar School 1807; Kingston County Grammar School 1853; Kingston High School 1871; Kingston Collegiate Institute 1872; Kingston Collegiate and Vocational Institute 1931.

Kingston Collegiate Institute. This cornerstone was dedicated by the Lieutenant Governor of Ontario, the Honourable George A. Kirkpatrick, on the occasion of the centennial of K.C.I. September 3, 1892.

Kingston Collegiate and Vocational Institute. This cornerstone was dedicated by His Excellency The Right Honourable Ramon John Hnatyshyn, Governor General of Canada on the occasion of the Bicentennial of K.C.V.I. November 12, 1992.

To Commemorate a Century's Work of the School. September 3, 1892.
*Maxima Debetur Pueris Reverentia*

To Commemorate a Second Century's Work of this School. September 4, 1992.
*Youth deserves the Greatest Respect*

**Location:** Kingston Collegiate & Vocational Institute, 235 Frontenac Street, Kingston, main foyer
**Type:** Wooden and metal plaques on wall
**Sponsor:** Kingston Collegiate Institute and Kingston Collegiate and Vocational Institute
**Dates Erected:** 1892 & 1992

*Additional Information:* Many Kingstonians remember the Kingston Collegiate Institute (KCI) before its demolition in 1959. It was a large brick building designed by architectural firm Power and Son in 1892 in the Romanesque Revival Style. Most of the information found on the largest plaque is repeated on a bronze version sponsored by the KCVI Alumni Association in 1984.

*Related Markers:* 40, 41

*Readings:* KCI 1921; Woods 1960; Horsey, Woods and Saunders 1970; KCVI 1973; Ritchie 1979; Ede 1992

*Early view of KCI.* J. George Hodgins, *Schools and Colleges in Ontario, 1792-1910,* (Toronto, 1910), p.59

*Children playing behind KCI in 1909. This view is looking from the present site of Victoria School towards Earl Street.* Department of Manuscripts and Archives, Cornell University

# Bellevue House

Map X – 7

Built about 1840, Bellevue House is one of the most interesting examples surviving in Canada of "Italian Villa" architecture, a style that was new in the country and novel in Kingston. This type of residence subsequently became popular in Canada. John A. Macdonald, later first Prime Minister of Canada, lived here with his family from August, 1848, to September, 1849. At that time the rising young lawyer was Member for Kingston in the Legislative Assembly of the Province of Canada.

*Bellevue House has been fully restored and furnished to reflect Macdonald's occupancy.* Photo David Kasserra

*Location:* Bellevue House, 35 Centre Street, Kingston
*Type:* Bronze plaque on wall
*Sponsor:* Historic Sites and Monuments Board of Canada
*Date Erected:* 1967
*Additional Information:* Macdonald was not at Bellevue House for an extended period but it was a very difficult time in his life. In August 1848, he moved from his house on Brock Street to this rented house, at the time considered distant from the city, with the hopes that the fresh air of the country would help improve his wife Isabella's ailing health. Within a month of moving to "Tea Caddy Castle," as John A. referred to it, their son died suddenly – just over a year old. Within the year, his law partnership with Alexander Campbell came to an end because Macdonald's focus on politics made it difficult to fulfil the obligations of his legal business. Isabella's ill health continued but Macdonald's income was insufficient to remain at Bellevue. In September 1849, Macdonald moved back into the city to 180 Johnson Street. Bellevue, a stone stucco covered house, was built for Charles Hales in the early 1840s, and has been attributed to architect George Browne.
*Related Markers:* 36, 37, 62, 123, 125, 126, 130, 157, 187, 195, 201, 202, 203
*Readings:* Creighton 1952; Creighton 1955; Angus 1966; Newman 1974; Angus 1984; Swainson 1979; Swainson 1989; DCB vol. 12; McKendry 1992; McKendry 1995.

Map X – 8

# John A. Macdonald

**Location:** Bellevue House National Historic Site, 35 Centre Street, Kingston, on the grounds
**Type:** Aluminum plaque on post
**Sponsor:** Kingston Historical Society
**Date Erected:** 1954
**Related Markers:** 36, 37, 62, 123, 125, 126, 130, 157, 186, 195, 201, 202, 203
**Readings:** Creighton 1952; Creighton 1955; Newman 1974; Angus 1984; Swainson 1979; Swainson 1989; DCB vol. 12.

The architect of Canadian Confederation in 1867, and the first Prime Minister of Canada, occupied this house, Bellevue, for a period from 1848.

*Sir John A. Macdonald (1815-1891) c1856, and his first wife Isabella (1809-1857) c1843.*
National Archives of Canada

# Hillcroft 1853

Map X – 9

Built in 1853 by a mayor of Kingston, Francis Hill, this house, during the 1860's and 1870's, was the residence of Alexander Campbell (1822-1892). A member of the Legislative Council of the Province of Canada and delegate to the Quebec Conference which led to Confederation, he was a life-long political associate of the Dominion's first Prime Minister, Sir John A. Macdonald. Campbell held several cabinet posts after Confederation, was knighted in 1879 and, from 1887 to 1892, was Lieutenant-Governor of Ontario.

*Location:* 26 Hillcroft Drive, Kingston
*Type:* Aluminum plaque on post
*Sponsor:* Ontario Heritage Foundation
*Date Erected:* 1957
*Additional Information:* On 17 August 1852 Francis M. Hill paid architect William Coverdale (1801-1865) £ 62 for the plans and specifications of a limestone house later described as a "neat antique villa" and "a very delightful suburban residence" (City Directory 1857-58). It is typical of a number of Coverdale's houses with round windows and tall round arched windows in pairs or triplets. Campbell is buried in Section C, Cataraqui Cemetery, near Sir John A. Macdonald's gravesite.
*Related Markers:* 166, 204
*Readings:* Angus 1966; McKendry 1995.

Photo David Kasserra

Map X – 10

# Government House 1832

*Location:* 245 Alwington Place, Kingston
*Type:* Aluminum plaque on post
*Sponsor:* Ontario Heritage Foundation
*Date Erected:* 1957
*Additional Information:* Alwington House, a stone temple-house (a two-storey centre portion with one-storey wings), had a fine Ionic portico that faced Lake Ontario.
*Related Markers:* 42, 163, 164
*Readings:* Angus 1966; Angus 1992; McKendry 1995.

Alwington House, which stood on this site, was completed in 1832 by Charles W. Grant, fifth baron of Longueuil. It was enlarged in 1841 to serve as the vice-regal residence during the period when Kingston was the capital of the united Province of Canada. Three governors general, Lord Sydenham, Sir Charles Bagot and Sir Charles Metcalfe, occupied the house. When the capital was removed to Montreal in 1844, Alwington was returned to Baron Longueuil. It was subsequently occupied by the Reverend J.A. Allen, author of scientific works and father of the Canadian novelist Grant Allen. Badly damaged by fire in 1958, it was demolished the following year.

*South view of Government House, also known as Alwington House.* Queen's University Archives

# Roselawn

Map X – 11

Built by architect William Coverdale for David John Smith in 1841, Roselawn stands as a reminder of the days when affluent Kingstonians erected magnificent country homes just beyond the city. Its proportions, roof pediments and arched openings reflect the then popular Classic Revival style. From 1851 to 1868 it was the residence of Sir Henry Smith, Solicitor General for Upper Canada and later Speaker of the Legislative Assembly of the Province of Canada. In 1970 Roselawn was acquired by Queen's University, which had originally sold the land in 1841.

*Location:* Donald Gordon Centre, 421 Union Street, Kingston, in the back courtyard
*Type:* Bronze plaque on wall
*Sponsor:* Historic Sites and Monuments Board of Canada
*Date Erected:* 1974
*Additional Information:* The attribution of William Coverdale as architect of Roselawn is now being questioned. (see McKendry 1992)
*Related Markers:* 174, 175, 191
*Readings:* Angus 1966; Canada 1974; Queen's University 1974; Neatby 1978; Gibson 1983; McKendry 1992; McKendry 1995.

*View of Roselawn in 1860.* From H.F. Walling. United Counties of Frontenac, Lennox and Addington, Canada West.

Map X – 12

# Donald Gordon Centre

*Location:* Donald Gordon Centre, 421 Union Street, Kingston, in the back courtyard
*Type:* Bronze plaque on wall
*Sponsor:* Queen's University
*Date Erected:* 1974
*Additional Information:*
Opened in 1974, this is Queen's University's year-round conference centre, containing meeting space, accommodation, reception and dining rooms. The core of the Centre is Roselawn, an elegant limestone country house built in 1841. It became the official residence of the Commandant of the National Defence College between 1948 and 1969. In 1970, Queen's University acquired the property.
*Related Markers:* 174, 175, 190
*Readings:* Angus 1966; Canada 1974; Queen's University 1974; Neatby 1978; Gibson 1983; Canadian Encyclopaedia 1985; McKendry 1992; McKendry 1995.

This centre for continuing education is a memorial conceived by the friends of Donald Gordon 1901-1969, an outstanding public servant whose innovative career bore the stamp of life-long learning. Banker of international distinction, a financier and leader whose vision steadied the nation's wartime economy and revitalized Canadian National Railways. Sagacious trustee, honorary graduate and generous benefactor of Queen's University.

*Roselawn (Donald Gordon Centre) in 1959.* George Lilley, Queen's University Archives

# Kingston Penitentiary

Map X – 13

Opened on 1 June 1835, Kingston Penitentiary is Canada's oldest reformatory prison. Its layout – an imposing front gate leading to a cross-shaped cellblock, with workshops to the rear – was the model for other federal prisons for more than a century. Its main structures constitute an impressive grouping of inmate-built 19th-century classical architecture in local stone. Kingston Penitentiary represented a significant departure from the way society had dealt with its criminals. Previously, jails were used primarily as places to hold convicts awaiting execution, banishment or public humiliation. The penitentiary imposed a severe régime designed to reform the inmate through reflection, hard work and the fear of punishment. "KP" employed the congregate system first developed at Auburn, New York, where inmates lived in small cells but worked together from dawn to dusk, all under a rigidly enforced rule of silence. Kingston Penitentiary stands as a powerful symbol of this country's commitment to the maintenance of law and order.

*Location:* 555 King Street West at Sir John A. Macdonald Boulevard, Kingston, east of the main entrance,
*Type:* 3 bronze plaques on concrete base
*Sponsor:* Historic Sites and Monuments Board of Canada
*Date Erected:* 1997
*Additional Information:* The north gateway was built 1840-1845 by convicts under the guidance of William Coverdale (1801-1865) who acted as penitentiary architect from 1834 to 1846, when he was replaced by Edward Horsey (1809-1869). The stone gate design in the Tuscan Order is modelled on a Roman triumphal arch symbolizing society's triumph over those who betray its values. See also p. 220.
*Related Markers:* 193
*Readings:* Edmison 1954; Curtis 1985; McKendry 1989; Patterson 1992; McKendry 1995; McKendry 1996.

*In this 1919 aerial view, a new south perimeter wall is being built next to the shore. The gasworks and the old south wall were later demolished when the south wing of the workshop was extended.* Corrections Canada Museum, Kingston

Map X – 14

# Portsmouth Village

*Location:* Aberdeen Park, King Street West and Yonge Street, Kingston
*Type:* Bronze plaque on post
*Sponsor:* Kingston Historical Society with the assistance of the Ontario Heritage Foundation and the Portsmouth Villagers.
*Date Erected:* 1999
*Additional Information:* See also p. 234.
*Related Markers:* 192, 194, 195, 196
*Readings:* Angus 1973b; McKendry 1996.

Originally part of Kingston Township, this area was granted to United Empire Loyalists in 1784. A village, first known as "Hatter's Bay," grew in response to the establishment of the Provincial Penitentiary in 1833, and was formally incorporated in 1858. King Street West was extended across a bay south of here in 1845, and a stone town hall, designed by William Coverdale, was erected on the reclaimed land in 1865. This common was named Aberdeen Park by 1900. Villagers worked in tanneries, breweries, shipyards, sawmills, as well as the penitentiary and nearby asylum, but economic opportunities declined in the late 19th-century. The village was annexed by the city of Kingston in 1952. Many interesting early stone, brick, and frame buildings have survived in this area.

*Portsmouth Town Hall, (now St John House) in 1999.* Photo David Kasserra

Map X – 15

# 97-101 Yonge Street

This building, designed by William Coverdale, architect, and erected for Isabella McIntyre in 1853 in the former village of Portsmouth, is a good example of a Kingston limestone house, typical of the period. It has been restored through the courtesy of Northern Telecom Limited.

*Location:* 97 Yonge Street, Kingston
*Type:* Bronze plaque on wall
*Sponsor:* City of Kingston
*Date Erected:* 1976
*Additional Information:* Captain John McIntyre who died in 1849, acquired three acres along the Portsmouth waterfront in 1841, and probably built this row house shortly after. His widow Isabella Fraser McIntyre and his eldest son Alexander, an engineer, lived in one of the units and rented out the others. (William Coverdale was not involved in designing this building.) Yonge Street was once the main street of the busy Village of Portsmouth.
*Related Markers:* 193
*Readings:* McKendry 1996

Photo David Kasserra

Map X – 16

# Hazeldell

**Location:** 225 Mowat Avenue, Kingston
**Type:** Bronze plaque on post
**Sponsor:** Parks Canada with the assistance of the Frontenac Historic Foundation
**Date Erected:** 1992
**Additional Information:** This building was a fine country house, outside Kingston on the outskirts of Portsmouth Village, when the extended Macdonald family moved here. The house belonged to Sarah Mackenzie, widow of George, under whom Macdonald had articled between 1830 and his death in 1834. It was leased from Mrs Mackenzie by Macdonald's brother-in-law, Professor Williamson. At this stage the Williamsons were stand-in parents for Macdonald's son, Hugh John who was living with them. Macdonald was, more often than not, resident in Quebec City during this period, especially when Parliament was in session. The stone house built in the 1840s, was altered (by adding a second storey) by William Coverdale in 1852.
**Related Markers:** 36, 37, 62, 123, 125, 126, 130, 157, 186, 187, 201, 202, 203
**Readings:** Creighton 1952; Creighton 1955; Newman 1974; Angus 1984; Swainson 1979; Swainson 1989; DCB vol. 12; McKendry 1996.

Sir John A. Macdonald, Father of Confederation, First Prime Minister of Canada
225 Mowat Avenue, built 1842.
In 1860 John A. Macdonald's mother came to live in this house together with her two daughters, Louisa and Margaret, and Margaret's husband Professor James Williamson. Mrs. Macdonald died here in 1862. Until 1865, when Louisa and the Williamsons moved from the house, this was Macdonald's legal residence as member of the Legislative Assembly for Kingston.

Photo David Kasserra

# Rockwood 1842

Map X – 17

Rockwood was built in 1842 as a country villa for John Solomon Cartwright (1804-1845). Designed by George Browne, architect of the Kingston City Hall, in a monumental phase of the Regency style, it is a stone structure covered with stucco but lined to suggest ashlar masonry. Cartwright began to practise law in Kingston in 1830 and in 1831 became president of the Commercial Bank of the Midland District. He was elected to the Legislative Assembly of Upper Canada in 1836 and of Canada in 1841. The government acquired this property in 1856 as a site for a "Criminal Lunatic Asylum." With another building erected in 1859, it became the nucleus of the present psychiatric hospital.

*Location:* On the grounds of Kingston Psychiatric Hospital, 752 King Street West, Kingston
*Type:* Aluminum plaque on post
*Sponsor:* Ontario Heritage Foundation
*Date Erected:* 1968
*Additional Information:* The other building mentioned in the plaque is Rockwood Lunatic Asylum (located to the rear of Rockwood Villa), designed in 1859 by architect William Coverdale and completed in 1870, five years after his death. A high stone structure in the classical style, the asylum was considered a state-of-the-art hospital modelled after Dr Kirkbride's 'linear plan.'
*Related Markers:* 193
*Readings:* Pratten 1969; Stewart 1973; McKendry 1992, 1993, 1995, 1996.

*Rockwood Villa.* Queen's University Archives

# CATARAQUI
## *and*
## ST MARY'S
## CEMETERIES

# Map XI

# Cataraqui and St.Mary's Cemeteries

1. Sundial Commemorating Kingston's Tercentennial
2. Tercentenary 1673-1973
3. Heathfield
4. Father of Confederation, Sir J.A.Macdonald 1815-1891
5. Sir John A. Macdonald 1815-1891
6. Sir John A.Macdonald 1815-1891
7. Father of Confederation, Sir Alexander Campbell
8. Angel of the Resurrection                    1822-1892
9. The Typhus Epidemic 1847

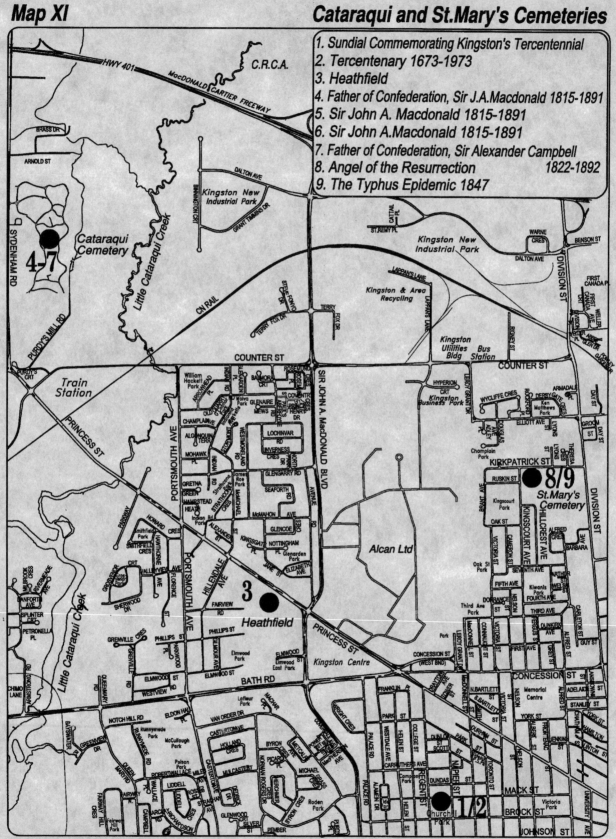

Map XI – 1

# Sundial Commemorating Kingston's Tercentennial

**Location:** Centre of Churchill Park; Brock, Napier, Mack, and Regent Streets, Kingston
**Type:** Stone sundial with a metal plaques
**Sponsor:** Victoria and Grey Trust Company
**Date Erected:** 1973
**Additional Information:** Designed by Jennifer McKendry, this memorial is about 20 feet high and constructed of local limestone. The monument is capped with a ball design inspired by the posts of local stone fences. The upper portion of the pier has two metal sundials on the south and east faces.
**Related Markers:** 72, 73, 200
**Readings:** Roy 1952; Preston 1959; Mika 1987; Osborne and Swainson 1988.

Presented to the City of Kingston to mark its tercentennial year and the 500th anniversary of the birth of Copernicus by The Victoria and Grey Trust Company, June 1973.

Photo David Kasserra

# Tercentenary 1673-1973

Map XI – 2

To mark Kingston's 300th Anniversary as a set-
tled community. Buried beneath this marker is a
Time Capsule containing material identified with
Kingston's history and the year long celebrations
of 1973 to be reopened in 2073. George N.
Speal, Q.C. Mayor; Walter W. Viner, Chairman;
John Clements, Committee Chairman.

*Location:* Churchill Park on a
boulder facing Brock Street
across from Graham Avenue,
Kingston
*Type:* Metal plaque on
boulder
*Sponsor:* City of Kingston
*Date Erected:* 1973
*Additional Information:* During
the reign of Louis XIV of
France, Fort Frontenac was
established in 1673 at Ontario
and Place d'Armes Streets.
*Related Markers:* 72, 73, 199
*Readings:* Roy 1952; Preston
1959; Mika 1987; Osborne
and Swainson 1988.

Photo David Kasserra

Map XI – 3

# Heathfield

**Location:** 1200 Princess Street, Kingston
**Type:** Aluminum plaque on post
**Sponsor:** Ontario Heritage Foundation
**Date Erected:** 1957
**Additional Information:** Despite being away from Kingston for much of the time due to his presence in Parliament and preoccupation with government business, Macdonald continued to maintain a residence in Kingston. Although the house was owned by Professor James Williamson, it was leased to Macdonald. As Margaret Angus explains, "To satisfy Louisa's insistence that she would live only in John A.'s house, Prof. Williamson, who owned Heathfield, rented the whole house to John A. as a home for Louisa. Margaret and James Williamson lived and boarded with Louisa. Since John A. was the official tenant he sat at the head of the table when he dined there, with Louisa at the foot." It was here that Macdonald's sister, Margaret Williamson, died in April 1876.
**Related Markers:** 36-37, 62, 123, 125-126, 130, 157, 186-187, 195, 202-203
**Readings:** Creighton 1952; Creighton 1955; Fleurette 1961; Angus 1984; Swainson 1979; Swainson 1989; DCB vol. 12.

The house which stood near this site was constructed prior to 1841, and purchased in 1865 by Prof. James Williamson of Queen's University. His wife, Margaret, was a sister of Sir John A. Macdonald, who became the first prime minister of the Dominion of Canada. Prof. Williamson leased the building to the Conservative leader, but retained a portion for his own use. Macdonald installed his unmarried sister, Louisa, in the house, and it served as his residence during his visits to Kingston 1865-1878. Later "Heathfield" was occupied by the Sisters of Providence of St. Vincent de Paul, and was demolished in 1964.

*Heathfield while occupied by The Sisters of Providence of St Vincent de Paul.* Queen's University Archives

# Father of Confederation, Sir John Alexander Macdonald 1815-1891

Map XI – 4

A delegate to the Intercolonial Conferences of 1864-1867 at which the basis was laid for the federal union of the British North American Provinces in a new nation. The grave is marked and maintained in perpetuity by the Government of Canada.

*Location:* Cataraqui Cemetery, 927 Purdy Mills Road, Kingston, at the Macdonald family gravesite, Section C off Beech Avenue
*Type:* Bronze plaque on post
*Sponsor:* Historic Sites and Monuments Board of Canada
*Date Erected:* 1980

# Sir John Alexander Macdonald 1815-1891

Map XI – 5

Prime Minister of Canada July 1867 – November 1873, October 1878 – June 1891. This marker was unveiled by the Government of Canada on the occasion of the 125th anniversary of Confederation.

*Location:* Cataraqui Cemetery, 927 Purdy Mills Road, Kingston, at the Macdonald family gravesite, Section C off Beech Avenue
*Type:* Bronze plaque on post
*Sponsor:* Government of Canada
*Date Erected:* 1993

*A ribbon and memorial card to commemorate Sir John A. Macdonald's death in 1891.* Special Collections, Queen's University

**Map XI – 6**

# Sir John A. Macdonald
# 1815-1891

**Location:** Cataraqui Cemetery, 927 Purdy Mills Road, Kingston, at the Macdonald family gravesite, Section C off Beech Avenue

**Type:** Metal plaque on stone base and flag

**Sponsor:** Parks Canada

**Date Erected:** 1999

**Additional Information:** Macdonald had promised his mother that he would be buried alongside her in Cataraqui Cemetery. Although he died in Ottawa on 6 June 1891, it took a number of days for the Ottawa ceremonies before he finally came home to Kingston by train for burial on 11 June. Macdonald is buried here with his father (died 1841), mother (1862), first wife (1857) and infant son (1848), sister Margaret (1876) and her husband Professor James Williamson (1895), and his sister Louisa (1888). Those family members who died before Cataraqui Cemetery opened in 1853 were transferred in 1865 from the Upper Grave Yard (known as Skeleton Park, and now McBurney Park) which was located at the end of Clergy Street East in Kingston. Beginning in 1892 there has been a memorial service

John A. Macdonald, a Father of Confederation and Canada's first prime minister, dominated the life of the new nation for a quarter century. Macdonald was a visionary statesman, a determined Conservative partisan, and a much-loved leader. His policies of westward expansion and of railways to the Atlantic and Pacific laid the basis of a successful transcontinental nation. Still prime minister, Macdonald died in Ottawa on June 6, 1891. A simple stone cross marks his grave, as he wished.

on the anniversary of Macdonald's death, initially organized by the Macdonald Club and later by the Conservative Party. Since 1970 the Kingston Historical Society has been responsible for the memorial service, which has been held at Cataraqui Cemetery, Macdonald's statue in City Park, Kingston City Hall and continuously at Macdonald's gravesite since 1980.

**Related Markers:** 36-37, 62, 123, 125-126, 130, 157, 186-187, 195, 201

**Readings:** Newman 1974; Swainson 1979; Swainson 1989; DCB vol. 12; KHS 1991; Grenville 1992; McKendry 2000.

*Sir John A. Macdonald's gravesite*
Photo David Kasserra

# Father of Confederation
# Sir Alexander Campbell
# 1822-1892

**Map XI – 7**

A delegate to the Intercolonial Conferences of 1864 (Charlottetown and Québec) at which the basis was laid for the federal union of the British North American Provinces in a new nation. This grave is marked by the Government of Canada.

**Location:** Cataraqui Cemetery, 927 Purdy Mills Road, Kingston, section C off of Beech Avenue

**Type:** Bronze plaque on post

**Sponsor:** Historic Sites and Monuments Board of Canada

**Date Erected:** 1980

**Additional Information:** Both Campbell and Macdonald were involved with the establishment of Cataraqui Cemetery and selected grave sites very close to each other. In life, they were even more closely connected. Alexander Campbell had joined Macdonald in 1839 as an articling student and later the two formed a law partnership from 1843 to 1849. Campbell was first elected to the Legislative Council of Canada as the representative for Cataraqui division in 1858. He was involved with developing confederation and was as at the 1864 conferences. Appointed as a senator in 1867, he held a number of ministerial appointments in Macdonald's governments. He was appointed Lieutenant Governor for Ontario in 1887 but died in office in 1892.

**Related Markers:** 166, 188

**Readings:** Anonymous 1892; DCB vol. 12; Swainson 1969; McKendry 2000.

Photo David Kasserra

Map XI – 8

# Angel of the Resurrection

*Location:* Corner of Kingscourt and Kirkpatrick Street in St Mary's Cemetery (main entrance 718 Division Street), Kingston
*Type:* Stone statue
*Sponsor:* James Cleary, Archbishop of Kingston
*Date Erected:* 1894

*Additional Information:* It is now thought that more than 1,600 victims of the typhus epidemic were buried on the grounds of Kingston General Hospital in 1847-1848. This mass grave containing the remains of Irish immigrants and local people lay unmarked and overgrown until 1894, when Archbishop Cleary donated a marble structure portraying the Angel of the Resurrection (also more commonly known as the Angel of Mercy) to mark the grave site. In 1966, to accommodate the expansion of Kingston General Hospital, some of the bodies were re-interred at St. Mary's Cemetery on Division Street. The Angel of the Resurrection was also moved to this location.
*Related Markers:* 137, 206
*Readings:* Flynn 1976; MacKay 1990; Towns 1990; Deslauriers 1995; O'Gallagher 1995.

On the 6th of August, 1894, this Monument was erected by James Vincent Cleary, Archbishop of Kingston, in memory of his afflicted Irish compatriots, nearly 1400 in number, who, enfeebled by famine, in 1847-8, ventured across the ocean in unequipped sailing vessels, in whose fetid holds they inhaled the germs of pestilential "ship-fever" and on reaching Kingston perished here, despite the assiduous attention and compassionate offices of the good citizens of Kingston. *May the Heavenly Father give them eternal rest and happiness in reward of their patient suffering and Christian submission to His holy will, through the merits of His divine Son, Christ Jesus our Lord. Amen.*

*The Angel of the Resurrection Monument in its former location at Kingston General Hospital.*
Kingston Whig-Standard, May 1950

# The Typhus Epidemic 1847

Map XI – 9

Though typhus had been epidemic periodically in Canada since the 1650's, the worst outbreak occurred in the summer of 1847. In that year some 90,000 emigrants embarked for Canada, most of them refugees from the potato famine then ravaging Ireland. Nearly 16,000 died of typhus, either at sea or after their arrival in Canada. Those stricken while passing through Kingston found shelter in makeshift "immigrant sheds" erected near the waterfront. Despite the efforts of local religious and charitable organizations, notably the Sisters of the Religious Hospitallers of St. Joseph and the ladies of the Female Benevolent Society, 1,400 immigrants died. Buried near the present General Hospital, their remains were re-interred here in 1966.

*Location:* Kingscourt and Kirkpatrick Streets in St Mary's Cemetery, (main entrance 718 Division Street), Kingston
*Type:* Aluminum plaque on post
*Sponsor:* Ontario Heritage Foundation
*Date Erected:* 1966
*Related Markers:* 137, 205
*Readings:* Flynn 1976; MacKay 1990; Towns 1990; Deslauriers 1995; O'Gallagher 1995.

*Religious Hospitallers of St Joseph caring for typhus victims, Kingston waterfront, 1847.*
Courtesy of Religious Hospitallers of St Joseph, St Joseph Province Archives

# THE LOYALIST PARKWAY

**Map XII**                                                    **The Loyalist Parkway**

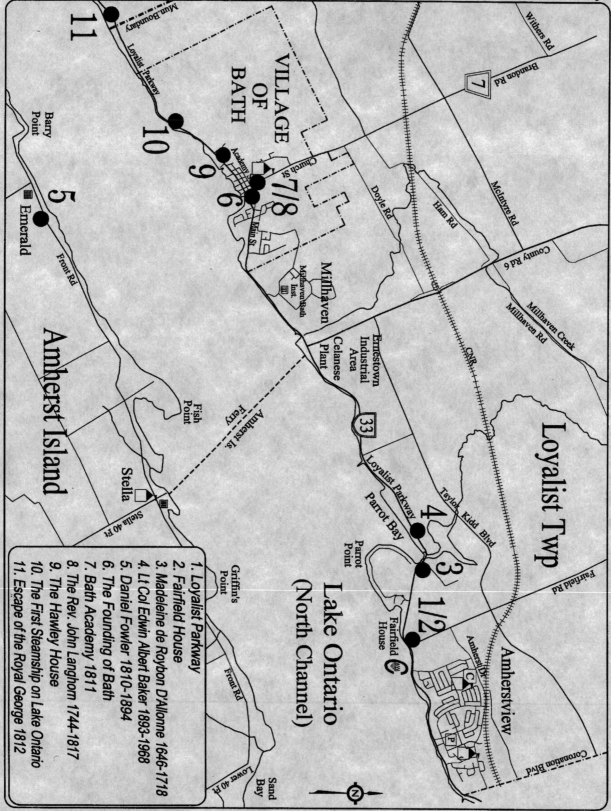

VILLAGE OF BATH

Millhaven

Barry Point

Emerald

Amherst Island

Front Rd

Fish Point

Amherst Is. Ferry

Stella

Stella 40 Ft.

Griffin's Point

Front Rd

Lower 40 Ft.

Sand Bay

Lake Ontario (North Channel)

Parrot Point

Parrot Bay

Loyalist Parkway

Fairfield House

Amherstview

Loyalist Twp

Celanese Plant

Ernestown Industrial Area

Millhaven Creek

Millhaven Rd

County Rd 6

McIntyre Rd

CNR

Ham Rd

Doyle Rd

Brandon Rd

Withers Rd

Fairfield Rd

Taylor Kidd Blvd

Amherst Dr

Coronation Blvd

7

33

Academy St

Church St

Main St

Millhaven/Bath Inst.

Mun.Boundary

Loyalist Parkway

1. Loyalist Parkway
2. Fairfield House
3. Madeleine de Roybon D'Allonne 1646-1718
4. Lt Col Edwin Albert Baker 1893-1968
5. Daniel Fowler 1810-1894
6. The Founding of Bath
7. Bath Academy 1811
8. The Rev. John Langhorn 1744-1817
9. The Hawley House
10. The First Steamship on Lake Ontario
11. Escape of the Royal George 1812

N

*Strategic & Long-Range Planning - DJMartin*

**Map XII – 1**

# Loyalist Parkway

*Location:* Across from Briargate Retirement Home, 4567 Highway No. 33 (Loyalist Parkway), Amherstview, on a boulder next to the Parkway gates on the south side of Highway No. 33
*Type:* Stone gateway, bronze plaque
*Sponsor:* Government of Ontario
*Date Erected:* 1984
*Additional Information:* The stone and iron gateway was designed by Kingston architect Lily Inglis.
*Related Markers:* 134, 210, 214
*Readings:* Richardson 1976; Waltman 1981; MCC 1985; MOT 1988.

Loyalist Parkway recalls those Loyalists of diverse backgrounds and races who, during the American Revolution, had in common a proud allegiance to His Majesty King George III. Coming to this Province from the United States, for the most part in 1784, they provided a foundation for our growth. This plaque commemorates the opening of the gateway and public highway in honour of the Loyalists on September 27, 1984 by Her Majesty The Queen in the presence of The Quinte Association, The United Empire Loyalists Association of Canada and other loyal citizens.

*The Loyalist Parkway running along the shore of Lake Ontario from the west end of Kingston to Adolphustown passes through historic Bath.* Photo David Kasserra

# Fairfield House

Map XII – 2

This is one of the few eighteenth-century Loyalist residences remaining in Ontario. William and Abigail Fairfield were among the first Loyalists to settle this area after the American Revolution. They arrived in 1784 and probably completed this farmhouse by 1793. Its symmetrical style and timber-frame construction evoke the architecture of the family's native New England. Except for its verandahs and french windows, added by 1860, Fairfield House survives much as it was built. It offers rare evidence of building techniques and interior detailing from the Loyalist era. By 1959, when it was donated for public preservation, Fairfield House had been in the family for six generations.

*Location:* 4574 Highway 33 (Loyalist Parkway), just west of Amherstview, at the entrance to Fairfield Park
*Type:* Aluminum plaque on post
*Sponsor:* Ontario Heritage Foundation with Loyalist Township
*Date Erected:* rededicated 1999
*Additional Information:* Provincial plaques have marked Fairfield House since the family's generous donation of the site to the Province. In 1985, when the house was opened to the public, a revised text matched new appreciations of the building. In August 1998, the St Lawrence Parks Commission, responsible for the property until then, transferred ownership from the Province to Loyalist Township, which has provided the present plaque. The heritage significance of the site itself starts with the 1784 first survey of lots for Loyalists. In time, the family's farm surrounded the house and extended to the north. In the early 1900s, Fairfield House started to be locally known as the "White House." The original road between Kingston and settlements to the west passed in front of Fairfield House until the Park was formed.
*Related Markers:* 134, 209, 214, 216
*Readings:* MacRae 1963; Waltman 1981; MCC 1985; Snyder 1991; Turner 1993; McKendry 1995.

*Facing Lake Ontario, the house is located in a popular park, and can be visited during the tourist season.* Loyalist Township

Map XII – 3

# Madeleine de Roybon D'Allonne c1646-1718

**Location:** South side of Highway No. 33 (Loyalist Parkway), approximately six kilometres west of Amherstview, just east of the Parrott Bay bridge
**Type:** Aluminum plaque on post
**Sponsor:** Ontario Heritage Foundation
**Date Erected:** 1970
**Related Markers:** 72, 73, 154
**Readings:** DCB vol. 2; Richardson 1976; Waltman 1981; MCC 1985.

Of noble French birth, de Roybon was the first European woman to own land in what is now Ontario. She came to Fort Frontenac (Kingston), probably in 1679, where she acquired property from René-Robert Cavelier de La Salle, governor and seigneur of the fort. In 1681 she loaned him money to finance his explorations, and about this time he granted her a seigneury extending westward from Toneguignon (Collins Bay). On this land she built a house, outbuilding and a trading post, grew crops and raised cattle. Marauding Iroquois, angry at the French for their campaign against the Senacas in 1686, destroyed de Roybon's establishment in August 1687 and took her prisoner. Released the following year, she lived in Montreal until her death.

*Plaque unveiling 14 June 1970. Shown from left to right are: Mr A.R. Hazelgrove of the Kingston Historical Society; the Rev. Jerome Rozon of St François d'Assise Eglise, Kingston; Mr Douglas Alkenbrack, MP (Frontenac-Lennox and Addington); Mr Glenn Herrington, Warden, Lennox and Addington; Mr Cecil Kidd, Reeve of Ernestown; Mr G.H. Blomeley of Kingston; Dr H.C. Burleigh of Bath; Mrs Margaret Angus, President, Ontario Historical Society; Mrs N.W. Hutchinson, President, Lennox and Addington Historical Society; and Mr Morris Whitney, MPP (Prince Edward-Lennox).* Ontario Heritage Foundation

# Lt Col Edwin Albert Baker
# 1893-1968

Map XII – 4

A passionate advocate of the rehabilitation and training of the blind, Baker was born nearby. In 1914 he enlisted in the Canadian Army and was blinded while in action in Belgium. He was hospitalized in England where he embraced the philosophy of self-reliance espoused by Sir Arthur Pearson, the prominent newspaper owner who was himself partially blind. Returning to Canada, Baker was instrumental in the formation of the Canadian National Institute for the Blind in 1918 and, as its General Secretary and Managing Director (1920-64), worked tirelessly to improve the medical, rehabilitative and educational services for veterans and the handicapped. He received many honours for his efforts and in 1951 was elected first president of the World Council for the Welfare of the Blind.

*Location:* Beulah United Church, 4949 Highway No 33 (Loyalist Parkway), about 6 kilometres west of Amherstview, just west of the Parrot Bay bridge
*Type:* Aluminum plaque on post
*Sponsor:* Ontario Heritage Foundation
*Date Erected:* 1979
*Readings:* Campbell 1965.

*CNIB founder Lt Col Edwin Baker (right) with King George VI (left) at the unveiling of the National War Memorial in Ottawa, May 1939.*
Queen's University Archives

Map XII – 5

# Daniel Fowler 1810-1894

*Location:* Concession Road No. 1, near Emerald, Amherst Island
*Type:* Aluminum plaque on post
*Sponsor:* Ontario Heritage Foundation
*Date Erected:* 1959
*Additional Information:* This plaque to Daniel Fowler was unveiled on 11 October 1959 by Charles Comfort (1900-1994), President of the Royal Canadian Academy of Arts and a well-known Canadian artist. According to noted art historian J. Russell Harper (*Painting in Canada*, 1966), Fowler stands in the forefront of "the leading English-born painters in Canada, who are superb craftsmen whose work inspired and influenced many younger artists in Ontario." Fowler was described as a gentle little bearded man who wore a skull cap and had delicate sharp features.
*Readings:* Comfort 1959; Smith 1976; Smith 1979; DCB vol. 12.

In this house Daniel Fowler, a well-known nineteenth-century Canadian artist, lived for over forty years. Born in England, he first took up law, but on the death of his father studied art under the English watercolour painter, J.D. Harding. As a result of ill health he came to Canada in 1843 and settled on this farm on Amherst Island. His subjects ranged from landscapes to still life, and his work was marked by originality and a strong sense of colour. In 1879 he became one of the first members of the Royal Canadian Academy.

*Self-portrait, c1886.*
National Gallery of Canada

# The Founding of Bath

Map XII – 6

Settlement of this village, one of Ontario's oldest communities, began in 1784 when discharged soldiers from Jessup's Rangers, a Loyalist corps, took up land grants in the vicinity. The sheltered harbour here provided easy access stimulating the growth of a community. Connected to Kingston by an early waterfront road, the hamlet, called Ernestown, contained a tavern, a church and an academy by 1811. A significant shipbuilding industry developed and in 1816 the *Frontenac*, the first steamboat in Upper Canada, was launched from a local shipyard. Two years later the settlement was officially renamed Bath. Incorporated as a village in 1859, it prospered as a commercial, shipping and industrial centre well into the 1870s. Today Bath's thriving past is reflected in its many distinctive 19th-century buildings.

*Location:* Centennial Park, Main and Fairfield Streets, Bath
*Type:* Aluminum plaque on post
*Sponsor:* Ontario Heritage Foundation
*Date Erected:* 1984
*Additional Information:* Bath's continuing development was hindered with the by-passing of the settlement by the York Road in 1832, the railway in the 1850s, and the decline in the importance of water transportation. Kingston was selected over Bath as the region's military centre, and Napanee was chosen as the county seat of Lennox-Addington. The village became a part of Loyalist Township in 1998.
*Related Markers:* 134, 209, 210, 215, 216, 217, 218
*Readings:* Arif 1976; Waltman 1981; MCC 1985; Foster 1996.

*Bath, on the Bay of Quinte, and Upper Gap to Lake Ontario c1830.*
By Thomas Burrowes. Archives of Ontario

Map XII – 7

# Bath Academy 1811

*Location:* 352 Academy Street, Bath

*Type:* Aluminum plaque on post

*Sponsor:* Ontario Heritage Foundation

*Date Erected:* 1959

*Additional Information:* In 1811, a fine two-storey, rough-cast Georgian style school was erected "for the instruction of youth in English reading, speaking, grammar and composition, the learned languages, penmanship, arithmetic, geography and other branches of Liberal Education" (*Kingston Gazette,* March 1811). The old academy was replaced in 1874 by a brick public school that was also demolished in 1910, and replaced by the present building.

*Related Markers:* 214

*Readings:* Arif 1976; Foster 1996.

On this site stood the Bath Academy, Lennox and Addington's earliest public school, founded in 1811 by means of local subscriptions. During the War of 1812 it was used for a time as a military barracks. Barnabas Bidwell, a radical political reformer and supporter of William Lyon Mackenzie, was its first teacher. His son, Marshall Spring Bidwell, who held similar views and became a leading member of the Legislative Assembly 1825-33, attended the academy. The institution was supported for many years by local settlers, but was merged into the common school system under the Public School Act of 1850.

*The historical plaque with the brick public school of 1910 in the background.* Photo David Kasserra

# The Reverend John Langhorn
# 1744-1817

Map XII – 8

Born in Wales, Langhorn was appointed missionary to Ernestown and Fredericksburgh townships in 1787. He thus became the first resident Anglican clergyman in the Bay of Quinte region, and the second in what is now Ontario. Although of somewhat eccentric character, he proved to be a tireless supporter of his faith during the twenty-six years he served in this area. He was largely responsible for the erection of St. Paul's Church at Sandhurst in 1791, St. Warburg's in Fredericksburgh in 1792 and the second St. John's at Bath in 1793-95. The hardships he endured undermined his health and Langhorn returned to England in 1813.

*Location:* 212 Church Street, Bath
*Type:* Aluminum plaque on post
*Sponsor:* Ontario Heritage Foundation
*Date Erected:* 1960
*Additional Information:* In 1793, the Rev. John Langhorn built a new wood-frame church on this site to replace a nearby log structure of 1787. The new building with its square 30 foot tower was located on land donated by William Fairfield, a United Empire Loyalist. The Reverend Langhorn's church was destroyed by fire in 1925 and replaced by the current church which resembles its predecessor.
*Related Markers:* 210, 214, 217
*Readings:* Arif 1976; Swainson 1991; Foster 1996; DCB vol. 5.

*St John's Church (of 1925) and graveyard.* Photo David Kasserra

Map XII – 9

# The Hawley House

*Location:* 531 Main Street, Bath
*Type:* Aluminum plaque on post
*Sponsor:* Ontario Heritage Foundation
*Date Erected:* 1959
*Related Markers:* 209, 214, 216
*Readings:* Arif 1976; Foster 1996.

This house, the oldest in the Bay of Quinte district, was built about 1785 by Captain Jeptha Hawley (1740-1813), a Loyalist from Arlington, Vermont. The Hawleys, an old Connecticut family, had sent several representatives, including Jeptha's father, to the legislature of that colony. Jeptha joined the Royal Standard in 1776, served under General Burgoyne and was later in charge of Loyalist refugees at Machiche, Quebec. In 1784 he settled here in Ernestown Township. The stone portion of this building was added between 1787 and 1799 as quarters for the Rev. John Langhorn, the district's first resident Anglican clergyman.

*An early view of the Hawley House.* Lennox and Addington Museum and Archives, N-60

# The First Steamship on Lake Ontario

Map XII – 10

In the early 1800's Kingston was a shipbuilding centre of note. The *Frontenac*, the first steamship to navigate Lake Ontario, was built here at Finkle's Point, Ernestown (now Bath), and launched September 7, 1816. Designed to carry freight and passengers, it was a boon to travellers, greatly reducing the difficulties and the cost of travel between Kingston and York (now Toronto). More sophisticated ships soon rendered the *Frontenac* obsolete and it was sold in 1825. Two years later it burned and sank in the Niagara River, but passenger steamships plied the lake for many years until rail and road travel became more effective.

*Location:* Finkle's Shore Park, 1 kilometres west of Bath, on the south side of Highway No. 33
*Type:* Bronze plaque on large stone cairn
*Sponsor:* Historic Sites and Monuments Board of Canada
*Date Erected:* 1924
*Additional Information:* See also p. 220.
*Related Markers:* 214
*Readings:* Cruikshank 1926; Mika 1987; Foster 1996.

*The Steamship Frontenac in 1827.* By James Van Cleve. Buffalo and Erie County Historical Society

Map XII – 11

# Escape of the *Royal George* 1812

*Location:* Highway No. 33, at County Road 21 approximately six kilometres west of the Bath, near the shore of Lake Ontario
*Type:* Aluminum plaque on post
*Sponsor:* Ontario Heritage Foundation
*Date Erected:* 1962
*Related Markers:* 93, 141
*Readings:* Anonymous 1812; Hitsman 1967; Malcomson 1998.

Opposite here is the gap between Amherst Island and the eastern tip of Prince Edward County. On November 9, 1812, the British corvette *Royal George* (22 guns), commanded by Commodore Hugh Earl(e), was intercepted off False Duck Islands by an American fleet, comprising seven ships under Commodore Isaac Chauncey. Pursued by the enemy, *Royal George* escaped through this gap into the Bay of Quinte's North Channel. The chase resumed in light winds the following day when she arrived safely in Kingston harbour. Chauncey, intent on capturing the largest British warship then on Lake Ontario, attacked her in the harbour but after exchanging fire with *Royal George* and shore batteries, was forced to withdraw.

*Pursuit of the Royal George, 10 November 1812.* Toronto Reference Library, T-15239

*Stone cairn with the Historic Sites and Monuments Board of Canada plaque, commemorating the Launching of the First Steamship.* See also p. 218.
Photo David Kasserra

*Historic Sites and Monuments Board of Canada plaque commemorating Kingston Penitentiary.* See also p. 192.
Photo David Kasserra

# APPENDICES

# Sir John A. Macdonald's Kingston

Few Canadian politicians have had such an impact on Canada as did Sir John A. Macdonald, architect of Confederation and the first Prime Minister of Canada. He was a determined Conservative who was able to bring politicians together, despite their diverse opinions, and to guide their decisions. His greatest achievement was the confederation of the colonies of the United Province of Canada (Ontario and Quebec), Nova Scotia and New Brunswick into the Dominion of Canada in 1867. His policies of westward expansion resulted in a transcontinental nation in 1871 and the construction of the Canadian Pacific Railway by 1885. As Prime Minister, he led the development of the country from the four provinces of the original Canada to seven provinces (adding Manitoba, 1870; British Columbia, 1871; Prince Edward Island, 1873), so that by the time he died in 1891 Canada was a country, which reached from sea to sea.

No Canadian Prime Minister is as closely associated with a Canadian community as Sir John A. Macdonald is with Kingston. Although born in Glasgow in 1815, Macdonald emigrated to Kingston with his family when he was only five years old. The Macdonald family (Hugh Macdonald and his wife Helen, along with their four children, Margaret, John A., James and Louisa) came to Kingston because Colonel Donald Macpherson, husband of Helen Macdonald's half-sister, was retired and living in Kingston.

Most aspects of Macdonald's life, particularly his role in Confederation and as Prime Minister, are well documented in a variety of books. The bibliographic references included with the Macdonald plaques provide the details. Macdonald's association with Kingston is well explained by Margaret Angus in *Sir John A. Lived Here* (Angus 1984).

Macdonald's early years of growing up and attending school, his legal training, and subsequent beginnings as an attorney are all related to Kingston. Macdonald's earliest years in Kingston are associated with 110-112 Rideau Street (62-63), a house which Macpherson had purchased in 1824. When only fifteen years old, Macdonald began training for the legal profession, an apprenticeship process during which he articled with George Mackenzie. By 1835 he had opened his first law office at 169-171 Wellington Street (37). Shortly after opening his law office, he took in two law students; Oliver Mowat and Alexander Campbell, both of whom later became Fathers of Confederation. Mowat became Premier of Ontario (149) and Campbell Lieutenant Governor of Ontario (166, 188, 204). Although away from Kingston for extensive periods of time in his role as Member of Parliament for Kingston, Macdonald retained his partnership in a law firm in Kingston until 1871. Between 1849 and 1860, Macdonald's office was at 343 King Street (36).

Macdonald's entry into political life began in 1843 when he was elected to the municipal council – a time when Kingston's City Hall was being constructed (22). In 1844 he was elected to represent Kingston in the parliament for the United Province of Canada. Although Macdonald always thought of Kingston as his home, once he began his life in politics, he was away from Kingston for increasing lengths of time. In the late 1840s, Macdonald and his family resided at Bellevue House (186) followed by 180 Johnson Street (126).

With the death of Macdonald's father in 1841, he was left as the head of the family. Part of his responsibilities was to ensure the appropriate living arrangements for his mother and sisters. By 1855 he had decided that he would no longer maintain a Kingston home for his wife and son but that they would live with him as he attended to government business. However, he still maintained close familial ties to Kingston, largely through leasing houses for his mother (died 1862) and sisters, Margaret (died 1876) and Louisa (died 1888).

These houses also served as his legal residence for purposes of his representation as MP for Kingston. Those houses which are still in existence have all been marked: 194 Johnson Street (125), Hazeldell (195), 79-81 Wellington Street (130), and 134 Earl Street (123). Heathfield (201), demolished in 1964, has also been marked.

Although Macdonald represented constituencies other than Kingston (Victoria, British Columbia, 1878-1882; Carleton, Ontario, 1882-1887), he continued to maintain his connection with Kingston. After a stroke in late May, Macdonald died in Ottawa on 6 June 1891. Following several days of ceremonies in Ottawa, Macdonald came home to Kingston. Macdonald had promised his mother that he would be buried alongside her in Cataraqui Cemetery. Macdonald's grave is marked by several plaques, all erected by the Government of Canada: one marking his grave as a Father of Confederation (202), one marking his grave as a Canadian Prime Minister (part of the celebration of the 125th anniversary of Canada's confederation) (202) and a third as part of a larger program by Parks Canada to mark the grave sites of Canadian Prime Ministers (203).

Following Macdonald's death in 1891, Kingstonians put forward a number of ideas to honour his memory. Of those that were implemented, the most tangible was the erection of a statue in City Park at the corner of West and King Street East (front and back covers; 157). A plaque was placed on the statue much later (157). Kingston and Macdonald were inextricably linked in the 19th century, a relationship which has been well remembered and marked in the 20th century. Every year on June 6th, the anniversary of Macdonald's death, the Kingston Historical Society organizes a memorial service in honour of Kingston's most famous son.

*"A" Battery standing guard at Sir John A. Macdonald's gravesite in 1891.*
Queen's University Archives

1. **The Macdonald family gravesite**, Cataraqui Cemetery (section C, Beech Avenue), *927 Purdy Mills Road* off Counter Street. (202, 203)

2. **The site of Heathfield**, Macdonald's residence during visits to Kingston 1865-1878. Plaque located at *1200 Princess Street*, west of Sir John A. Macdonald Boulevard. (201)

3. **Hazeldell**, home of Macdonald's mother who died there in 1862. *225 Mowat Avenue* between Johnson Street and King Street West. (195)

4. **Bellevue House** National Historic Site, where Isabella and John Macdonald lived 1848-1849. Restored villa, grounds, and interpretative centre at *35 Centre Street* between Union Street and King Street West. (186, 187)

5. **Statue** of Sir John A. Macdonald, 1895, in *City Park* near the corner of King Street East and West Street. (157, 223, front & back covers)

6. **House** rented by Macdonald 1878-1889. *134 Earl Street* at Sydenham Street. (123)

7. **Macdonald's legal residence** 1856-1860 as a member of the Legislative Assembly for Kingston. *194 Johnson Street* near Sydenham Street. (125)

8. **Isabella and John Macdonald's house** from 1849-1852, and where their son Hugh John was born in 1850. *180 Johnson Street* between Sydenham and Bagot Streets. (126)

9. **House** leased by Macdonald for his sister Louisa and brother-in-law Professor Williamson 1876-1878. *79-81 Wellington Street* between William and Johnson Streets. (130)

10. **Macdonald's first law office** 1835-1839 *171 Wellington Street* between Brock and Princess Streets. (37)

11. **Macdonald's law office** from 1849-1860. *343 King Street East* between Brock and Princess Streets. (36)

12. **Kingston City Hall** at *216 Ontario Street*. Macdonald was an alderman from 1843-1846. See the medallion for the laying of the cornerstone (22, second floor near Mayor's office), as well as the oil full-length portrait of Macdonald painted in 1863 by William Sawyer (1820-1889) in Memorial Hall.

13. **House** owned by Macdonald's relatives, the Macphersons, and where he lived as a young lawyer in the 1830s. *110-112 Rideau Street* between Bay and North Streets. (62-63)

*Sir John A. Macdonald in the early 1880s.*
National Archives of Canada, C-8447

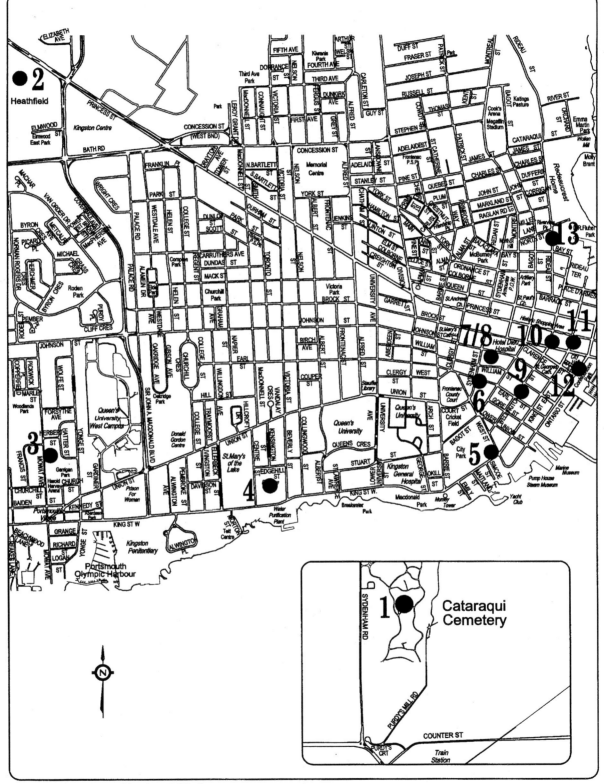

*Strategic & Long-Range Planning - DJMartin*

225

# Chronology
# of Kingston's History

## Based on the
## Monuments, Memorials, & Markers
## Included in this Book
### [Additional Information not from Markers]

**1608** [Samuel de Champlain founds Quebec, establishing the colony of New France.]

**1615** [Champlain travels in the Kingston area.]

**1673** On 30 June the Governor of New France, Count Frontenac, establishes a French trading post at Cataraqui. In 1973 Kingston celebrated its tercentenary.

**1675** Sieur de La Salle builds Fort Frontenac at Cataraqui and establishes a seigneury.

**1681** Madeleine de Roybon D'Allonne establishes a seigneury near present-day Collins Bay, but it is destroyed by the Iroquois in 1687.

**1689** Fort Frontenac is abandoned to the Iroquois.

**1695** Fort Frontenac is reoccupied and rebuilt.

**1735** Hon. René Boucher is born at Fort Frontenac.

**1756-63** [The Seven Years War between Britain and France has implications for Kingston.]

**1756** General Montcalm uses Fort Frontenac as a base to attack and destroy the British fort at Oswego.

**1758** Lt Col Bradstreet leads a British force that captures Fort Frontenac and partly demolishes it.

**1760** Major Robert Rogers takes possession of Fort Frontenac which remains unoccupied.

**1763** [British proclamation following the Peace of Paris creates the Province of Quebec.]

**1776-83** [The American Revolution gives rise to the Loyalist migration to Canada.]

**1783** Major John Ross, commanding officer of the 2nd Battalion, The King's Royal Regiment of New York, with a large military force occupies Cataraqui and partly rebuilds Fort Frontenac in preparation for the arrival of the Loyalists.

The King's Mills consisting of both saw and grist mills are built at Kingston Mills. A number of saw and grist mills are built on the site during the 19th century.

The Crawford Purchase of Indian lands secures most of Eastern Ontario for settlement.

An early land survey in Ontario is begun in the Kingston area.

**1784** Captain Michael Grass leads a party of Loyalists to Cataraqui, some of whom stay in the townsite while the majority settle in the first township, later named Kingston Township.

Molly and Joseph Brant are granted lots in Kingston, but Joseph moves to Brantford with the Six Nations, some of whom settle at Deseronto.

**1785** The Rev. John Stuart, the first Anglican priest in Ontario, arrives at Cataraqui and establishes the first school the following year.

A graveyard is established by the Rev. John Stuart that becomes St George's graveyard in 1792; its present name, St Paul's Churchyard, is taken from St Paul's Church founded in 1845 and built on the site.

Capt Jeptha Hawley, Loyalist, builds his house in Bath, Ernestown (now Loyalist) Township.

**1786** Bath, a Loyalist community established in 1784 west of Kingston, is named. The Bath Road, one of the earliest roads in Ontario, that connects Kingston with the communities to the west along Lake Ontario to Adolphustown was recognized in 1984 by being declared by Queen Elizabeth the Second, the Loyalist Parkway.

**1787** The Rev. John Langhorn, the second Anglican priest in Ontario, ministers to the Loyalist townships west of Kingston.

Fort Frontenac is renamed Tête de Pont barracks and Cataraqui renamed King's Town, which becomes Kingston the following year.

**1787-88** Pittsburgh Township is surveyed and opened for Loyalist settlement.

**1789** A naval dockyard and base for the Provincial Marine is established at Point Frederick.

**1791** [The Constitutional Act splits the Province of Quebec into Lower and Upper Canada.]

**1792** The first St George's Church is built. The second church of 1825 is built on a different site and in 1862 becomes St George's Cathedral.

The Kingston Grammar School is established; in 1807 it becomes the Midland District Grammar School.

Lieutenant Governor John Graves Simcoe and his Executive Council are sworn-in at St George's Church and hold their first formal meeting at Kingston.

**1793** Fairfield House is built by a Loyalist family west of Amherstview.

**1794** The first Masonic Lodge, Ancient St John's No 3, is founded in Kingston.

**1796** Molly Brant, consort of Sir William Johnson and sister of Joseph Brant, dies and is buried in St Paul's churchyard.

**1800** The Rev. Robert McDowall founds the Presbyterian Church at Sandhurst, west of Kingston; he becomes the first moderator in 1820, and a founder of Queen's University in 1840.

**1801** [The Kingston market is established.]

**1808** St Joseph's Roman Catholic Church is built on the corner of Bagot and William Streets. It becomes a school in 1859 and is demolished in 1891.

**1810** [The *Kingston Gazette* and the first printing office established in Kingston.]

**1811** Bath Academy is founded, the first common school in Lennox and Addington.

**1812-14** [The War of 1812 establishes Kingston as a major military centre.]

**1812** The *Royal George* is chased into Kingston harbour by an American fleet which is driven-off by the shore batteries.

**1813** Fort Henry is built on Point Henry in defence of the naval dockyard at Point Frederick. It is replaced in 1832 by a new fortification.

Sir James Lucas Yeo, in command of a Royal Naval detachment, arrives at the naval dockyard and proceeds to build warships in order to control Lake Ontario.

**1814** *HMS St Lawrence*, 112 guns, is launched, becoming the most powerful ship on the Great Lakes.

**1816** The *SS Frontenac* is launched just west of Bath; it is the first steamship on Lake Ontario.

**1817** The Rush-Bagot Treaty is signed demilitarizing the Great Lakes.

**1818** [The *Kingston Chronicle*, Kingston's second newspaper is founded.]

**1819** [Establishment of the Female Benevolent Society of Kingston.]

**1820** The Stone Frigate is built to store naval supplies at the Royal Naval Dockyard.

Sir Oliver Mowat is born in Kingston; he is premier of Ontario, 1872-96, and Lieutenant Governor, 1897-1903.

[St Andrew's Presbyterian Church is built.]

**1822** Charles Sangster, a significant Canadian poet, is born at Point Frederick.

Sir Alexander Campbell, a subscription governor of the Kingston General Hospital and Lieutenant Governor of Ontario, 1887-92, is born in Kingston. He is buried in Cataraqui Cemetery in 1892.

A parish house for St Joseph's Church is built and acts as a home for Bishop Macdonell when he is in Kingston; in 1846 it becomes the Notre Dame Convent, a primary school, and later a secondary school for girls. Today it forms part of the Kingston Public Library.

**1824** Captain John Strange builds his stone house on the corner of King and Barrack Streets. His grandson, Lt Col Courtlandt Strange, becomes a long-time president of the Kingston Historical Society.

Thomas Molson opens his brewery between West and Simcoe Streets, followed with another further west on the lakefront in 1831.

**1825** [The cornerstone of the present St George's Anglican Cathedral is laid.]

**1826** Bishop Alexander Macdonell is appointed Roman Catholic Bishop of Kingston and Regiopolis.

The Rev. John Barclay, first minister at St Andrew's Presbyterian Church, is remembered with a large stone monument in Kingston's second graveyard, now McBurney Park.

**1829** [Cataraqui Bridge is opened connecting Kingston to Pittsburgh Township.]

**1832** The Rideau Canal is completed.

The construction of a new Fort Henry, on the same site as the fort of 1813, begins following ten years of planning by two Ordnance Board commissions and four years of preparation by Royal Engineers.

Alwington House is completed as the residence for Baron Longueuil; it becomes Government House, the vice-regal residence of the Governor General from 1841 to 1844.

**1833** Kingston Penitentiary is established as the Provincial Penitentiary; it receives its first inmates in 1835 and thus becomes Canada's oldest penitentiary.

**1834** [*The British Whig* begins publication as a weekly.]

The Kingston Mechanics' Institute is founded; its books are transferred to the new Kingston Public Library in 1895.

**1835** John A. Macdonald opens his law practice in Kingston at 171 Wellington Street, and is admitted to the Bar of Upper Canada the following year. During these years he lives at 110-112 Rideau Street.

Sir Richard Cartwright, the grandson of the Hon. Richard Cartwright (one of Kingston's first residents), is born in the Cartwright House (191 King St E.) of 1832; he becomes Minister of Trade and Commerce, 1873-1878.

The Kingston General Hospital is completed but not opened due to a lack of funds.

**1836** Construction begins on Summerhill, the residence of Archdeacon George Okill Stuart, son of the Rev. John Stuart; it becomes the first permanent building of Queen's University in 1853.

[D.D. Calvin begins his timber business on Garden Island; it closes in 1914]

**1837** [Queen Victoria comes to the throne and rules until her death in 1901.]

[Rebellion breaks out first in Lower Canada and then in Upper Canada.]

Regiopolis College is founded and its building cornerstone laid by Bishop Alexander Macdonell in 1839. The college, a training school for priests and located at 123 Sydenham Street, is closed in 1869 but reopens in 1896 at 243 King St E. as a Roman Catholic boys' secondary school and later moves to its present location in 1915 at 130 Russell St, where it is now a co-ed high school.

**1837-38** During the Rebellions the local militia is concentrated in Kingston to replace the British regular troops who are sent to Lower Canada.

Lt Col Sir Richard Bonnycastle, Royal Engineers, is in charge of the completion of Fort Henry when the Rebellions break out; he organizes the local militia and prepares the defences of Kingston against a rebel attack.

**1838** [Kingston becomes a town with Thomas Kirkpatrick as first mayor.]

**1840** [Act of Union creates the United Province of Canada uniting Upper and Lower Canada.]

The first Board of Trustees of Queen's College (granted a Royal Charter in 1841 and now known as Queen's University) meets in St Andrew's Presbyterian Church.

**1841** Kingston becomes the first capital of the new province.

Governor General, Lord Sydenham, moves into Government House, but dies before the end of the year and is buried in a vault under St George's Church.

The first parliament meets in the vacant hospital; some of the members are housed in Summerhill.

Queen's College is established by Royal Charter.

Roselawn, a country villa, is built; it later becomes the home of Sir Henry Smith, Solicitor General of Upper Canada and Speaker of the House (1851-1868), and in 1974 the Donald Gordon Centre, a conference centre for Queen's University

**1842** Sir Charles Bagot is appointed Governor General and moves into Government House, where he dies the following year.

**1842** Queen's College opens for classes at 67 Colborne Street.

Rockwood Villa is built for John and Sarah Cartwright west of Portsmouth village; in 1856 the estate is sold for the site of an insane asylum.

**1842 continued** Rockwood Lunatic Asylum is built 1859-70; Kingston Psychiatric Hospital is built in 1959.

Hazeldell, a country villa, is built in Portsmouth Village. From 1860 to 1865 it was John A. Macdonald's legal residence and the home of his mother, who died there, and his sisters, Louisa and Margaret, and Margaret's husband, Professor James Williamson.

**1843** John A. Macdonald is elected to the Kingston Town Council; in the same year he marries Isabella Clark.

Architect George Browne supervises the building of City Hall; it is completed in 1844.

Sir Charles Metcalfe arrives as Governor General.

The cornerstone of St Mark's Anglican Church, Barriefield, is laid; the church opens in 1844.

The Commissariat Stores on Point Henry are completed, joining the Advanced Battery, built 1836, to Fort Henry.

The cornerstone of St Mary's Roman Catholic Cathedral is laid; the building is completed in 1848.

Artist Daniel Fowler settles on Amherst Island.

**1844** John A. Macdonald is elected to the House of Assembly of Upper Canada representing Kingston.

The government of the United Province of Canada leaves Kingston for Montreal.

**1846** Kingston is incorporated as a city; John Counter is first mayor.

The Oregon crisis spurs a military response in Kingston: four Martello towers, the Market Battery in front of City Hall, and two ditch towers completing the defences of Fort Henry are built 1846-48.

Edward Horsey designs and builds Elizabeth Cottage as his home and office; it is converted to a double house in 1883. It is now a retirement home for women.

**1847** The Kingston Gas Light Company is proposed and founded the next year; gas lamps are used until 1947.

John A. Macdonald is appointed to the Executive Council.

[Kingston is connected by telegraph.]

**1847-48** A wave of immigrants, fleeing from the Irish famine, arrive in Kingston. More than 1,400 die of typhus and are buried near the Kingston General Hospital, where a monument, the Angel of Resurrection, is erected in 1894. In 1966 the monument is moved to St Mary's Cemetery.

**1848** John A. and Isabella Macdonald move into Bellevue House, an 1840s "Italian Villa," where his young son dies.

[The St Lawrence Canals are completed, the final work of Canada's first "Seaway."]

**1849** John A. Macdonald, after dissolving his partnership with Alexander Campbell, moves his law office to 343 King St East where, in 1854, he takes on a new partner Archibald J. Macdonell.

John A. Macdonald moves his family from Bellevue to 180 Johnson Street where his second son, Hugh John, is born.

*The British Whig* begins daily publication; its direct descendant, the *Kingston Whig Standard,* is Canada's oldest continuous daily newspaper.

[The Municipal Councils Act is passed, legislating democratic local government.]

The Kingston General Hospital is incorporated.

**1850** The City of Kingston and the Townships of Kingston and Pittsburgh inaugurate the basic form of municipal government still in effect.

John Marks is elected reeve of Pittsburgh Township. From then until the amalgamation with the City of Kingston on 1 January 1998 a total of 48 residents serve as reeve, 9 of whom serve as wardens of Frontenac County.

**1851** [Sydenham Street Methodist (now United) Church is designed by William Coverdale and opened for service in 1852.]

**1852** John A. Macdonald moves his family to Brock Street. With his appointment as Attorney General in 1854 he moves to Toronto, the seat of government, in 1855. He rents 194 Johnson Street, where his mother and two sisters live until 1860, as his legal Kingston residence in order to retain his Kingston constituency.

**1852 continued** Robert Sutherland, a Jamaican of African origin, graduates with a BA degree from Queen's; after his death in 1878 he becomes the university's first major benefactor.

**1853** The Kingston County Grammar School (formerly the Midland District Grammar School) moves into new quarters (now Sydenham Public School); it becomes the Kingston High School in 1871.

Hillcroft, a country villa, is built for Francis Hill, mayor of Kingston; later it becomes the home of Sir Alexander Campbell, a political associate of Sir John A. Macdonald.

**1855** The Kingston Observatory, the first in Ontario, is established.

Henry Wartman Richardson, son of grain merchant James Richardson, is born; Henry becomes president of the family firm from 1906 to 1918 and together with his wife, Alice Ford, become major benefactors of the Kingston General Hospital.

A Faculty of Medicine is established at Queen's College (now University) and within 50 years four medical buildings are built.

John Meagher, head of the family that founded Meagher's Distillery Limited of Montreal, one of Canada's largest producers of liqueurs, builds a stone residence at 85 Barrack Street.

[James Morton purchases the Ontario Foundry and builds locomotives; under a variety of owners and names the production of locomotives continues for over 100 years.]

**1856** The Custom House and Post Office are designed and completed three years later.

[Kingston is connected to Toronto and Montreal by the Grand Trunk Railway.]

**1857** John A. Macdonald becomes Premier of the Province of Canada; that same year his wife, Isabella, dies.

**1858** The Village of Portsmouth is incorporated; a town hall is built in 1865. In 1952 the City of Kingston annexed Portsmouth.

The Frontenac County Court House is opened, complete with jail and jailer's house.

**1859** The Wolfe Island Township Hall is erected.

The first association of Canadian newspaper publishers is held in Kingston.

**1860** John A. Macdonald moves his office to 93 Clarence Street.

**1862** The Orphans' Home is opened by the Widows' Friend Society on the corner of University Avenue and Union Street. In 1927 it was acquired by Queen's to become part of the Students' Memorial Union. It burnt in 1947.

**1863** The 14th Battalion of Infantry is formed from a number of volunteer militia companies and in the same year is given the name The Princess of Wales' Own Rifles in honour of the new Princess of Wales (the future Queen Alexandria). Today, known as the Princess of Wales' Own Regiment (PWOR), it continues as one of Canada's oldest serving militia units.

**1864** The Charlottetown and Quebec constitutional conferences are held; three Kingstonians are present: John A. Macdonald, Oliver Mowat, and Alexander Campbell.

**1865** James Williamson purchases Heathfield, a country house built before 1841, and leases part of it to John A. Macdonald who makes it his official residence until 1878; his sister Louisa also lives there. His other sister, Margaret Williamson, dies there in 1876.

**1866** The Fenian Raids take place; the PWOR are called out to make a show of force at Cornwall.

Hawthorn Cottage, Pittsburgh Township, is built; in 2000 it becomes part of the newest branch of the Kingston Frontenac Public Library.

**1867** The Dominion of Canada is formed on 1 July; John A. Macdonald is appointed Prime Minister, a Privy Councillor, and a Knight Commander of the Bath. He also remarries. One hundred years later, Confederation Park, opposite City Hall, is opened on 1 July. Also, a stone emblem commemorating Canada's centennial is constructed by the Girl Guides and Boy Scouts in front of Murney Tower.

**1867** Sir Edouard Percy Cranwill Girouard is born in Montreal, educated at the Royal Military College, and commissioned in the Royal Engineers in 1888; he builds railways throughout Africa.

**1870** The last British troops to be garrisoned in Kingston are withdrawn; a total of 33 British regiments have garrisoned Fort Henry since 1813.

**1871** The first units of the Permanent Force of Canada are formed with "A" Battery, Garrison Artillery, stationed in Fort Frontenac and Artillery Park.

[The Kingston and Pembroke Railway is incorporated and construction begins in 1872.]

**1872** The Market Battery is demolished; and on the site a park is built in 1876. In 1885 with the building of the Kingston and Pembroke Railway station it becomes Kingston's "Inner Station" until 1961. In 1967 the area is redesigned and renamed Confederation Park.

The Kingston High School is renamed the Kingston Collegiate Institute.

**1875** Jenny Trout becomes the first woman to be licensed to practise medicine in Canada. She helps to fund the Kingston Women's Medical College.

**1876** The Military College opens on Point Frederick with 18 students; in 1878 it becomes the Royal Military College (RMC). In 1948 it becomes a tri-service institution and in 1959 achieves degree-granting status. On the occasion of RMC's centenary the original dockyard bell is returned by St Mark's Church, Barriefield.

Sir John A. Macdonald rents half of 79-81 Wellington Street for his sister and widowed brother-in-law.

**1877** George Monro Grant is appointed principal of Queen's College, a position he holds until his death in 1902. More than any other person Grant made Queen's the great university it becomes, as he lays the ground work for the conversion of the Presbyterian college into the non-denominational "Queen's University at Kingston" in 1912.

[The Kingston Street Railway begins operations; the system is electrified in 1893.]

**1878** Sir John A. Macdonald moves his sister and brother-in-law to 134 Earl Street, where his sister dies in 1888.

For the first time Sir John A. Macdonald loses an election in Kingston (he is elected in Victoria, BC).

**1881** [A telephone system is established in Kingston.]

**1883** The Women's Medical College of Kingston is founded and located in the City Hall. It closes its doors in 1894.

**1885** James Armstrong Richardson is born in Kingston; he becomes a benefactor of Queen's and chancellor for ten years.

The Canadian Artillery from Kingston takes part in the Northwest Rebellion; the Princess of Wales' Own Rifles garrison Fort Henry.

**1886** The first hockey game is played in Kingston between Queen's and RMC.

An astronomical observatory is constructed at RMC.

**1887** Sir John A. Macdonald is again elected in Kingston, his legal residency is 134 Earl Street, even though he is living in "Earnscliffe" in Ottawa after 1883.

[The city acquires the Kingston Water Works Company.]

**1888** [Electricity is introduced in Kingston.]

**1890** Sir John A. Macdonald lays the cornerstone for the Kingston Dry Dock, a federal repair facility. It is leased in 1910 by the Kingston Shipbuilding Company, which builds ships until 1968. Today it is part of the Marine Museum complex.

**1891** Sir John A. Macdonald is buried in Cataraqui Cemetery.

**1892** The Religious Hospitallers of St Joseph, who came to Kingston in 1847 to care for the sick and orphaned immigrants, open the Hotel Dieu hospital in the original Regiopolis College building.

Kingston Collegiate Institute moves to its present location at 235 Frontenac St.

Sir George Airey Kirkpatrick, son of the first mayor of Kingston, is appointed lieutenant governor of Ontario. In 1903 a fountain is dedicated to him in front of the Frontenac County Court House.

**1893** [The Kingston Historical Society is founded.]

**1893 continued** The School of Mining and Agriculture is founded at Queen's, the forerunner of the Faculty of Applied Science formed the next year.

The Canadian Artillery, for its efforts in 1885, becomes the Royal Canadian Field Artillery (RCA).

**1895** A memorial statue to Sir John A. Macdonald is unveiled in City Park; [the portion of City Park in the area of Murney Tower is named Macdonald Park.]

**1899** The South African War begins. The RCA from Kingston and the PWOR both participate; the PWOR gains the battle honour "South Africa 1900."

**1904** A nurses' residence opens at the Kingston General Hospital, where nurses' training had been conducted since 1886. Later the building is named the Ann Baillie Building.

**1906** The RCA in Fort Frontenac becomes the Royal Canadian Horse Artillery (RCHA).

**1908** [*The Story of Old Kingston* by Agnes Maule Machar is published.]

**1909** [The city purchases the Kingston Light, Heat & Power Company.]

**1914** [Kingstonians strongly support the war effort at home and abroad during the First World War.]

The 21st Battalion, formed from a nucleus of the PWOR, is mobilized and proceeds to France in 1915. It has a magnificent war record (18 battle honours) including taking part in the battle of Vimy Ridge, where it erects a memorial cross to its fallen. It brings the cross back to Canada.

The RCHA proceeds overseas as part of the 2nd Canadian Division and takes part in 13 major battles, many in support of the British Army.

Fort Henry becomes an internment camp for enemy aliens, mostly former citizens of the Austro-Hungarian Empire who had emigrated to Canada before 1914.

**1915** The 1st Canadian Division is formed; it is the first Canadian formation into battle, suffering 52,000 casualties. It is activated during the Second World War, suffering 14,000 casualties. Since 1945 it has been

twice activated as part of the Regular Army, but as of 1999 it has been removed from the Order of Battle.

**1916** The Kingston Historical Society installs its first known plaque to the memory of the Reverend John Stuart in St George's Cathedral.

**1917** [LaSalle Causeway is opened, replacing the Cataraqui Bridge.]

**1918** The Canadian Institute for the Blind is formed under the direction of Lt Col Edwin Albert Baker, who was blinded during the First World War.

**1919** The Frontenac Club, a gentleman's club formed in 1908, erects a plaque to its ten war dead.

**1921** The County of Frontenac erects a memorial window and a plaque for those from the county who died in the First World War.

The City of Kingston renovates part of City Hall into Memorial Hall in honour of Kingston's dead in the First World War.

**1923** The RMC Memorial Arch is erected by ex-cadets to the fallen from the college beginning with the Emin Pasha Relief Expedition, 1887-1890; the Arch continues as the memorial for fallen cadets for all campaigns in which cadets have served since 1876.

**1925** The Imperial Order of the Daughters of the Empire erect a Cross of Sacrifice to the fallen of the First World War in Macdonald Park; it becomes Kingston's centre of remembrance on 11 November.

Kingstonian Samuel D. Chown plays an important role in the formation of the United Church of Canada.

**1927** Queen's University opens the Students' Memorial Union, a club for male students, as its war memorial to students and faculty who fell in the First World War. After the Second World War the building is destroyed by fire and a new building erected containing a War Memorial Room with two plaques listing the over 350 fallen in both World Wars.

**1929** [The Great Depression begins; life in Kingston is greatly affected during the 1930s.]

**1930** The RCHA erects a stone memorial to their fallen. In 1996 a 25 pounder gun is

**1930 continued** added to the site in recognition of the 125 anniversary of the founding of the Royal Regiment of Canadian Artillery, Canada's first regular troops.

**1931** The 21st Battalion Association erects a magnificent memorial to its 830 war dead.

The Kingston Collegiate Institute becomes the Kingston Collegiate and Vocational Institute (KCVI) with the addition of a technical and commercial teaching wing. In 1992 the school celebrates 200 years of existence as well as 100 years of being located on the same site.

**1936** The restoration of Fort Henry begins under the direction of Ronald Way who originates the idea of the Fort Henry Guard. Later he is in charge of the creation of Upper Canada Village and the recreation of the Fortress of Louisbourg.

**1938** Fort Henry opens on 1 August as a military museum following two years of restoration as federal-provincial works project. The Fort Henry Guard, a military interpretative unit, is on parade for the first time; one year later 30 members of the Guard volunteer for military service.

**1939** [King George VI and Queen Elizabeth visit Kingston.]

[Canada declares war on Germany on September 10; Kingstonians support the war effort at home and abroad during the Second World War.]

**1940** The Stormont, Dundas and Glengarry Highlanders (SD&G), mobilized in June, concentrate at Kingston's fair grounds; "A" Company is formed from the PWOR. For its contribution to the SD&G the PWOR is granted a badge of distinction on its Regimental Colour, in addition to the 21st Battalion's ten battle honours.

Fort Henry again becomes an internment camp, first for aliens and then for prisoners-of-war. It does not reopen as a military museum until 1948.

**1945** A plaque is placed in Richardson's Feed Mill to commemorate in that site in 1940 the formation of *HMCS Cataraqui*, Kingston's Royal Canadian Naval Reserve Division.

**1946** A Book of Remembrance is placed in Memorial Hall listing the names of Kingstonians who served in the Second World War. Kingston's monument to them takes the form of the Kingston Community Memorial Centre erected in the fair grounds in 1950.

**1952** [The Kingston Historical Society begins its annual publication of *Historic Kingston*.]

**1953** [The coronation of Queen Elizabeth II takes place.]

**1957** [The Agnes Etherington Art Centre is founded with André Bieler as its first director.]

**1959** [The St Lawrence Seaway is opened.]

**1961** A memorial entrance to McNaughton Barracks at Canadian Forces Base, Kingston is erected to the memory of fallen members of the Corps of Royal Canadian Electrical and Mechanical Engineers (today the Electrical and Mechanical Engineering Branch.)

**1962** A memorial entrance to Vimy Barracks at Canadian Forces Base, Kingston is erected to the memory of fallen members of the Royal Canadian Corps of Signals (today the Communications and Electronics Branch).

**1965** [The Kingston Historical Society and the Kingston Whig-Standard publish a *Catalogue of Historic Sites and Monuments of Kingston and District*.]

**1967** A stone memorial is erected in City Park to the memory of those who gave their lives in the Royal Canadian Air Force and the Commonwealth Air Forces during both World Wars.

[St Lawrence College opens.]

**1971** [The first volume of *Buildings of Architectural and Historic Significance* appears as part of the City's efforts to protect heritage buildings from demolition or unsympathetic alterations.]

**1973** Kingston celebrates its tercentennial. A commemorative sundial is built and a time capsule is buried in Churchill Park. City Hall is restored.

**1976** [Sailing Olympics are held in Kingston. The Marine Museum of the Great Lakes is opened.]

**1984** Kingston celebrates the bicentennial of Loyalist settlement.

**1991** Queen's University celebrates its 150th anniversary.

**1994** A stone cairn is erected at the site of the former ship-building works to the veterans of the Royal Canadian Navy and the Merchant Navy, in particular their service in the Second World War.

**1995** A stone memorial is erected in City Park to those who served in the Far East and Pacific Theatres of War, 1941-1945.

**1998** [On 1 January the City of Kingston, Kingston Township, and Pittsburgh Township are amalgamated into one municipality.]

*The Kingston Historical Society's (KHS) Portsmouth Village plaque unveiling, 1 July 1999, Aberdeen Park, Kingston. Left to right: Mayor Gary Bennett; Anne Milina, President of the Portsmouth Villagers; William Baiden, representative of one of the founding families of Portsmouth Village; Brian Osborne, Vice-President of the KHS and; Jennifer McKendry, representing the KHS Plaque Committee. (See also p. 193)*

Photo David Kasserra

# Bibliography

THE READER'S ATTENTION is particularly drawn to the annual publication of the Kingston Historical Society, *Historic Kingston,* "the most important of ongoing publications" and "a publication of impressive quality," as characterized by Donald Swainson and Brian Osborne in *Kingston: Building on the Past.* Although the Kingston Historical Society published its "Reports and Proceedings" in 1923, it was not until 1952 that continuous publication of *Historic Kingston* began. The Society has published this journal, largely papers presented to the Society, on an annual basis since then. The first ten volumes (1952-1962) have been reprinted in one bound indexed volume - *Historic Kingston* (Belleville: Mika, 1974). To assist researchers, the volumes have been indexed at different stages: 1952-1972 (1973), 1973-1977 (1977), 1978-1985 (1985), 1986-1996 (1996). Although selected articles have been listed below by author, there are many more on a variety of aspects of Kingston's history.

**Allen 1992** Allen, M. Peter. "The Earliest Surveys in Frontenac County." *Historic Kingston* 40: 49-57.

**Anderson 1963** Anderson, Allan J. *The Anglican Churches of Kingston.* Kingston: By the Author.

**Angus 1966** Angus, Margaret. *The Old Stones of Kingston: Its Buildings before 1867.* Toronto: University of Toronto Press.

**Angus 1967** Angus, Margaret. "Lord Sydenham's One Hundred and Fifteen Days in Kingston." *Historic Kingston* 15: 36-49.

**Angus 1972** Angus, Margaret. "The Old Stones of Queen's, 1842-1900." *Historic Kingston* 20: 5-13.

**Angus 1973a** Angus, Margaret. *Kingston General Hospital: A Social and Institutional History.* Vol. I. Montreal: McGill-Queen's University Press.

**Angus 1973b** Angus, Margaret. "Portsmouth Village." *Historic Kingston* 21: 37-49.

**Angus 1981** Angus, Margaret. "Summerhill in the 19th Century: Its Uses and Users." *Historic Kingston* 29: 122-136.

**Angus 1984** Angus, Margaret. *John A. Lived Here.* Kingston: Frontenac Historic Foundation.

**Angus 1991** Angus, Margaret. *Cornerstones and Plaques, Queen's History in Names.* Kingston: Queen's Alumni Association.

**Angus 1992** Angus, Margaret. "Alwington House." *Historic Kingston* 40: 20-32.

**Angus 1994** Angus, Margaret. *Kingston General Hospital: A Social and Institutional History.* Vol. II. Kingston: Kingston General Hospital.

**Anonymous 1812** Anonymous. "The American Attack on Kingston, 10th November 1812 (from the *Kingston Gazette*)." *Historic Kingston* 6: 50.

**Anonymous 1892** *In Memoriam: Sir Alexander Campbell, KCMG, born March 9, 1822 died May 24, 1892.* Toronto: n.p.

**Anonymous 1950** Anonymous. "No Plaques on Monument of Sir John A. Macdonald to Tell of his Great Contribution to Canada." *Kingston Whig-Standard,* 24 February 1950.

**Anonymous 1956** Anonymous. "Documents: the Kingston Historical Society (from the Minute Book of the Society)." *Historic Kingston* 5: 46-48.

**Anonymous 1957** Anonymous. "Documents: Excerpts from the Minute Book of the Kingston Historical Society." *Historic Kingston* 6: 46-49.

**Anonymous 1958** Anonymous. "Lieutenant-Colonel C.M. Strange." *Historic Kingston* 7: 3-4.

**Anonymous 1962** Anonymous. "Sir Oliver Mowat Plaque Dedicated." *Kingston Whig-Standard*, 5 July 1962.

**Arif 1976** Arif, Muhammad. *History and Architecture, Village of Bath, Ontario: Buildings of Architectural and Historical Significance.* Kingston: Queen's University.

**Bator 1997** Bator, Paul A. *Ontario's Heritage.* Toronto: Ontario Heritage Foundation.

**Bazely 1997** Bazely, Susan M. "Molly Brant: Koñwatsi'tsiaéñni: Who Was She Really?" *Historic Kingston* 45: 9-21.

**Benedict 1997** Benedict, Ernie. "Koñwatsi'tsiaéñni, a Prayer." *Historic Kingston* 45: 22.

**Bennett 1981** Bennett, Carol and D.W. McCuaig. *In Search of the K & P: The Story of the Kingston and Pembroke Railway.* Renfrew, ON: Renfrew Advance.

**Bindon 1978** Bindon, Kathryn M. *Queen's Men, Canada's Men: The Military History of Queen's University, Kingston.* Kingston: Trustees of the Queen's University Contingent, Canadian Officers' Training Corps.

**Boss and Patterson 1995** Boss, W. and W.J. Patterson. *Up the Glens: Stormont, Dundas and Glengarry Highlanders 1783-1994.* Cornwall: The Old Book Store.

**Bowering 1991** Bowering, Ian. "The Art and Mystery of Brewing in Kingston." *Historic Kingston* 39: 26-32.

**Bradford 1988** Bradford, Robert D. *Historic Forts of Ontario.* Belleville, ON: Mika Publishing.

**Bradstreet 1759** Bradstreet, J.A. *Impartial Account of Lieutenant Colonel Bradstreet's Expedition to Fort Frontenac to Which are Added a Few Reflections on the Conduct of that Enterprise, and the Advantages Resulting from its Success.* Reprint ed., Toronto: Rous and Mann, 1940.

**Breck 1993** Breck, Wallace G. "A Hectic Decade at Fort Frontenac." *Historic Kingston* 41: 7-21.

**Brock 1968** Brock, T.L. "H.M. Dockyard, Kingston, Under Commissioner Robert Barrie, 1819-1834." *Historic Kingston* 16: 3-22.

**Campbell 1965** Campbell, Marjorie Wilkins. *No Compromise: The Story of Colonel Baker and the CNIB.* Toronto: McClelland & Stewart.

**Canada 1974** Canada. Indian and Northern Affairs. *Official opening of the Donald Gordon Centre and Commemoration of Roselawn.* Kingston: Queen's University.

**Canada 1980a** Canada. Department of National Defence. *The Official History of the Royal Canadian Air Force.* Toronto: University of Toronto Press.

**Canada 1980b** Canada. Department of National Defence. *Canadian Airmen and the First World War.* n.p.

**Canada 1986** Canada. Department of National Defence. *Creation of a National Air Force.* n.p.

**Canada 1992** Canada. Department of National Defence. *To Serve Canada: A History of the Royal Military College Since the Second World War.* Ottawa: Department of National Defence.

**Canada 1994** Canada. Department of National Defence. *Crucible of War, 1939-1945.* Ottawa: Canada Communication Group.

**Canadian 1995** Canadian Land Force Command and Staff College. *Fort Frontenac, Yesterday and Today.* 4th ed. Kingston: n.p.

**Canadian Encyclopaedia 1985** Marsh, James ed. 3 vols. Edmonton: Hurtig, 1985.

**Careless 1967** Careless, J.M.S. *The Union of the Canadas: The Growth of Canadian Institutions, 1841-1857.* Toronto: McClelland & Stewart.

**Carruthers 1975** Carruthers, James, R. "The Little Gentleman: The Reverend Doctor John Stuart and the Inconvenience of Revolution. Kingston: MA Thesis, Queen's University.

**Carter 1983** Carter, Margaret. *Early Canadian Court Houses.* Ottawa: Parks Canada.

**Cartwright 1912** Cartwright, Sir Richard. *Reminiscences by the Right Honourable Sir Richard Cartwright.* Toronto: W. Briggs.

**Christie 1950** Christie, Mary Katherine. *Sir Alexander Campbell.* Toronto: University of Toronto Press.

**City of Kingston** *Buildings of Architectural and Historic Significance.* 6 vols. Kingston: City of Kingston, 1971-1985.

**Cohoe 1978** Cohoe, Margaret. "Sir John A. Macdonald Memorializations and the Red Rose League." *Historic Kingston* 26: 58-69.

**Cohoe 1979** Cohoe, Margaret. "The Observatory in City Park 1855-1800." *Historic Kingston* 27: 78-91.

**Cohoe 1984** Cohoe, Margaret. "Kingston Mechanics' Institute, 1834-1850." *Historic Kingston* 32: 62-74.

**Cohoe 1985** Cohoe, Margaret. "Kingston Mechanics' Institute To Free Public Library." *Historic Kingston* 33: 42-55.

**Cohoe 1995** Cohoe, Margaret. "Kingston's Memorial Hall." *Historic Kingston* 43: 3-16.

**Comfort 1959** Comfort, Charles. "Daniel Fowler, R.C.A., 1810-1894." *Historic Kingston* 8: 50-53.

**Cossar 2000** Cossar, Bruce. "Uniting and Dividing: The Church Union Movement in Kingston." *Historic Kingston* 48: forthcoming.

**Creighton 1952** Creighton, Donald. *John A. Macdonald, The Young Politician.* Toronto: Macmillan.

**Creighton 1955** Creighton, Donald. *John A. Macdonald, The Old Chieftain.* Toronto: Macmillan.

**Crickard 1996** Crickard, Fred W., Michael L. Hadley, and Rob Huebert, eds. *A Nation's Navy: In Quest of Canadian Identity.* Kingston: McGill-Queen's University Press.

**Crothers 1973** Crothers, Katherine Connell. *With Tender Loving Care: A Short Story of the K.G.H. Nursing School.* Kingston: n.p.

**Cruikshank 1924** Cruikshank, Ernest Alexander. *First Session of the Executive Council of Upper Canada, Held in Kingston July 8 to July 21, 1792.* Toronto: n.p.

**Cruikshank 1926** Cruikshank, Ernest Alexander. *Notes on the History of Shipbuilding and Navigation on Lake Ontario up to the Time of Launching of the Steamship Frontenac, at Ernestown, Ontario.* Toronto: n.p.

**Cruikshank 1984** Cruikshank, Ernest Alexander. *The King's Royal Regiment of New York.* Toronto: Ontario Historical Society, 1931; reprint ed., Toronto: G.K.Watt, 1984.

**Cuneo 1959** Cuneo, John R. *Robert Rogers of the Rangers.* New York: Oxford University Press.

**Curtis 1985** Curtis, Dennis, Andrew Graham, Lou Kelly and Anthony Patterson. *Kingston Penitentiary: The First 150 Years, 1835-1985.* 2nd ed. Ottawa: Correctional Service of Canada.

**Dale 1993** Dale, Clare, A. *The Palaces of Government: A History of the Legislative Buildings of the Provinces of Upper Canada, Canada and Ontario, 1792-1992.* Toronto: The Library.

**Davidson 1981** Davidson, George. "The Construction of Murney Tower, George Davidson's Diary of 1846." *Historic Kingston* 29: 42-52.

**DCB** *Dictionary of Canadian Biography.* 14 vols., Toronto: University of Toronto Press, 1966-1998.

**Denison 1955** Denison, Merrill. *The Barley and the Stream, The Molson Story.* Toronto: McClelland & Stewart.

**Dent 1885** Dent, John Charles. *The Story of the Upper Canadian Rebellion, Largely Derived from Original Sources and Documents.* Toronto: C.B. Robinson.

**Deslauriers 1995** Deslauriers, Jessie. *Hotel Dieu Hospital Kingston, 1845-1995: The House of Tender Mercy Continuing to Serve.* Kingston: Hotel Dieu Hospital.

**Downie 1993** Downie, Mary Alice and M.A. Thompson, eds. *Written in Stone: A Kingston Reader.* Kingston: Quarry Press.

**Eccles 1959** Eccles, W.J. *Frontenac, The Courtier Governor.* Toronto: McClelland & Stewart.

**Ede 1992** Ede, Ronald A. "A Bicentennial Look at Kingston Collegiate and Vocational Institute. *Historic Kingston* 40: 33-48.

**Edmison 1953** Edmison, J. Alex. *St. Andrew's Presbyterian Church, Kingston, Ontario and Queen's University.* Kingston: St. Andrew's Church and Queen's University.

**Edmison 1954** Edmison, J. Alex. "The History of the Kingston Penitentiary." *Historic Kingston* 3: 26-35.

**Edmison 1960** Edmison, J. Alex. "Kingston and the Founding of the Canadian Press Association." *Historic Kingston* 9: 46-56.

**Errington 1988** Errington, Jane. *Greater Kingston: Historic Past, Progressive Future.* Burlington: Windsor Publications.

**Evans 1992** Evans, A. Margaret. *Sir Oliver Mowat.* Toronto: University of Toronto Press.

**Fetherling 1993** Fetherling, Douglas. *A Little Bit of Thunder: The Strange Inner Life of the Kingston Whig-Standard.* Don Mills, ON: Stoddart.

**Fitsell 1982** Fitsell, J.W. "Captain Sutherland and his Dream." *Historic Kingston* 30: 3-17.

**Fitsell 1985** Fitsell, J.W. "The Meagher Family and House." *Historic Kingston* 33: 86-90.

**Fitsell 1987** Fitsell, J.W. *Hockey's Captains, Colonels and Kings.* Erin, ON: Boston Mills Press.

**Fleurette 1961** Mary Fleurette, Sister, S.P. *Centenary of the Institute of the Sisters of Providence of St. Vincent de Paul, 1861-1961.* Kingston: Providence Mother House Heathfield.

**Flynn 1963** Flynn, Louis J. "The Early Years of the Kingston Historical Society 1893-1906." *Historic Kingston* 11: 35-46.

**Flynn 1964** Flynn, Louis J. "In Retrospect: the Kingston Historical Society since 1906." *Historic Kingston* 12: 19-26.

**Flynn 1973** Flynn, Louis. *At School in Kingston 1850-1973.* Kingston: Frontenac, Lennox, and Addington County Roman Catholic Separate School Board.

**Flynn 1976** Flynn, Louis. *Built on a Rock: The Story of the Roman Catholic Church in Kingston 1826-1976.* Kingston: Roman Catholic Archdiocese of Kingston.

**Fort Henry** *Old Fort Henry.* Kingston: St. Lawrence Parks Commission, n.d.

**Foster 1996** Foster, Jane. *Bath, On the Bay of Quinte.* Napanee, ON: Lennox and Addington County Museum.

**Fryer 1987** Fryer, Mary Beacock. *Volunteers and Redcoats, Rebels and Raiders: A Military History of the Rebellions in Upper Canada.* Toronto: Dundurn Press.

**German 1990** German, Tony. *The Sea is at Our Gates: The History of the Canadian Navy.* Toronto: McClelland & Stewart.

**Gibson 1983** Gibson, Frederick W. *Queen's University. Volume II, 1917-1961. To Serve, and Yet be Free.* Kingston: McGill-Queen's University Press.

**Glazebrook 1929** Glazebrook, G.P. de T. *Sir Charles Bagot in Canada, a Study of British Colonial Government.* New York: Oxford University Press.

**Gray 1951** Gray, D.M. *A History of the Construction of the Rideau Canal.* Kingston: n.p.

**Gregorovich 1994** Gregorovich, John B., ed. *Commemorating an Injustice: Fort Henry and Ukrainian Canadian "Enemy Aliens" during the First World War.* Kingston: Kashtan Press.

**Grenville 1988** Grenville, John H. "Kingston's Reaction to the Rebellion of Upper Canada: Bonnycastle and the Role of the Militia." *Historic Kingston* 36: 66-88.

**Grenville 1992** Grenville, John H. "In Memoriam: Kingston Mourns Sir John A. Macdonald." *Historic Kingston* 40: 93-105.

**Grimshaw 1993** Grimshaw, Louis E. "Fort Frontenac: Over Three Centuries of Service." *Historic Kingston* 41: 22-35

**Gundy 1955** Gundy, H.P. "Growing Pains: The Early History of the Queen's Medical Faculty." *Historic Kingston* 4: 14-25

**Gundy 1958** Gundy, H.P. "The Sir George Kirkpatrick Memorial Fountain." *Historic Kingston* 7: 64-67.

**Hacker 1974** Hacker, Carlotta. *The Indomitable Lady Doctors.* Toronto: Clarke & Irwin.

**Halford 1994** Halford, Robert G. *The Unknown Navy: Canada's World War Two Merchant Navy.* St. Catharines: Vanwell Publishing.

**Hamilton 1971** Hamilton, W.D. *Charles Sangster.* New York: Twayne Publishers.

**Hamilton 1988** Hamilton, W.D. *Charles Sangster and His Works.* Toronto: E.C.W. Press.

**Hawkins 1967** Hawkins, James, Mrs. *History of Wolfe Island.* n.p.

**Hazelgrove 1974** Hazelgrove, A.R. "Robert Sutherland: Queen's First Black Student." *Historic Kingston* 22: 64-69.

**Hill 1991** Hill, E. Jean M. *Breaking Down the Walls: Nursing Science at Queen's University.* Kingston: School of Nursing, Queen's University.

**Hitsman 1967** Hitsman, J.M. "Kingston and the War of 1812." *Historic Kingston* 15: 50-60.

**Horsey 1937** Horsey, Edwin. *Cataraqui, Fort Frontenac, Kingstown.* Kingston. (unpublished manuscript)

**Horsey 1938** Horsey, Edwin. *Kingston a Century Ago.* Kingston: Kingston Historical Society.

**Horsey, Saunders and Woods 1970** Horsey, Edwin, Samuel Woods and W.J. Saunders. *A Century and a Half of Secondary School Education in Kingston, 1792-1942.* Kingston: n.p.

**Hughes 1986** Hughes, V.A. "The Kingston Observatory." *Historic Kingston* 34: 99-102.

**IODE 1950** Imperial Order Daughters of the Empire. *The Imperial Order Daughters of the Empire: Golden Jubilee, 1900-1950.* Toronto: n.p.

**IODE 1954** Imperial Order Daughters of the Empire. *Imperial Orders Daughters of the Empire: I.O.D.E. Canada: What It Is and What It Does.* n.p.

**Jackson 1953** Jackson, Harold McGill. *Rogers' Rangers: A History.* Ottawa, n.p.

**Johnston** Johnston, Murray. *Canada's Craftsmen at 50! CFB Borden, ON.:* EME Branch. n.d.

**KCI 1921** Kingston Collegiate Institute. *Times of K.C.I. 1920-1921.* Kingston: Kingston Collegiate Institute.

**KCVI 1973** Kingston Collegiate and Vocational Institute. *Historical Times.* Kingston: n.p.

**Kennedy 1955** Kennedy, C.H. *The Kingston General Hospital: A Summary of its Growth, 1835-1954.* Kingston: n.p.

**Kerry 1962** Kerry, Colonel A.J. and McDill, Major W.A. *The History of The Corps of Royal Canadian Engineers.* 2 vols. Ottawa: The Military Engineers Association.

**Kingston City Hall 1974** *Kingston City Hall.* Kingston: City of Kingston.

**KHS 1968** *A Catalogue of Plaques, Tablets, Markers, Memorials and Museums in Historic Kingston and in The Circulation Area of the Kingston Whig-Standard.* 2nd ed. Kingston: *Kingston Whig-Standard* in Association with the Kingston Historical Society.

**KHS 1991** Kingston Historical Society. Complied by Cohoe, Margaret M. *Sir John A. Macdonald, 1815-1891. A Remembrance to Mark the Centennial of his Death, 6 June 1891.* Kingston: Kingston Historical Society.

***Kingston Whig-Standard* 1950** "Action Regarding Monument of Sir John A. Seems Remote." *Kingston Whig-Standard.* 4 May 1950.

**Kirkconnell 1920** Kirkconnell, Watson. "Fort Henry, 1812-1914." *Queen's Quarterly* 20 (July): 78-88.

**Lavell 1936** Lavell, W.S. "The History of the Present Fortifications at Kingston." *Ontario Historical Society Papers and Records* 31: 155-177.

**Le Sueur 1964** Le Sueur, W.D. *Count Frontenac.* Toronto: University of Toronto.

**Litt 1997** Litt, Paul. "Historical Markers in Canada: Pliant Clio and Imutable Texts: The Historiography of a Historical Marking Program." *The Public Historian* 19 (Fall 1997): 7-28.

**Long 1955** Long, Charles E. "A Sketchy History of St. Paul's Church." *Historic Kingston* 4: 40-46.

**Luciuk 1980** Luciuk, Lubomyr Y. *Internment Operations: The Role of Old Fort Henry in World War I.* Kingston: Delta Educational Consultants.

**Luciuk 1988** Luciuk, Lubomyr Y. *A Time for Atonement: Canada's First National Internment Operations and the Ukrainian Canadians, 1914-1920.* Kingston: Limestone Press.

**Machar 1908** Machar, Agnes Maule. *The Story of Old Kingston.* Toronto: Musson.

**Mack 1992** Mack, Donald Barry. "George Monro Grant: Evangelical Prophet." Ph.D. dissertation, Queen's University.

**MacKay 1990** MacKay, Donald. *Flight from Famine: The Coming of the Irish to Canada.* Toronto: McClelland & Stewart.

**MacKay 1977** MacKay, D.S.C. "Kingston Mills 1783-1830." *Historic Kingston* 25: 3-14.

**McKendry 1989** McKendry, Jennifer. "The Early History of the Provincial Penitentiary, Kingston, Ontario." *Bulletin of the Society for the Study of Architecture in Canada* 14 (December): 93-105.

**McKendry 1992** McKendry, Jennifer. "A Residence Fit for any Gentlemen in the Country: Three Kingston Villas by George Browne." *Canadian Art Review/Revue d'art Canadienne* 19: 68-78.

**McKendry 1993** McKendry, Jennifer. "An Ideal Hospital for the Insane? Rockwood Lunatic Asylum, Kingston, Ontario." *Bulletin of the Society for the Study of Architecture in Canada* 18 (March): 4-17.

**McKendry 1995** McKendry, Jennifer. *With Our Past Before Us: Nineteenth-Century Architecture in the Kingston Area.* Toronto: University of Toronto Press.

**McKendry 1996** McKendry, Jennifer. *Historic Portsmouth Village, Kingston.* Kingston: By the Author.

**McKendry 1998** McKendry, Jennifer. *Early Photography in Kingston.* 2nd ed., enl. and rev. Kingston: By the Author.

**McKendry 2000** McKendry, Jennifer. *Weep Not For Me: An Illustrated History of Cataraqui Cemetery, Kingston.* 2nd ed., enl. and rev. Kingston: By the Author.

**Mackenzie-Naughton 1946** Mackenzie-Naughton, J. D. *The Princess of Wales' Own Regiment (M.G.).* Kingston: Princess of Wales' Own Regiment (M.G.).

**MacRae 1967** MacRae, Marion and Anthony Adamson. *The Ancestral Roof: Domestic Architecture of Upper Canada.* Toronto: Clarke & Irwin.

**MacRae 1983** MacRae, Marion and Anthony Adamson. *Cornerstones of Order: Courthouses and Town Halls of Ontario, 1784-1914.* Toronto: Clarke & Irwin.

**Malcomson 1998** Malcomson, Robert. *Lords of the Lake: The Naval War on Lake Ontario, 1812-1814.* Toronto: Robin Brass Studio.

**Maracle 1997** Maracle, Donald. "Speech of Donald Maracle, Chief, Mohawks of the Bay of Quinte, for the Molly Brant Commemoration held Sunday, August 25, 1996." *Historic Kingston* 45: 3-8.

**MCC 1985** Ministry of Citizenship and Culture. *Loyalist Settlements, 1783-1789: The Land.* Toronto: Ministry of Citizenship and Culture.

**Meacham 1972** Meacham, J.H. *Illustrated Historical Atlas of Frontenac, Lennox and Addington Counties.* Toronto: 1878; reprint ed., Belleville, ON: Mika Publishing, 1972.

**Mecredy 1984** Mecredy, Steven D. "Simcoe House." *Historic Kingston* 32: 75-84.

**Mecredy 1989** Mecredy, Steven, D. "The Fort Nobody Wanted: The Restoration of Fort Henry Fifty Years Ago, 1936 to 1938." *Historic Kingston* 37: 59-83.

**MGO 1838** *Militia General Order: The Lieutenant Governor and Major General Commanding, Feels Much Pride in Congratulating the Brave and Gallant Militia of Upper Canada.* Toronto: R. Stanton.

**Mika 1987** Mika, Nick and Helma. *Kingston Historic City.* Belleville, ON: Mika Publishing.

**Mitchell 1986** Mitchell, G.D. *RCHA - Right of the Line: An Anecdotal History of the RCHA from 1871.* Ottawa: RCHA History Committee.

**Mitchell 1992** Mitchell, Michael ed. *Ducimus: The Regiments of the Canadian Infantry.* Ottawa: The Queen's Printer.

**Moir 1962** Moir, John S. ed. *The History of the Royal Canadian Corps of Signals.* Ottawa: Corps Committee.

**Molson's 1972** Molson's Brewery Limited. *Molson's: 81 Years Older than Confederation* Montreal: Molson's Brewery Limited.

**Moorehead 1987** Moorehead, Earl. "Murney Point: Its Evolution Within a Civilian/Military Dialectic." *Historic Kingston* 35: 64-86.

**Morang 1902** Morang, George N. *Pro Patria: A Song of the British Empire.* Toronto: Robert White.

**Morton 1964** Morton, W.L. *The Critical Years: The Union of British North America, 1857-1873.* Toronto: McClelland & Stewart.

**Morton 1981** Morton, Desmond. *Canada and War: A Military and Political History.* Toronto: Butterworths.

**MOT 1988** Ministry of Transportation. *Loyalist Parkway Master Plan.* 2 vols. Kingston: Ministry of Transportation.

**Neatby 1978** Neatby, Hilda. *Queen's University. Volume I, 1841-1917: To Strive, to Seek, to Find, and Not to Yield.* Kingston: McGill-Queen's University Press.

**Newman 1974** Newman, Lena. *The John A. Macdonald Album.* Montreal: Tundra Books.

**Nicholson 1962** Nicholson, G.W.L. *Canadian Expeditionary Force, 1914-1919: Official History of the Canadian Army in the First World War.* Ottawa: Queen's Printer.

**Nicholson 1967** Nicholson, G.W.L. *The Gunners of Canada: A History of the Royal Regiment of Canadian Artillery.* 2 vols. Toronto: McClelland & Stewart.

**O'Brien 1975** O'Brien, Robert A. *Frontenac at Cataraqui, 1673-1973.* Belleville: Mika Publishing.

**O'Gallagher 1995** O'Gallagher, Marianna. *Eyewitness: Grosse Isle, 1847.* Sainte-Foy, QC: Livres Carraig Books.

**Osborne and Ripmeester 1995** Osborne, Brian and Michael Ripmeester. ""Kingston, Bedford, Grape Island, Alwick: the Odessey of the Kingston Mississauga." *Historic Kingston* 43: 84-111.

**Osborne and Swainson 1988** Osborne, Brian and Donald Swainson. *Kingston: Building on the Past.* Westport, ON: Butternut Press.

**Parks Canada 1976** Parks Canada. *Canadian Historic Sites #15, Occasional Papers in Archaeology and History.* Ottawa: Ministry of Indian and Northern Affairs.

**Parks Canada 1998** Canadian Heritage. *Register of Designations of National Historic Significance: Commemorating Canada's History, Ontario.* Ottawa: Parks Canada.

**Passfield 1982** Passfield, Robert Walter. *Building the Rideau Canal: A Pictorial History.* Toronto: Fitzhenry & Whiteside in association with Parks Canada.

**Patterson 1985** Patterson, Neil A. "Molson's Brewery in Kingston." *Historic Kingston* 33: 81-85.

**Patterson, 1981** Patterson, William J. "Fort Henry, Military Mistake or Defiant Deterrent." *Historic Kingston* 29: 31-40.

**Patterson 1989** Patterson, William J. *Lilacs and Limestone: An Illustrated History of Pittsburgh Township 1787-1987.* Kingston: Pittsburgh Historical Society.

**Patterson 1993** Patterson, William J. *Courage, Faith and Love: The History of St. Mark's Church, Barriefield, Ontario.* Barriefield, ON: St. Mark's Church.

**Patterson 1997** Patterson, William J. "Outside the Walls: The Story of Quarrying and Farming at Kingston Penitentiary." *Historic Kingston* 45: 46-73.

**Perley 1896** Perley, Henry, F. *The Dry Dock at Kingston, Ontario.* Kingston: n.p.

**Pratten 1969** Pratten John S. "The Early History of Rockwood Hospital." *Historic Kingston* 17: 50-68.

**Preston 1956** Preston, Richard A. "A Clash in St. Paul's Churchyard." *Historic Kingston* 5: 30-44.

**Preston 1959** Preston, Richard A. *Kingston Before the War of 1812: A Collection of Documents.* Toronto: Champlain Society, University of Toronto.

**Preston and Lavell 1963** Preston R.A. and W.S. Lavell. "A Story in Stone: A Few Interesting Facts About Murney Redoubt." *Historic Kingston* 11: 47-51.

**Preston 1969** Preston, Richard A. *Canada's RMC: A History of the Royal Military College.* Toronto: University of Toronto Press.

**Preston and Lamontagne 1958** Preston, R.A. and Leopold Lamontagne. *Royal Fort Frontenac.* Toronto: Champlain Society, University of Toronto.

**Queen's University 1974** Queen's University. *Donald Gordon Centre for Continuing Education.* Kingston: n.p.

**Queen's University 1979** *Queen's University at Kingston, Faculty of Medicine 1854-1979: 125 Years dedicated to Education and Service.* Kingston: Queen's University.

**Queen's University Alumni Association 1990** Queen's University Alumni Association. *Queen's University: The First One Hundred and Fifty Years.* Newburgh, ON: Hedgehog Productions.

**Queen's University Alumni Association 1995** Queen's University Alumni Association. *Queen's Goes to War: "The Best and the Worst of Times."* Kingston: Queen's University Alumni Association.

**Rahmer 1973** Rahmer, F.A. *Dash to Frontenac. An Account of Lt.- Col. John Bradstreet's Expedition to and Capture of Fort Frontenac.* Rome: By the Author.

**Rea 1974** Rea, James Edgar. *Bishop Alexander Macdonell and the Politics of Upper Canada.* Toronto: Ontario Historical Society.

**Read 1988** Read, Colin. *The Rebellion of 1837 in Upper Canada.* Ottawa: Canadian Historical Association.

**Regiopolis College** Regiopolis College. *The Annual.* Kingston: n.p., n.d.

**Reid 1983** Reid, Sean. "The Rt. Rev. A. Macdonell and the Education of the Catholic Settlers of Upper Canada." *Historic Kingston* 31: 18-31.

**Richardson 1992** Richardson, George W. *Queen's Engineers: A Century of Applied Science 1893-1993.* Kingston: Queen's University, Faculty of Applied Science.

**Ritchie 1979** Ritchie, J.H. "From Pioneer School-house to K.C.V.I." *Historic Kingston* 27: 5-15.

**Robb 1963** Robb, W.H. "Charles Sangster, Canada's and Kingston's Poet." *Historic Kingston* 11: 30-34.

**Robertson 1900** Robertson, J. Ross. *The History of Freemasonry in Canada from its Introduction in 1749.* 2 vols.. Toronto: George Morang.

**Rogers 1769** Rogers, Robert. *Journal of Major Robert Rogers: Containing an Account of the Several Excursions He Made Under the Generals Who Commanded Upon the Continent of North America During the Late War.* Dublin: R. Archeson.

**Rollason 1982** Rollason, Brian, ed. *County of a Thousand Lakes: The History of the County of Frontenac.* Kingston: County of Frontenac.

**Ross** Ross, Arthur Edward. *The History of St. Andrew's Church, Kingston, Ontario, 1673-1973.* Kingston: By the Author, n.d.

**Roy 1952** Roy, James. *Kingston: The King's Town.* Toronto: McClelland & Stewart.

**Rushbrook 1977** Rushbrook, Audrey E. *Turning the Historic Kingston Dry-Dock into a Maritime Museum.* Kingston: Kingston Marine Museum.

**Ryerson 1843** Ryerson, Egerton. *Some Remarks Upon Sir Charles Bagot's Canadian Government.* Kingston: Desbarats and Derbishire.

**Scammell 1914** Scammell, E.H. *Rush-Bagot Agreement.* Hamilton: Girffin & Richmond.

**Shultz 1993** Shultz, Michael E. "Kingston's Own Regiment: A Capsule History." *Historic Kingston* 41: 64-67.

**Scrope 1844** Scrope, G.P., ed. *Memoir of the Life of the Right Honourable Charles, Lord Sydenham, G.C.B.: With a Narrative of His Administration in Canada.* 2nd ed. London: J. Murray.

**Shortt 1926** Shortt, Adam. *Lord Sydenham.* Toronto: Oxford University Press.

**Slim 1972** Slim, William. *Defeat into Victory.* London: Cassell.

**Smith 1976** Smith, George L. *Daniel Fowler, R.C.A., 1810-1894: Genealogy, Autobiography, Source Material.* Brights Grove, ON: George L. Smith.

**Smith 1979** Smith, Frances. *Daniel Fowler of Amherst Island, 1810-1894.* Kingston: Agnes Etherington Art Centre, Queen's University.

**Smith 1987** Smith, Arthur Britton. *Kingston! Oh Kingston!* Kingston: By the Author.

**Snell 1964** Snell, Dick. "He Makes a Present of Our Past." *Imperial Oil Review* 48 (June) 22-27.

**Sneyd 1962** Sneyd, Robert Brown. *A Canal in the Wilderness of the Rideau: Its Origin and Construction.* Toronto: University of Toronto Press.

**Snyder 1991** Snyder, Barbara. "A Closer Look at the Fairfield Family and Their Homestead." *Historic Kingston* 39: 15-21.

**Spankie 1914** Spankie, R.M. *Wolfe Island, Past and Present.* Kingston: By the Author.

**Spurr 1982** "Sir James Lucas Yeo, a Hero on the Lakes." *Historic Kingston* 30: 30-45.

**Stanley 1950** Stanley, G.F.G. *A Short History of Kingston as a Military and Naval Centre.* Kingston: Royal Military College.

**Stanley 1968** Stanley, G.F.G. "The Rush-Bagot Agreement, 1817." *Historic Kingston* 16: 77-79.

**Stanley 1972** Stanley, G.F.G. "Bishop Alexander Macdonell." *Historic Kingston* 20: 90-105.

**Stanley 1976** Stanley, G.F.G. "Kingston and the Choice of Canada's Capital." *Historic Kingston* 24: 18-37.

**Stewart 1991** Stewart, J. Douglas. "Great Princes Affected Great Monuments: George Browne's Molson Mausoleum and its Antecedents." *Bulletin of the Society for the Study of Architecture in Canada* 16 (Dec): 98-110.

**Stewart and Wilson 1973** Stewart, J. Douglas and Ian Wilson. *Heritage Kingston.* Kingston: Agnes Etherington Art Centre.

**Swainson 1968** Swainson, Donald. "Richard Cartwright Joins the Liberal Party." *Queen's Quarterly* 75 (Spring 1968): 124-133.

**Swainson 1969** Swainson, Donald. "Alexander Campbell: General Manager of the Conservative Party (Eastern Ontario Section)." *Historic Kingston* 17: 78-92.

**Swainson 1971** Swainson, Donald. "George Airey Kirkpatrick: Political Patrician." *Historic Kingston* 19: 28-40.

**Swainson 1972** Swainson, Donald. ed. *Oliver Mowat's Ontario.* Toronto: Macmillan.

**Swainson 1979** Swainson, Donald. *Macdonald of Kingston: First Prime Minister.* Don Mills, ON: Thomas & Nelson.

**Swainson 1989** Swainson, Donald. *Sir John A. Macdonald: The Man and the Politician.* Kingston: Quarry Press.

**Swainson 1990** Swainson, Donald. "James Richardson: Founder of the Firm." *Historic Kingston* 38: 95-110.

**Swainson 1991** Swainson, Donald, ed. *St. George's Cathedral: Two Hundred Years of Community.* Kingston: Quarry Press.

**Syme 1969** Syme, Ronald. *Frontenac of New France.* New York: William Morrow.

**Thomas 1989** Thomas, Earle. "Molly Brant." *Historic Kingston* 37: 141-149.

**Thomas 1996** Thomas, Earle. *The Three Faces of Molly Brant.* Kingston: Quarry Press.

**Towns 1990** Towns, Colleen M. "Relief and Order: The Public Response to the 1847 Famine Irish Immigration to Upper Canada." MA Thesis. Kingston: Queen's University.

**Travill 1982** Travill, A.A. "Early Medical Co-education and Women's Medical College, Kingston, Ontario: 1880-1894." *Historic Kingston* 30: 68-69.

**Tulchinsky 1976** Tulchinsky, Gerald, ed. *To Preserve and Defend, Essays on Kingston in the Nineteenth Century.* Montreal: McGill-Queen's University Press.

**Tulloch 1981** Tulloch, Judith. *The Rideau Canal: Defence, Transport and Recreation.* Ottawa: Parks Canada.

**Turner 1992** Turner, Larry. *Rideau Canal Bibliography, 1972-1992.* Smith Falls, ON: Friends of the Rideau.

**Turner 1993** Turner Larry. *Ernestown: Rural Spaces, Urban Places.* Toronto: Dundurn Press.

**Turner 1995** Turner, Larry. *Rideau.* Erin, ON: Boston Mills Press.

**Uffen 1982** Uffen, Robert J. *From Plowshares to Swords.* Kingston: Royal Military College of Canada.

**Walkem 1897a** Walkem, R.T. "Notes on Fort Frontenac and the Old Fortifications of Kingston." *Queen's Quarterly* 4 (April): 290-300.

**Walkem 1897b** Walkem, R.T. "Old Fortifications on Point Frederick and Henry, Kingston." *Queen's Quarterly* 5 (July): 53-61.

**Waltman 1981** Waltman, Marla Susan. *From Soldier to Settler: Patterns of Loyalist Settlement in Upper Canada, 1783-1785.* Kingston: n.p.

**Wilson 1976** Wilson, Ian E. "Molly Brant: An Appreciation." *Historic Kingston* 24: 55-58.

**Wilson 1977** Wilson, Barbara M. *Ontario and the First World War, 1914-1918: A Collection of Documents.* Toronto: Champlain Society for the Government of Ontario, University of Toronto Press.

**Wishart 1997** Wishart, James. *Producing Nurses: Nursing Training in the Age of Rationalisation at Kingston General Hospital 1924-1939.* Kingston: Kingston General Hospital.

**Woods 1960** Woods, Samuel. "Kingston Collegiate Institute." *Historic Kingston* 9: 57-63.

**Young 1921** Young, A.H. ed. *The Parish Register of Kingston, Upper Canada, 1785-1811.* Kingston: British Whig.

# The Authors

**John H. Grenville** has long been involved with historic sites. Beginning at Fort Henry as Curator and Historical Research Officer, continuing with the development of public programs at the Halifax Citadel and now at Bellevue House National Historic Site as Area Superintendent, John is also National Historic Sites Program Manager for Parks Canada in Eastern Ontario. He has been a member of the Kingston Historical Society for close to 30 years, currently as Chair of the Society's Plaque Committee.

**David C. Kasserra,** born in Kingston, grew up in Kingston and Brockville. He holds a BA Honours in History from Queen's University, and a BSc Honours in Marine Biology from the University of Guelph. A recent graduate and first time author, David continues to pursue opportunities that allow him to educate others in history and aquatic biology. David is presently living in Bath, Ontario, with his wife Christine, their dog, two cats, a horse and a tank of fish.

**Jennifer McKendry** is the author of *With Our Past before Us: 19th-Century Architecture in the Kingston Area* (University of Toronto Press). Dr McKendry, an architectural historian, a lecturer, and a photographer is currently preparing a book, *Into the Silent Land: Historic Graveyards and Cemeteries in Ontario.* She has presented numerous illustrated papers to the Kingston Historical Society on regional architecture and history.

**William J. Patterson**, MA (History) Queen's University, is a former director of Fort Henry and Upper Canada Village, and a retired Canadian Armed Forces Brigadier-General. He is the author of five published works: *Joyful is Our Praise: The History of Trinity (Bishop Strachan Memorial) Church, Cornwall, 1784-1984; Lilacs and Limestone: The Illustrated History of Pittsburgh Township, 1787-1987; Courage, Faith and Love: The History of St Mark's Church, Barriefield, Ontario; Portland, My Home: An Illustrated History of Portland Township; A Regiment Worthy of Its Hire: The Canadian Guards, 1953-1970.*

**Edward H. (Ted) Storey**, BA, BPHE Queen's University; MSc, PhD University of Illinois, is a retired university professor. He has held teaching and administrative posts at Illinois, Wisconsin-Green Bay, Penn State, and Ottawa Universities. He served on the Historic Sites and Monuments Board of Canada 1980-1987. He has written numerous policy and planning papers and reports for federal, provincial, and municipal governments.

# Index of Markers